PRIVILEGES OF WAR

281 st AHC

Bandit Crew Chief
67113

Bandit 24
AKA "Fat albert"
Norm Kaufman

Jay Hare

PRIVILEGES OF WAR

A Good Story of American Service in Vietnam

by

THOMAS A. ROSS

Paul Ross

"DE OPPRESSO LIBER"

AMERICAN
HERITAGE
PUBLISHING

Atlanta, Georgia

American Heritage Publishing
Atlanta, Georgia

Privileges of War

Published by
American Heritage Publishing
5710 Mt. Repose Lane, NW
Norcross, Georgia 30092-1428

First Edition

Book design by Jill Dible
Cover design by Antonio DeRose
Cover graphics of helicopter and troops from "God's Own Lunatics" by and courtesy of Joe Kline

For legal and other reasons, some names in this book have been changed.

Library of Congress Control Number: 2004093313

ISBN: 0-9754859-0-3

Printed in the United States of America

DEDICATION

To the more than three million who served with honor, and, especially,
to each of the more than fifty-eight thousand who died or
were declared missing in action in the Republic of South Vietnam.

To my teammates on Special Forces Detachment A-502
and those encountered while there.

To those who wear an American military uniform today.
Thank you for your service.

To the country, family, and friends who give me the freedom
and purpose to live and enjoy life.

CONTENTS

THIS IS A REAL STORY. It is told by a real soldier about one of the most incredible moments in the Vietnam War. It is a story of the energetic innocence of youth, the craving to be a patriot, the anguish of war fought on the other side of the world. Yet, even in the despair amongst demons of horrific proportions, heroes were bred.

On one mission of mercy to save others, Tom Ross shows us what it means to be a positive American. He makes us all proud. He doesn't ask that you understand all the real pain of triumph and fear that he experienced. He only hopes that you won't forget what happened, or the men and women to whom it happened.

Tom Ross's *Privileges of War* makes me glad to have served in Vietnam and proud to be an American.

Max Cleland
CPT U.S. Army, Ret.
Author, Strong at the Broken Places
Former U.S. Senator (1997–2003)

MORE THAN THIRTY-FIVE years have passed since I left the compound of Special Forces Detachment A-502 in the Republic of South Vietnam. After nearly a year of service with the team, I returned to the United States, where I was released from active military service. Within days of returning to my Northwest Florida home, I drafted the outline and the first few pages of this book, immediately titled *Privileges of War*.

My goal was to tell the stories of some remarkable occurrences that I witnessed while serving in Vietnam. In telling those stories, I was forced to tell my own. None of my actions were beyond the training or scope of what was expected from any other Special Forces officer. However, as my tour of duty unfolded, I was privileged to meet and work with Americans who did far more than they were asked or required to do.

Occasionally, names and call signs have been changed by request or simply because they were never known or have been erased by the passage of time. While the names and faces of some individuals encountered in Southeast Asia have become difficult to recall or even forgotten, the experience of serving with them and the inspiration of their deeds will remain with me forever.

INTRODUCTION

WHILE SERVING AS AN officer and military advisor with the U.S. Army Special Forces, the elite unit known as the Green Berets, it was my honor to experience the privileges of war.

Privileges of War is a collection of positive stories about wartime service during one of the most negative and controversial periods in American history. While the stories told here are relatively simple and straightforward, they are also powerful, with the potential of changing viewpoints, opinions, and even lives.

Soldiers did not commit the U.S. military to war in Vietnam. However, they did bear the brunt of that commitment both on Vietnamese battlefields and in their own hometowns when they returned. Not only did soldiers fight battles against an enemy who hated them, but upon returning home they often faced fellow countrymen who seemed to hate them as well.

Few of the Americans who served in Southeast Asia were pot-smoking, cursing, killing machines, as they have so often been portrayed. It is my opinion that the great majority of the more than three million men and women who spent time in Vietnam were decent people who believed deeply in the principles of freedom. Whether or not they agreed with government policies regarding the war, they had demonstrated their patriotism or respect for constitutional law by responding as either an enlistee or a draftee. They either wanted to serve in Vietnam and found a way to get there, or they had absolutely no desire to be there but went anyway. Most of them were young, either still in or scarcely out of their teens when they were asked to shoulder heavy responsibility and face life-and-death situations, many of them on a daily basis. I know. I was there. I was one of those soldiers, and *Privileges of War* is my story—a firsthand account of the many acts of selfless heroism and courage that I witnessed during my tour of duty.

Many of the books about Vietnam currently in print tell provocative stories with messages that are often dark and brooding. While many ugly and brutal events took place in Vietnam—with the atrocities at My Lai being perhaps the most notorious and most widely known—good things happened too.

This book tells a very different story about the war in Vietnam and the people who served in it. *Privileges of War* treats neither the politics of the war nor the conflict itself, but depicts some of the people who were there and shows the spirit-lifting manner in which they served. This detailed, action-filled account gives readers a real, often frightening idea of what it was like to be on the ground or in the air over the Vietnamese jungle during that conflict. The stories related in *Privileges of War* could be about a relative, friend, or acquaintance you know who served in Southeast Asia. These are factual accounts of persons who could have, or maybe even do, live on your street or in your home. Most of the people portrayed in this book are warm, very real, and wonderfully full of life. Many were individuals who could smile and display a bright sense of humor under the most difficult circumstances. The people I encountered never failed to meet their challenges in the face of danger. In fact, many raced into danger headlong, often placing their personal safety at risk to help or protect others. They served with honor and distinction and were people of whom this country can be very proud.

The American public deserves to hear all the stories, not just the ugly ones. In this book, I tell some of the many bright stories of dedication and patriotism that I was privileged to witness. While I do not present them as a goody-goody gloss of ugly occurrences that took place in Vietnam, I do feel that a vital piece of the American historical puzzle is missing. Stories of heroism, courage, and commitment demonstrated by U.S. troops and other Americans in Vietnam deserve to be told as well.

Many of the men and women who served in Vietnam are still reluctant to discuss their wartime experiences for fear they might be viewed negatively or might offend others. In the thirty-five years since I served there, I have frequently encountered other veterans, who exist in every socioeconomic level of our society. Because this war was so divisive, and the controversy over it so bitter, many veterans of that time remain secretive about their service, unwilling to discuss or mention it even with those closest to them. My greatest sorrow has been encountering spouses or children who have said far to often, "He has never spoken to me about the time he spent in Vietnam."

My deep and sincere hope is that *Privileges of War* helps dispel some of the myths that have swirled up around our involvement in Vietnam, redefine the image of the Vietnam veteran, and encourage other men and women who served there to begin to tell their own stories. In so doing, I hope the tethered pride and hidden honor they have felt compelled to conceal for so many years can at last be released. I also hope this book helps our country take a significant step forward, finally dealing openly and honestly with the painful and complicated legacy of the Vietnam War.

When I started writing, this book was for my wife and our children. I wanted them to know why I went to Vietnam, what I did there, and what I saw others do. However, as the book developed, the last of those three things became its focus; its purpose grew far more important. The book took flight in a quiet and very personal way—for my country, a country I love—to share yet untold, uniquely American stories.

My deep and honest belief is that the men and women portrayed in this book asked nothing for themselves beyond the opportunity to serve their country and help the people of South Vietnam in their struggle for freedom. This book provides the reader with the opportunity to share American smiles and laughter, while feeling fears and torment as U.S. servicemen and women fought a war for which support was deteriorating in their own country. The reader can also witness courage and selflessness as a small band of these individuals, risking their own lives, race into enemy territory in a daring attempt to rescue the enslaved families of a remote mountain village.

Ultimately, the purpose of this book is to give readers the opportunity to discover, as I did, the privileges of war.

ABBREVIATIONS

AHC	Attack Helicopter Company
AO	Area of Operation
ASAP	As soon as possible
CAV	Cavalry
CIB	Combat Infantryman's Badge
CIDG	Civilian Irregular Defense Group
CO	Commanding officer
COC	Combat orientation class
FAC	Forward air controller
FDC	Fire direction center
HE	High explosive
KIA	Killed in action
LLDB	Luc Luong Dac Biet (Vietnamese Special Forces)
LRP	Long-range patrol
LT	Lieutenant (pronounced "ell-tee" in conversation)
LZ	Landing zone
MEDCAPS	Medical Civic Action Program
MIA	Missing in action
NCO	Noncommissioned officer
NVA	North Vietnamese Army
OCS	Officer Candidate School
PIO	Public information officer
Psy Ops	Psychological operations
ROK	Republic of Korea
S2	U.S. Intelligence
S3	U.S. Operations
SF	Special Forces
SFC	Sergeant first class
Sit Rep	Situation report

SPC4	Specialist fourth class
Spooky	Modified C-47 aircraft
SRAO	Supplemental Recreational Activities Overseas
TAOI	Team Area of Influence
TAOR	Team Area of Responsibility
UH-1	Huey helicopter
VC	Viet Cong
WIA	Wounded in action
XO	Executive officer

PART I

Along the Way

CHAPTER 1

No Ticket Home

MIDDAY, JANUARY 1968 — *This looks as if it could be the beginning of a fantastic tropical vacation,* I thought. The magnificent scenery below certainly made the thought a plausible one.

With an index finger, I eased my sunglasses up above my eyes in order to have an untinted view of the spectacle passing beneath me. The landscape was even more beautiful with its natural colors revealed.

We were flying low over sparkling blue-green water that flashed and glittered as it rolled and danced gently onto a long, narrow, light-brown beach. A natural piping of lush green palm trees swayed slowly in warm tropical breezes. Coral heads blossomed from beneath the crystal-clear water, and bright green mangroves grew thick along waterways that led to winding inland rivers. Occasionally, the beach dissolved into massive rock outcroppings, which rose up to meet us. Off in the distance, inland mountains were visible against a bright blue sky, which played host to a few randomly scattered, fluffy white clouds.

The panorama before me, a true masterpiece of nature, was surely meant for the cover of an exotic travel brochure. It was exactly the way I imagined Tahiti would look.

As any other healthy young male might, I had daydreams of some day traveling to a faraway tropical island, which I would share with at least one stunningly beautiful woman. Now, barely a few hundred feet below me, was at least part of the dream: the tropical island. The view was so hypnotically captivating that I thought I could even hear the rhythmic beating of island drums. I began to wonder, *Will the rest of the dream come true?*

Still peering beneath my sunglasses as we crossed over the shoreline, I could see what appeared to be a native village in the distance. Here and there, over and through the thick growth of tropical vegetation, I caught an occasional glimpse of shapes that perhaps were island huts. As we neared them, and then swooped almost directly over them, I saw that the hutlike shapes weren't really huts at all. Rather, they were large military tents that had absolutely nothing to do with a romantic island village, Tahitian or otherwise. We were arriving in Nha Trang, and the tents were part of a military base camp position for a U.S. Army artillery battery.

The imagined sound of island drums faded quickly from my mind as I once again became conscious of the synchronized *whop, whop, whop* sound of the churning helicopter blades above me. I let my sunglasses fall back to the bridge of my nose and settled back into my seat.

◆ ◆ ◆

In reality, this scene wasn't the start of a fantastic vacation at all, and no beautiful woman waited on the beach to welcome me with a cold tropical drink. The unexpectedly beautiful terrain I had just flown over was at a point where the coastline of the Republic of South Vietnam met the South China Sea.

After almost two years of intense military training, I had finally received orders in late January 1968 that directed me to service in the much-talked-about country of South Vietnam. Now I was just one in the very long line of approximately 3 million men and women who had received or would receive similar orders, whether they wanted them or not. The helicopter on which I was a passenger was a military shuttle on its way to Nha Trang from Cam Ranh Bay, an arrival and departure point for U.S. troops serving in Vietnam. Most of us on the shuttle had been in Vietnam for only a day or two—just long enough to be officially processed "in-country."

Since volunteering for this duty, my eventual assignment with the Fifth Special Forces Group, a Vietnam-based unit, had been one I looked forward to with considerable anticipation. I had trained hard for the assignment and had tried to prepare myself, both mentally and physically, for the day I would become a part of the Vietnam War. But the day that began to unfold wasn't at all what I had envisioned. I had expected a dark and ominous place, not a place that looked as though it might be a vacation destination or part of a pleasantly remembered daydream.

When we reached Nha Trang, I was to report to Fifth Group Headquarters, where my assignment as a military advisor, one appropriate for my rank of first lieutenant, would be revealed. The flight north along the coast didn't take long, only about twenty minutes. Shortly after flying over the artillery battery we reached the outer edge of Nha Trang and began our landing approach to the airbase and runway zero-five.

During the approach to Nha Trang Air Base, and even as the chopper came to rest on the pad at the edge of the base runway, it was still a little difficult to believe that we had been flying over Vietnam. Maybe I had seen too many old black-and-white war movies. My image of Vietnam was of a dark, war-torn place in varying shades of gray. Surely, too, recent war damage would be easily visible, with smoke rising over a not-too-distant battlefield. Instead, the sky before me that day was clear and bright, and the landscape was a mixture of colors as vibrant and beautiful as any back home in Florida.

◆ ◆ ◆

The helicopter blades were still spinning over my head as I jumped down onto the runway. Once on the ground, it didn't take long for me to realize that I had indeed reached Southeast Asia. As soon as I carried my duffel bag far enough away from the chopper for the smell of exhaust to dissipate, a distinctly new odor filled my nostrils. Coming from every direction and permeating the air, it seemed to be a mixture of fish and fowl being cooked together and was as foreign to me as the ground on which I now stood. The odor wasn't particularly offensive, but it was definitely new and distinctively different. I had never smelled air like that before. Other sights and sounds around me offered additional evidence that I really was in a country halfway around the world from home. Asian people were performing various tasks as their supervisors shouted directions in a language I recognized as Vietnamese.

As I stood there looking, listening, smelling, absorbing it all, little doubt remained about my exact location. Suddenly, about the only things that didn't seem foreign to me were the military equipment and the familiar humidity, which reminded me of Pensacola.

Turning a 360-degree circle, I continued to survey my new surroundings with every one of my five senses more acute than I could ever recall. *So this is it . . .* I remember thinking. *This is the place creating so much controversy back home.*

Then, as I began to mentally prepare myself for the twelve months ahead, I watched troops as they came and went, moving all around the runway. I wondered if any of those who were arriving felt the same strangeness that I did. As for those who were departing, I could only guess about their feelings. Some looked very excited and obviously glad to be going home; others looked very worn and tired, while still others appeared totally expressionless. *Does even one of these men feel he has accomplished anything during his tour of duty?* I wondered, examining the passing faces. I was searching for the slightest evidence that any of these men might have felt as if he had accomplished even the smallest good—but I just couldn't tell.

Watching as the last man in one group boarded a homeward-bound shuttle, I began to wonder what my own feelings of accomplishment would be twelve months from now. *Will my presence here have made a difference? With the dissension over the war growing back in the States, will anyone ever know or even care that I was here?* Of course, I had no way to know the answers. But making a personal contribution and accomplishing some good had been among my reasons for coming— to do something, anything, that would make a difference to someone, even if that someone were only me. Having volunteered for this assignment, I didn't want my time in Vietnam to be meaningless or inconsequential, especially if it cost me my life.

While I couldn't at that point know why the men around me had come to Vietnam, as 1968 unfolded I would learn much about others who were there. In many cases their presence in Vietnam was no more complicated than a simple, but strong, patriotic desire to make a contribution, to make a difference.

In my case, the desire to make a difference had been so strong that, counter to my parents' pleas, I decided to leave college and join the service. Now that I was actually standing on foreign soil, ready to begin making that contribution, my mind began to race and fill with thoughts and questions. *Had I made the right decision? Was I really where I wanted to be?* And *Now that I've reached Vietnam, will I make it back here in twelve months to catch the return shuttle to Cam Ranh Bay and my flight home?* I purged these thoughts from my consciousness almost as quickly as they had developed. I didn't want to consider the prospect that I might be killed, however real that possibility. I know my father had considered it, though, because on the day I left home his eyes were filled with tears when we said good-bye. He was a big man and a veteran of World War II, and I had only seen him that way once before: the day his father died.

✦ ✦ ✦

After carrying my duffel bag to a pickup area at the edge of the runway, I stood it on end and used it as a stool while waiting for the jeep that would take me to headquarters. Continuing to watch the activity around me, I reflected on my decision to join the service and volunteer for duty in Vietnam. I can still remember sitting there on that scuffed, olive–drab green duffel bag that I had been carrying from base to base for over two years. With my tour of duty about to begin, my thoughts also turned to my evolution from college student to professional soldier. Many things had happened since making the decision to enter the service, a decision that had been spontaneous and one that would change my life forever.

As I sat on the hot runway apron under a relentlessly blazing Southeast Asian sun, there was no way to avoid recalling the single event that compelled me to interrupt my college education and choose military service. It occurred one evening in January 1966 while at my parents' home for dinner. My mother and sister were busy preparing the meal, and my father and I were watching the evening news on television. When a news segment began that reported on an unfortunate gunshot taken by a young Marine began, I was unexpectedly drawn to what was happening. The incident struck me so intensely that I would never forget it or its subsequent effect on me. The broadcast marked a specific point in time that brought maturity, decisiveness, and focus to what had otherwise been a carefree college student's life.

✦ ✦ ✦

In 1966, reports regarding the Vietnam War were typically the lead story or major report for almost every news program on the three television networks, ABC, CBS, and NBC. That unforgettable evening I sat and watched a report focusing on three young American Marines. They appeared to be about my age, and two of them were desperately trying to drag another Marine out of the line of fire after he had been seriously wounded.

Suddenly, and without any warning as I watched the struggle to save the downed Marine's life, I felt as if I had been struck by a loud, crackling bolt of lightning. The experience was remarkably intense and was accompanied by a wave of goose bumps that swept over my body. More than just watching a TV broadcast, the moment might be more accurately described as an epiphany.

In an instant there was a connection with the desperate situation of the young Marines, and I found myself yelling at the television screen, "Get him out of there!"

I had been stunned by the awareness and reality of what was occurring so far away from the safety of my family's home. I was immediately embarrassed by the thought that other young American men were fighting and dying while I attended school and enjoyed fraternity parties.

Television depicted countless other reports of war action, but none had affected me as powerfully as that one. Perhaps it was their terrible situation or the look on their faces, I don't know. For whatever reason, I remembered thinking that I could no longer stay at home to attend college and date girls while others did what I now felt I should be doing also.

Other men in my family had served their country or community. My father, who had flown in B-17s with the Eighth Army Air Force in Europe during World War II, survived being shot down over Europe. My grandfather had worked long shift hours as a metallurgist, turning out needed supplies for the same war effort. My great-grandfather served as a town marshal. Unfortunately, his service had cost him his life. After responding to a call for help, he had been surprised and killed.

I certainly had no desire to be killed as my great-grandfather was, but considering the contributions to their country and communities of other men in my family, I couldn't imagine doing any less than they had done. So, with absolute certainty, I knew I could not ignore what I had just seen on television. As the TV anchorman turned to other news, a quote came to mind that I had read only a few days earlier in research for one of my college classes. Daniel Webster had written, "There is no evil we cannot face or fly from, but the consciousness of duty disregarded." That quote summed things up for me. The decision was made. I would leave school and join the service as soon as possible.

✦ ✦ ✦

Now, with two years of exceptional military training behind me and about to enter a war I had only watched on television, perhaps my reflection was prompted by a need to confirm that the decision to leave school had been the correct one. By the time the jeep arrived to take me to Fifth Group Headquarters, no question or doubt remained. I was confident that I was exactly where I needed to be and that I had indeed made the correct decision, one that would introduce me to some extraordinary men and women whose deeds I would remember for a lifetime.

I'm not sure what I would have done if I had concluded my decision was the wrong one. It was obviously too late to ask for a ticket home.

CHAPTER 2

Uncommon Warriors

WITH MY GEAR LOADED into the jeep, the driver made a quick U-turn and headed for 5th Special Forces Group Headquarters. Continuing to survey my new environment as we drove along the runway, I noticed an insignia on one of the buildings near the flight line. "Intruders" was emblazoned diagonally across the red-and-white-on-blue painted crest. Across the bottom of the crest was the unit's motto, "Hell from Above." Another sign on the building indicated that the insignia belonged to the 281st Attack Helicopter Company. *Air warriors*, I thought as we passed by the building. I had no idea yet about their role in the war nor any consideration that they would one day risk their lives to save mine.

Helicopters were the workhorses of the Vietnam War. They were the primary means of delivering troops and supplies to the battlefield. The derring-do of U.S. helicopter pilots and crews were already legendary in the States. They were professional airmen from whom you could expect courageous actions on a routine basis. During the next couple of days, however, I would be amazed to learn that job description had nothing to do with the level of an individual's personal courage. This would prove especially true for those holding what were often accepted as routine and often mundane noncombat positions.

✦ ✦ ✦

The ride by jeep from the airstrip at Nha Trang Air Base to Fifth Group Headquarters was taking longer than it might have ordinarily. Barricades had been erected and placed in strategic locations to restrict rapid movement through the city.

"We had a hell of a battle here the other night, sir," the driver said. "They say at least two battalions hit us. It was a damn mess. The Cong were running around everywhere, so our guys put these things in the road in case they tried to roll in with heavier stuff."

The "Cong" the driver referred to were Viet Cong, South Vietnamese who sympathized with our North Vietnamese enemies. They fought against the South and its allies, which, of course, included the United States.

"Tet, huh?" I grunted, noting some of the damage caused by the recent battle.

"Yes, sir. They came out of the damn woodwork."

✦ ✦ ✦

I had arrived in Vietnam in the middle of the 1968 Tet Offensive, a major surprise attack mounted by almost seventy thousand North Vietnamese and Viet Cong soldiers. The attack, launched during Tet, the lunar New Year, violated a holiday truce and occurred virtually simultaneously all over the country. In a single night, the war moved from the jungle and rural villages to the heart of over a hundred Vietnamese cities and towns, some previously thought to be impregnable. Nha Trang had been one of the first coastal cities hit as its inhabitants prepared for a celebration of the New Year, the Year of the Monkey.

According to superstition, the monkey is considered a harbinger of bad luck. Certainly in this case it was. During the Tet Offensive,

South Vietnam and its allies lost thousands of troops, hundreds of American soldiers among them. However, the Viet Cong and North Vietnamese who launched the attack lost thousands more.

While dissension had been growing regarding the war in Vietnam, the Tet Offensive would dramatically change public opinion in the United States and around the world. Events surrounding this offensive would cause antiwar resistance to intensify significantly. On that note, my tour of duty began.

✦ ✦ ✦

As we wound our way through the narrow streets, I began to be concerned about our safety. The driver had his M-16 lying across his lap, but I was unarmed because I hadn't been issued a weapon yet.

"Are we okay riding around through here?" I asked.

"Yes, sir," he said. "We're fine. Not much has happened during the last couple of days, but they're still active and probe us at night."

These words had barely passed his lips when we rounded the next corner and he slammed on the brakes. Our tires screeched, the driver's M-16 flew off his lap, and loose gravel scattered, causing dirt and dust to boil up around us as we slid to an abrupt sideways stop.

We had driven up on a group of South Vietnamese soldiers who had just begun firing into an abandoned building where some Viet Cong soldiers were believed to be hiding. The bursts of gunfire were ear-splitting as they echoed between the surrounding buildings. Someone wasn't a very good shot, because rounds ricocheted all around us. We both rolled out of the jeep and onto the street. The driver grabbed his M-16 and took cover on the side of the jeep closest to one of the buildings where we were stopped. I wasted no time crawling around to join him.

"This is crazy!" I said. "I haven't been here an hour, and I am not ready to get shot!"

"Well, you're right in the middle of it now, LT (pronounced 'ell-tee')."

"Yeah, so it seems. Let's get *out* of the middle of it. Okay?"

"I'm with you, sir."

"Okay, let's go."

We jumped up and ran toward the doorway of a nearby building. Inside an alcove, we stood shoulder to shoulder with our backs pressed against the wall.

I had come to Vietnam to fight, and now here I was, surrounded by gunfire, dodging bullets, and without a weapon. As I leaned out cautiously to see what was happening, I noticed a woman, apparently American, taking pictures from behind a truck. While the truck provided some cover, she was directly in the middle of the action. She continued taking pictures as she moved from place to place, presumably for a better angle on her subject.

"Who is that?" I asked.

Leaning out to look around me, the driver said, "I don't know, but I've seen her around. She's with the media, I think, and must work for a newspaper or something."

The gunfire stopped when yelling came from inside the abandoned building. Shortly, three men with their hands raised high in the air emerged tentatively from the building. The men, who appeared to be Viet Cong or NVA (North Vietnamese Army), were obviously concerned about the reception they would receive once outside. Their reluctance to come out was not without sound reason. The South Vietnamese soldiers began imposing street justice, jumping on them and beating them violently.

With things seemingly under control again, we remounted the jeep and pulled out. As we drove around all the activity, the female journalist was still busily snapping pictures. As she moved to another position she looked up, and for a moment we made eye contact. *Pleasantly attractive . . . and bold!* I thought.

"What is someone like that doing here?" I asked the driver.

"You've got me, LT, but she's sure easy to look at," he answered, a broad grin moving across his face.

As we drove away, it occurred to me that both the driver and I had reacted to the presence of the young female journalist in typically male fashion. We had observed and commented on her physical appearance rather than the more serious consideration of what she was doing, which was covering a war, a serious and clearly dangerous job. While I had noted the boldness in her effort to document the capture of the enemy solders, there was more to consider in assessing her actions. She was the only woman on the street and she was unarmed. However, except for me, every male on the street was armed, some heavily.

Many, many lessons were to be learned in Vietnam, a war brought into American living rooms by journalists similar to the one I had observed. For me, my arrival in Nha Trang constituted the first day of class; my first instructor had been the female journalist, whose lesson covered well the courage of women. Before I returned home, however, many others would reinforce her lesson.

✦ ✦ ✦

The rest of the ride to Fifth Group Headquarters was uneventful. When we finally arrived at the compound, I went in and reported for duty. After my paperwork was checked and verified, the clerk directed me to the supply area to draw my equipment. He said he would have my assignment confirmed by the time I finished collecting my gear over at supply.

✦ ✦ ✦

"Here ya go, LT. It's a brand-new piece," the supply sergeant said as he placed the familiar, sleek black M-16 rifle on the counter.

When I picked it up, it looked the same as the one I had been assigned in the States, but with one important difference: the one in the States had been used for training, while this one had been assigned for warfare. I rolled the weapon around in my hands and pulled the bolt back to make sure the firing chamber was empty.

The M-16 had always reminded me more of a space gun than a military rifle. Its design, the use of synthetic material rather than wood for its housing and stock, and its light weight almost made it look and feel like a toy.

As I held my new weapon, for a moment I could see the old .22-caliber rifle my grandfather had given me when he first taught me to shoot. I could hear still his admonition after handing it to me. "Now that I've taught you to shoot and given you this rifle," he said, "please don't ever disappoint me by wasting a life, any life."

When released, the bolt on my new M-16 slapped forward, I hoped my grandfather would understand the purpose for which it would be used.

✦ ✦ ✦

My arrival in Vietnam in 1968 came with a clear purpose: Use the weapons of war to defend and fight with the people of South Vietnam in their effort to stave off Communism and survive as a country.

Looking back with all we know now, some may perceive that purpose as naïve. But at that time, I was certain we were defending freedom and protecting the rights of others. Preventing a weak country from being taken over by the Communists and fighting against the spread of its influence seemed a just and noble purpose. As children, both in school and at home, we had been taught that Communism represented a great evil. Only six years had passed since the Cuban missile crisis, a potential doomsday confrontation with the Communist Soviet Union. We were well-versed in the domino theory, which suggested that if Vietnam fell to Communism, all of the countries surrounding it would fall as well.

The Chinese and Russians, our Cold War enemies, were supporting the North Vietnamese. If we didn't defend South Vietnam and its people, who else could confront such formidable powers? Both Russia and China were openly committed to the spread of Communism. In the United States, the word "communism" was equated with loss of freedom, just as the word "cancer" was equated with loss of life. At the time, it all made sense to me.

✦ ✦ ✦

Picking up the ammunition clips that went with my M-16, I continued through the supply area. After gathering the rest of my gear it was time to pick up my orders and learn my assignment.

"A-502, sir," the personnel specialist said as he handed me the envelope containing my orders.

"Where's 502?" I asked.

"Out in the valley. 502 is responsible for defense for Nha Trang area as well as the northern defense for Cam Ranh Bay."

As I turned to leave, he added, "Take care of us, sir."

"No problem. I'll keep an eye on you," I said confidently, even though I had no idea where I was going or exactly what I would be doing.

With my orders in one hand, my M-16 in the other, and a pack over my shoulder, I left to find transportation to detachment A-502's main camp.

✦ ✦ ✦

Outside, in the compound, I used the envelope containing my orders to shade my eyes from the bright sunlight. Searching the compound for the shuttle ride that was to take me to 502, I noticed a jeep in a pickup area not far away.

I was pleasantly surprised to see a good friend and fellow officer, First Lieutenant Bill Phalen, already waiting in the jeep. He was alone in the vehicle, sitting on the passenger's side.

"It's going to be tough to drive from that side, isn't it?" I asked.

Bill laughed when he saw me and said, "What the hell are you doing here?"

"I was told this jeep would take me to my unit. So, are you my driver?" I asked.

Totally ignoring my effort to ruffle him, he asked, "Where have they got you going?"

"A-502. Where are they sending you?"

"502!"

"You're kidding! You mean we're going to be together? Do they know what they're doing?" I asked.

✦ ✦ ✦

Bill and I had gone through Special Forces training together, and we had both been assigned to the Third Special Forces Group at Fort Bragg during and after that training. It was nice to be so far from home and recognize a very familiar and friendly face. I threw my gear in the back of the jeep, and we waited for a driver.

"How long have you been here?" I asked.

"I got in yesterday. It looks as if we just missed some really big fireworks."

"That's what I hear."

"Someone told me last night that when the VC (Viet Cong) and NVA hit, every unit in Nha Trang got in on the action. Even the clerks and mechanics were involved."

"What? Was it that bad?" I asked.

"Yeah. I was told they had a pretty rough time," Bill said.

Recounting events of the past few days, Bill shared with me what he had been told about the Tet attack.

"Evidently, what happened was a little unexpected, at least in this area. A large combined force of VC and NVA infiltrated into the city and they struck from inside. Then, another fairly large unit attacked, coming in along Highway 1. That's the main drag. They hit early in the morning, and the battle lasted for a day or so. The fighting got to be house-to-house at one point," Bill said.

"Yeah, well, that part of it may not be over yet," I told him. "I watched them drag three guys out of an abandoned building on my way over from the airstrip earlier this afternoon."

"Really?"

"Yeah. I thought I was going to be shot before I reported for duty. It was unbelievable," I commented.

"No, you haven't heard the unbelievable part yet," Bill said. "One of the officers over in Operations told me that during a fight for one location, a truck came roaring back for ammunition. When the truck slid into the headquarters compound, the driver jumped out and yelled that they needed more ammunition and reinforcements. Everyone within the sound of the driver's voice ran for his M-16, but by that time most of the field-experienced people were already gone and involved in the fight. So, this is where the unbelievable part begins."

"Okay, go ahead," I said, waiting for the punch line.

"Well, since there were few field types left to respond, when they heard both the commotion and call for reinforcements, clerk typists and mechanics from the motor pool grabbed their weapons and ran for the truck. Hell, even the damn cooks ran and jumped on the truck!"

"You're joking."

"No. Can you believe it? Clerk typists, mechanics, and cooks . . . I guess you do what you have to do," Bill said.

Bill's observation of doing what you have to do would prove to be prophetic many times over during our tour with A-502.

During a visit to headquarters a few days later, lunch in the mess hall gave me the opportunity to speak to one of the cooks who had been involved in the opening Tet skirmishes. He described how he and his makeshift reinforcement unit fought their way— block-by-block and house-to-house—through the city streets, which were illuminated only by the red-orange glow of artillery flares.

"They were shooting at us from every direction, sir. Rounds were ricocheting off of everything, and we never knew where the next burst of fire would come from. On top of that, with the echoing gunfire, we weren't always sure where they were. Hell, I just kept waiting to get hit," he said. "It was bad! All I could think about was getting home to my wife and baby," he added. The cook's voice betrayed the emotion stirred by telling his story.

"Why were you out there?" I asked.

"I was on the late shift or early shift, depending on your point of view. Anyway, when I heard them yelling for reinforcements, I knew our guys needed help and I just took off. I'm not sure I can explain it. I just knew I needed to be out there. Nuts, huh?"

Amazing, I thought.

"Damn!" he exclaimed. "You know, I think I wore my apron the whole time. What kind of soldier is that?" he asked.

"The best," I said. "The very best."

◆ ◆ ◆

After the cook, I encountered a clerk in the S2 (Intelligence) Office who, as a result of Tet, was now a combat veteran. He was anxiously awaiting the presentation of his CIB award. The CIB (Combat Infantryman's Badge) is given to U.S. Army soldiers who have been in combat. When asked about involvement in the recent action, his story was similar to the cook's. He was a reluctant but courageous participant.

"It was some bad shit, sir," the young clerk typist said. "I heard them calling for reinforcements when the truck came in for more supplies. But, hell, I'm just an ordinary analyst and typist, not an A-Team member. That's not what I signed up for, sir. I'm not a chicken or anything. I wanted to be in the Special Forces," he said.

"I understand," I said, wanting him to know I didn't think he was a chicken.

"But, you know, when I heard all that yelling for help, how could I stay here? I had to go. I was really afraid I might die, but I just had to go. Ya know, sir?"

"I do," was my reply to what I found to be remarkable character.

"I can't wait to write my father. He was in World War II, and the last thing he said to me before I left home was—" then he made a strange facial expression and, imitating his father's voice, continued—"'What the hell is a man with a typewriter going to do?'"

I couldn't help laughing at the impression of his father. He laughed as well and then added, "But, you know, sir . . . we saved the city," he said proudly.

"Yes, you did. You surely did," I said, amazed by his tale—amazed at the incredible courage he and his fellow clerks, mechanics, and cooks had displayed in the face of admitted fear.

Reflecting on the actions of the headquarters support personnel, I could only hope to match their deeds and their courage when the time came for me to act. While they had all received Special Forces training and were well qualified, they had never really expected to see the heat of house-to-house street fighting. Yet when the call for help came, these men threw down their domestic accoutrements, pencils, wrenches, and spatulas to take up the weapons of war. They may have been "ordinary" clerks, mechanics, and cooks . . . but, on that day, they were also uncommon warriors with extraordinary courage.

CHAPTER 3

The Team and
Tri Trung Dung

WAITING IS PART OF military service. The military doesn't consider these times wasted, though, and might simply apply a dictionary definition to them: periods to remain stationary in readiness or expectation of pending events. Regardless of how they are defined, in Vietnam long periods of boredom or quiet could be abruptly ended by the heart-stopping eruption of gunfire or the ear-pounding explosions of incoming artillery, mortar, or rocket-propelled grenades.

While there was no concern about incoming munitions in our current situation, Bill Phalen and I were well into a stationary period as we sat in a jeep in front of Fifth Group Headquarters. We were anxious to get to our new camp, Special Forces Detachment A-502, and were waiting for the driver who would take us there. As we sat, I looked out across the mint-green flats just west of group headquarters and up into the mountains that rose with authority from the flat valley floor. The only thing that betrayed the deceptive tranquility of the postcard setting was the barbed wire through which I observed the view.

While working in an environment where you could be killed at any moment, you tried not to consider the horrible prospect of that reality. However, occasionally I felt the icy chill of that possibility, and the feeling was not pleasant. As unsettling as my personal experiences were, I know my confrontation with the prospect of dying in combat was nothing compared to what others had to endure, often on a daily basis.

Many of the soldiers who served in Vietnam lived throughout countless days during their tour with the horrible, gut-wrenching fear of death. Having experienced the feeling myself gave me tremendous respect for the courage and fortitude of those who had to deal with it daily. As unlikely as it seemed at the time, one of my confrontations with the specter of death would occur in the mountains that were providing the impressive backdrop to the vista across the valley flats before me. Strangely, my friend Phalen would also encounter the specter in the very same mountain complex.

✦ ✦ ✦

While we continued to wait for our driver, I pulled my orders out of a large manila envelope. According to those documents, I had been assigned to A-502 as its S2 and S3 (Intelligence and Operations) officer. That was a bit strange, since a Special Forces "A" team, such as 502, normally only had twelve men with no slot for either an S2 or S3 officer. The next larger team, a "B" team, did have those slots, and both positions were normally staffed by captains, who were a complete rank above me.

Because my assignment at 502 was an unusual one, exactly how it was going to work was unclear. *502 must be modified in some way,* I thought. Then, recalling what a Special Forces training sergeant had once told me—"anything can happen next and you better be ready for it"—I was prepared to do whatever would be asked of me.

Musing over the strange assignment, I muttered out loud, "This is really bizarre."

"What?" Bill asked.

"I've been assigned as S2 and S3 of an 'A' team."

"That may not be so strange. I've heard 502 has a large AO (Area of Operation). Someone told me they have thirty or forty men and several outposts."

"I don't know. I suppose we'll find out soon enough," I said.

At about that time, a driver approached with another soldier who was to ride shotgun in the passenger seat as armed protection, just as occurred on stagecoaches in years gone by. Typically, during stage-coach days, the shotgun rider carried a double-barreled shotgun, thus the nickname. However, our shotgun carried an M-16 with several pouches full of ammunition. After confirming that our destination was A-502 the two men mounted the jeep, and we were quickly on our way out the main gate.

◆ ◆ ◆

Passing outward-bound through the Fifth Group gate meant that, for the first time in Vietnam, Bill and I were leaving personal security and relative safety behind. But since the headquarters had been established in Nha Trang in February 1963, though, we weren't the first; many men had passed through the gate ahead of us.

As dry, choking dust swirled behind the jeep on the road to A-502, neither of us had any idea what to expect. One of the few things the clerk at headquarters had shared with me about my assignment was that I would be replacing an officer who had been wounded during the Tet attack. So, we would clearly be going to a location that had seen recent action.

◆ ◆ ◆

Any remaining doubt about my presence in Southeast Asia vanished on the road to A-502. Less than a mile from the Fifth Group gate we passed a beautifully constructed Buddhist temple, colorfully painted in bright yellow and red with black Chinese characters adorning its columned facade. Two white ascending dragons faced each other and formed a large arch over the temple gates. Unquestionably, the dis-tinctive architecture was Asian.

As we continued on, we once again encountered the recently erect-ed barricades that were designed to slow enemy movement into Nha

Trang. Upon entering the city, Vietnamese lettering appeared on buildings and signs everywhere. Small cars, open three-wheeled motorized taxis, motor scooters, bicycles, and human-drawn carriages crowded the busy narrow streets. The steam and aroma of what I now recognized as Oriental cuisine rose from the cooking pots of street vendors and restaurants as we made our way through the city. I was surprised to see that business and life seemed to be going on with what appeared to be a great degree of normalcy, despite the recent battles.

On the north side of the city, a huge white Buddha sat on a tasseled pillow atop a decorated pedestal on a small hill. Even Buddha appeared unscathed by what had happened during the past few days. Neither the statue nor its ornate pedestal bore any signs of the war-related damage that was clearly visible in other parts of the city. Wearing a thin smile, Buddha continued to watch over Nha Trang from his commanding position, just as he had for years.

Occasionally, Bill and I turned and continued to admire the tremendous icon to Buddhism even after we had driven far beyond it. While it grew smaller in the distance, before this night was over we would have a much closer view of the dramatic statue and the hill on which it sat. Our purpose there would become the same as the Buddha's.

Continuing west beyond the city, we drove into the rural farming area where the cars and taxis of the city were replaced by slow-moving carts drawn by huge, black water buffaloes. While they were large and lumbering, the animals were relatively docile and were almost always led by young Vietnamese boys who carried a stick to guide the slow-moving beasts. The Americans often referred to the boys, who seemed to like the nickname, as "cowboys."

Small, picturesque hamlets appeared here and there while the fronds of tall thin palm trees in and around each hamlet waved gently in warm easterly breezes off the South China Sea. Rice paddies that appeared to extend to the base of distant mountains lined both sides of the road and shimmered like a vast inland sea. It was still difficult to associate the unexpected striking beauty of this Southeast Asian country with the controversial war that was tearing it apart. But war it was, and as we passed by one particular hamlet that fact became all too evident. Even though we were moving fairly quickly in order not to provide an easy target for any VC or NVA soldiers still hiding in the area, a nauseating stench blew through the jeep.

"My God! What is that smell?" I asked.

The driver responded immediately, "There was a big battle here the day before yesterday. Your team was involved in it and had to call in air support. They dropped napalm all along here, and enemy soldiers trying to get away from it jumped into the drainage ditches, but that didn't help. They were smoked [killed], and I'm not sure that all of the bodies have been hauled out yet."

Associating the beautiful country of Vietnam with the horrors of war was no longer difficult for me. Clarity came with the foul smell of death.

◆ ◆ ◆

During the long ride to A-502, the driver would occasionally talk over his shoulder, offering information he felt we might find interesting. He told us that he made this trip many times before and had become somewhat of a historian on the area. As with his account of the hamlet battle, he was quite willing to share his knowledge and began telling us about Tri Trung Dung (Camp Trung Dung), where A-502 was located.

"Trung Dung is inside an old Vietnamese fort," he said, "complete with a moat. According to the locals, the fort was built under the Nguyen Anh dynasty around 1793. It was occupied later by the French when they were here in South Vietnam. The fort was strategically situated north of Cam Ranh Bay and west of Nha Trang near the village of Dien Khanh. That's where we're headed, Dien Khanh."

Motioning as he spoke over the sound of the jeep's engine, the driver pointed and continued with his history lesson. "From that key location, the fort's occupants could help defend the seaport cities by patrolling that pass over there that runs to the south toward Cam

Ranh Bay and the one we're in, the major pass to the east. It runs back to Nha Trang."

The driver also shared with us the fort's more recent history, saying that the Seabees, a navy engineering unit, had built and occupied the camp prior to the A-Team moving in. 502 inherited the facilities when the Seabees moved to work at a new location. He said he thought we would find our accommodations to be above average.

After winding our way out through the valley that held a rich history dating back more than four thousand years, we finally arrived at Dien Khanh Village, then the fort and camp Trung Dung.

The fort, known to locals as the Citadel, was situated on the western edge of the village of Dien Khanh. It was the second oldest such structure in Vietnam. As we approached and then passed through the thick massive walls of the eastern gate, the old fort looked more like a Hollywood set than a modern military installation.

After passing through the gate at Tri Trung Dung, the driver took us to the A-502 teamhouse, where we unloaded our gear and thanked him for the ride and history lesson. Over the teamhouse doorway was a rectangular green sign with large orange letters painted on it that read "A-502," our address and home for the next twelve months.

◆ ◆ ◆

Before reaching the teamhouse door, we were met by Major Wilbur Lee, the team's CO (commanding officer) and First Lieutenant Bill Lane, the team's XO (executive officer).

Major Lee was tall with chiseled features, looking like someone whose image could be used on a Special Forces recruiting poster. I knew Lee as a captain back at Fort Bragg where he had a reputation for being a stern but experienced and extremely professional officer.

◆ ◆ ◆

Will Lee was an interesting man whose life story like his appearance could have been straight out of Central Casting. He was orphaned at an early age and dropped out of high school when he was sixteen years old. Forging his birth certificate, Lee enlisted in the Marine Corps and was eventually sent to Korea where he saw heavy combat duty. His involvement in intense combat action resulted in his being wounded on three separate occasions.

After Korea, Lee switched military branches and joined the U.S. Army, where he obtained an appointment to OCS (Officer Candidate School), ultimately earning a commission as a second lieutenant. Then, leaving active military duty to attend college, he graduated with a degree in civil engineering. When the Vietnam War began to escalate, this high school dropout, now an educated, combat-experienced army officer, responded to his patriotic urges. After applying for and receiving Special Forces training at Fort Bragg, where I met him, he was sent to Vietnam. Will Lee was a pragmatic man who had met life on its own terms and had succeeded under extremely difficult circumstances. I was glad to see him. Serving under his command would be a good experience.

✦ ✦ ✦

Bill Lane, Lee's XO, was warm and articulate, with a slight New York accent that was particularly distinct to me as a southerner. After spending time with him, it was easy to realize that Bill was an intelligent man who had set high standards for himself. Even dressed in a camouflaged military uniform, Lane had panache. As he turned to take us into the teamhouse, I noticed a flash just below his waist. The bright silver flash had come from his sidearm—a chrome-plated sawed-off shotgun. When he went through the door ahead of us, I leaned over to Phalen and said, "I hope we get one of those."

Bill just laughed and pushed me through the doorway.

✦ ✦ ✦

Even though he had only been in Vietnam a short time, Lane was already combat-experienced. Tet had made thousands of Americans combat-experienced overnight. Bill had been involved in the battle at the hamlet we passed on the way to Trung Dung. After fighting off and on for nearly twenty-four hours, he and the CIDG (Civilian Irregular Defense Group) unit he was advising became trapped in a graveyard across the road. Deciding that he and his men weren't going to become permanent residents of the graveyard, he called for the air support we were told about. A converted C-47 initially responded to Bill's call for help. The modified airship, often referred to as "Spooky," belched a hailstorm of blazing munitions from sets of Gatling-style miniguns. Spooky was followed later by a pair of F-105s that dropped the earth-scorching, battle-ending napalm from which enemy soldiers had tried to escape.

✦ ✦ ✦

After showing us our quarters, Lane gave us some time to unpack our gear and get settled, then took us on a tour of the camp. He took his time showing us around the interior of the historic fort, which had also been occupied by units of the French Foreign Legion when they were in Vietnam. It was in the shape of an irregular hexagon with arrowhead-type points at each corner. The expanse of the Dien Khanh Citadel was astounding, covering an area of approximately thirty-six thousand square meters. Built in Vauban military-style architecture, which was popular in Western Europe during the seventeenth and eighteenth centuries, the walls of the Citadel were approximately eleven feet high and massively thick. The outside of the wall was vertical with the interior portion terraced into two levels. This dual level formed a fighting platform for men and equipment.

Cannons had originally been mounted on each of the Citadel's corners or arrowheads. Lane showed us one of those cannons, which now decorated the center square in the assembly area of the camp's compound. The cannon had been salvaged from the moat that ran around the fort. The moat was approximately four to five meters deep and about ten meters wide.

Our tour of the Citadel was really quite interesting. The more I saw of the old fort, the more it looked like the set of an old Humphrey Bogart movie. You could almost hear the marching footsteps and clattering equipment of French Foreign Legion troops as they moved through the compound to man their posts. While my impression of their presence was imagined, others experienced visions of Legion troops, seemingly continuing their long-past responsibilities to protect the fort.

✦ ✦ ✦

One night months later, as I sat atop the Citadel wall watching the flickering candles in the village across the moat, a Vietnamese soldier who was on guard duty approached me from the near utter darkness. In spite of our broken use of each other's native language, we were able to communicate reasonably well. After some ice-breaking exchanges, the soldier said that when he first saw me he thought I might be a French legionnaire. When I asked what he meant, he said that he had seen French soldiers on guard duty before, but as he drew close to them they disappeared. Whether supernatural phenomenon or a result of too much Ba Mui Ba, a favored Vietnamese beer, or simply a ghost story designed to pass time while on guard duty, the tale was an amusing one that made my assignment to A-502 more interesting and memorable.

✦ ✦ ✦

In addition to its present-day housing of A-502, the fort was also home to several South Vietnamese military units as well as a small village that provided accommodations for the locals who were needed to service the walled behemoth.

As we made our way back to and through the A-502 compound, we were introduced to several of our team members. They were short and tall, black, white, and Hispanic, with a rich blend of heritage and background. It was a remarkable All-American team.

There were many on our team, but a true standout on the roster was the top sergeant, Jose (Joe) Vasquez, who was responsible for the NCOs (noncommissioned officers). Sergeant Vasquez was a tall man of medium build with high cheekbones, an olive complexion, and jet-black hair. While his ancestry was Portuguese, in appearance he had the strong looks and bold features of an American Indian. As might have been the case with a Native American chief, he commanded his men with a firm but caring hand. And, as with many Americans whose heritage was actually foreign, Sergeant Joe Vasquez was extremely patriotic and passionate about his service. He was an easy man to like and respect.

Military courtesy requires that noncommissioned officers and enlisted men salute commissioned officers upon meeting. While there was a swipe at an implied salute by each of the men we encountered, there were also the immediate offers of a handshake and varied verbal welcomes to the team. I was impressed by the warmth and firm grip of each encounter and realized that a silent but very strong bond immediately formed with each man. Special Forces and other special operations soldiers often advise or work in small teams of two or three. In a very real way each man's survival depends on the other. Regardless of the team's direction of movement, every man is expected to protect his teammate's vulnerable backside, often referred to by clock position as his "six." Each man trusts that the other will protect him with his life. That unique commitment and sense of brotherhood could be felt in the handshake of each team member.

The men of A-502 were exceptional, as, by military standards, were the accommodations. The buildings were wooden, with tin roofs. The outside walls were sandbagged for protection against attack, and one of the rooms in the teamhouse, the main living area, even had air conditioning—far beyond my most optimistic considerations. One day, after commenting about the quality of the team's accommodations, one of the sergeants quickly responded, "Sir, any grunt can sleep on the ground, but a professional will make the best of a bad situation."

While the team had been creative in upgrading the quality of its living conditions, Fifth Group Headquarters had been equally creative in its design of A-502's mission, a huge and important responsibility.

The detachment was originally authorized as a standard twelve man Special Forces A-Team in March 1964. Later, in October of that year, team members were actually assigned to the unit. Then, in December 1964, Detachment A-502 was made operational, with a stated mission of providing security for the Fifth Special Forces Group Headquarters and the Nha Trang Air Base. As a result, the team was located and quartered with a unit of the South Vietnamese LLDB (Luc Luong Dac Biet—Vietnamese Special Forces), which was strategically located within A-502's TAOR (Team Area of Responsibility).

In 1965, Fifth Group Headquarters determined the need for two A-Teams in the Nha Trang area, but each with different responsibilities. Fifth Group's decision to create a second team resulted in the authorization and establishment of Detachment A-503, which would assume the original responsibilities of A-502. Team leader, First Lieutenant Ken Day, and the team sergeant, Master Sergeant Art Fields, would remain with 502, taking on new responsibilities. Because of their familiarity with the original mission, key members of A-502 were assigned to the new team. 502's XO, First Lieutenant Oscar Hobby, became the CO and Team Leader of the new A-503. He selected Sergeant First Class, Paul Soublet as team sergeant.

Released from its original assignment, A-502 was given an even greater mission: responsibility for the security of the entire Nha Trang area. Overnight, the team's AO and responsibilities became significantly greater. With the acceptance of its new mission, A-502 would begin to write its history as the largest-ever Special Forces A-Team.

As we stood at the heart of Tri Trung Dung, Bill Phalen and I had just become a part of the Vietnam War and A-502's history. We were beginning tours of duty that would expose our teammates and us to the worst and, surprisingly, the best of the human experience.

CHAPTER 4

Ghosts and Guardians on Buddha Hill

WITH OUR TOUR OF the old Vietnamese fort and A-502's position within it complete, Lieutenant Lane began walking us back toward the teamhouse. Still noting the quality of living conditions the team had established for itself, I chuckled to myself as we passed small landscaped areas planted with brightly colored flowers. As it turned out, Major Ngoc (pronounced "Noc"), the Vietnamese camp commander, had the flowers planted for his wife, Kim, and official dignitaries who occasionally visited Trung Dung. The small patches of floral color brought some measure of civility to the military base-camp.

First surprised by the beauty of the country, I was now equally astonished by the appearance and quality of facilities at the camp where I would serve my tour of duty. I had expected to sleep on the ground in the jungle or, at best, on the ground in a tent or bunker in the jungle—and I would indeed do that many times before returning home. However, as we reentered the teamhouse where we were greeted by cool, refreshing air-conditioning, Phalen and I were about to learn that there would be no sleep that night.

Our welcome and tour officially completed our camp orientation. Lane immediately settled down to business and said that we would get our feet wet quickly. He explained the serious concerns about the recently initiated Tet offensive. The enemy actions had been unexpected, and no one was quite sure what they might do next. So, in order to provide additional early warning and protection for Nha Trang installations, our team had been assigned the task of providing security at a number of key locations in our AO. That night Phalen and I would be going out with one of the security units.

During our briefing, we heard that the Vietnamese unit to which we were being attached would be set up on a small hill overlooking the city of Nha Trang. Two other current team members would be assigned with us on the strategically located terrain feature. We were told that our night could be active because the enemy knew the strategic value of the hill, having briefly occupied it as a command and control center during the recent attack. Bill and I would be on the hill to assist in the direction of allied support in the event the VC or NVA units made another attempt to move into the city. Our presence there would also put us in a position to move in quickly behind the enemy if they approached down Highway 1, as they had a few nights before.

✦ ✦ ✦

A few evenings earlier, I had been enjoying a thick, juicy steak in a restaurant at the top of the Space Needle in Seattle, Washington, prior to catching my flight to Vietnam. As I looked out over Seattle that night, the lights twinkled and sparkled in the crisp winter air. Now, only days later, my location and landscape had changed dramatically. That night, I would be looking out over the lights of Nha Trang, which would be flickering and blinking in a very different type of atmosphere.

Nearly everyone who went to Vietnam would experience a similar and abrupt change in surroundings. For some, the transition either to or from the war zone could prove difficult, or at least challenging.

✦ ✦ ✦

We arrived on the hill just before dark, but even before we reached it, I knew exactly where we were going as the icon grew larger ahead of us: Buddha Hill.

When actually on the hill, the huge statue became even more impressive. In a sitting position, Buddha was at least forty or fifty feet tall. Possibly the only thing more dramatic than Buddha himself was the view he commanded. The glittering South China Sea and the city of Nha Trang, which was spread across the valley floor, appeared to present themselves as offerings to Buddha's imposing presence.

With darkness growing, Bill and I walked the hilltop with our two new teammates, two sergeants, who familiarized us with the position. Time has erased the names and faces of these two men, but not the lifetime impression of their character. The two sergeants had been involved in the fighting of the past few days and had been on the hill for the last two nights. They knew the area very well and showed us key areas from which they expected the enemy might attack. Once confident that Bill and I were comfortable with the layout of the hill, they took us to meet our South Vietnamese counterparts and their units.

During our meeting with the Vietnamese, it was decided that we four Americans would be stationed at equal intervals around the top of the hill, amongst the Vietnamese units. Plans were also established to react in various ways depending on enemy encounters. With plans set for the night, the four of us moved out to take up our positions.

Walking to my overnight location on the hill I realized, *This is it; this is where it all truly begins.* I lifted my M-16 and checked to be sure that the chamber was loaded.

✦ ✦ ✦

As darkness settled over the city, the hill took on a near-surreal appearance. The sky, a rich mixture of deep blues and vivid purples highlighted by faint yellows and oranges, served as backdrop for the huge white Buddha. Even Buddha himself was reflecting the beautiful colors of the Southeast Asian night sky. To find such beauty in the midst of such oppressive danger still was strange to me.

The brightly painted dragons that undulated down both sides of the steps leading up to Buddha faded into the darkness as night cloaked the hill and the valley below us. The only things clearly visible from the hilltop were the flickering lights from the city and the candlelight that made its way through the foliage between the hilltop and the village around the base of the hill. Candles and small cooking fires also flickered here and there across the expansive valley floor.

Vietnamese families in the villages around the hill were preparing their evening meals. The smell of dinner swirled in the humid night air and mixed with a warm salty sea breeze that blew in off the South China Sea. Along with the now-familiar aroma of Vietnamese food, the gentle sea breezes also carried the chatter of Asian conversation from the village below. Over the indiscernible voices, the gong of heavy bronze bells echoed back and forth across the darkened valley.

With the darkness restricting my vision, my other senses grew sharper, as did my dependence on them for information that might protect me. I could hear the rattling of equipment and the snapping of twigs along with a plethora of other unidentified sounds. The most recognizable sound was the crack of gunfire as it occurred throughout the valley.

Until that night, the only thing the sound of gunfire meant to me was that someone was involved in a training exercise. Before, the worst that was to be feared from the sound of rattling equipment or snapping twigs was the sudden appearance of an "aggressor" from an opposing training unit who might shoot me with a blank cartridge. That night, however, I was only too well aware that if I was shot, it wouldn't be with blanks.

As time passed and more gunfire occurred, I learned to distinguish differences in the types of weapons being fired. Sometime between 10 and 11 o'clock one of the sergeants walked over and squatted next to me. He was young, in his early twenties, but seemed relaxed and confident. He said he had come to check on me to make sure I was okay. As we looked out into the darkness together, a burst of gunfire could be heard in the distance.

"Did you hear that, LT?" he asked. Pointing into the darkness he continued, "That's where the bad guys are. Those were AK-47s. You can tell by that distinctive sharp crack."

AK-47s were automatic rifles that had been supplied to the Viet Cong and North Vietnamese by both the Chinese and the Russians.

Then there was another flurry of gunfire.

"Carbines and M-16s!" the sergeant said confidently. "Those are ours. Our guys are after their guys now. Go get 'em!" he said softly, encouraging our troops as they engaged in an unseen battle somewhere out in the darkness.

Later, as we sat and watched illumination flares and listened to gunfire from another distant skirmish, the young sergeant told me about the recent attack on Nha Trang. Much of what he told me I had already heard, but I responded as if hearing it for the first time. One aspect of the battle, though, was news to me.

"We've been told," he said, "that several of the enemy soldiers were high on opium and they had pinned notes to themselves. The notes were found on some of the bodies of those killed during the attack. They read, 'We volunteered to die.'"

"You're kidding."

"No, it's true. They were real fanatics, and I'm sure there are others," he said.

Needless to say, that report was chilling. They were like Japanese kamikazes, only on the ground. That was information I didn't need to hear my first night out in the field: I could be facing a fanatical enemy who doesn't care whether he lives or dies. *How do you fight an opponent like that, one that doesn't care about dying?* I wondered.

As if reading my thoughts, the sergeant said, "Keep your eyes open, LT," before he vanished into the darkness on his way back to his position.

✦ ✦ ✦

With each new sound of gunfire, I became more and more alert to the presence of objects closer to me. The movement of nearby figures occasionally interrupted the flicker of candles and fires in the distance. I even became conscious of changing patterns in the darkness itself, changes which also indicated movement.

As illumination flares lit the night, ghostly shadows appeared to march up the hill toward our position.

Is that an approaching VC patrol? I asked myself. I simply couldn't tell, and neither of the sergeants was around to see what I was observing. With the four of us widely spread out around the hill, I began to feel very alone.

I raised my rifle, snapped the safety off, eased my finger onto the trigger, and waited. My heart pounded with the anticipation of a life-or-death firefight. The sights of my rifle and my attention were focused on the shadows created by the eerie pink glow of the flares that drifted slowly toward the valley floor. After the flares went out, I waited for the enemy soldiers to emerge from the darkness and prayed that I would see them before they saw me. Even though an ocean breeze persisted, the night was hot and perspiration dripped down my forehead. I reached up and wiped the sweat away so it wouldn't get in my eyes. I fought to control my increased breathing so my first shot would be true.

Fear gripped my body as never before when I realized my life could be ended in a blaze of muzzle flashes from yet unseen enemy weapons. As I lay there waiting for whatever was to happen next, I recalled a statistical rumor shared among young officers back in the States. According to the unverified statistic, new lieutenants in Vietnam combat positions were only expected to live about two weeks. As the repugnant thought echoed around in my consciousness, another very important thought occurred to me: I was already involved in a battle, one that I needed to win quickly. I needed to fight to control my imagination and the accompanying and justifiable fear. An active imagination was distracting me, and fear was causing me to lose focus and concentration. I knew those things alone could cause me to react inappropriately or make a mistake that might contribute to the loss of my life. When and if the VC did appear, I would need to be calm and focus on what needed to be done.

Get your act together, I told myself.

♦ ♦ ♦

During my early days in Vietnam, I often felt the constricting grip of fear. Every man and woman had to learn to live and deal with it in his or her own way.

Sometime during the night on Buddha Hill, as I worked to control my emotions, I remembered a discussion in one of my college classes about fear. Someone read a passage that had remained with me; the passage suggested that we experience fear as an alert to warn us about evil or harm. Samuel Johnson wrote that the purpose of fear, "like that of other passions, is not to overbear reason, but to assist it."

Taking the remembered passage and its meaning to heart was how I learned to live and deal with fear. Whenever I began to experience it, I would quickly gather reason and sort through what was and was not real. That process became an indispensable survival tool until experience gave me the confidence to understand fear, and to live with it and use it.

Professional soldiers readily admit to experiencing fear. Acknowledging fear is not a sign of weakness; rather it is a sign of intelligence and confidence, and an understanding of the serious nature of their profession. Interestingly enough, what really scares a professional soldier is another soldier who is unwilling to say he has experienced fear. In my opinion, a soldier has two reasons for denying fear: He is either lying or he is crazy. In either case, the professional soldier has no need for this type of individual.

In my case, the adaptation to daily life in a combat zone affected my entire body. On occasions when the hair on my neck would begin to stand on end, I knew immediately that one of my senses had detected something important that required my attention. Then I would become keenly aware of my surroundings, knowing that I needed to be completely alert.

✦ ✦ ✦

With the extinction of each illumination flare, when on one appeared, I would relax and take my finger off the trigger and reengage the safety.

Maybe around midnight, the other sergeant, whom I hadn't seen since we separated, walked over and squatted next to me.

"Ya doin' okay, LT?" he whispered.

"Yeah . . . a little jumpy, but I'm fine," I whispered.

"That'll go away after a while," he assured me. "Don't worry about it."

"Good. The sooner, the better," I said. "I don't like the feeling."

✦ ✦ ✦

Off and on, throughout the rest of the night, the two sergeants, Bill, and I would walk the entire perimeter of our hilltop location. We checked to ensure that all of the Vietnamese soldiers we were advising were awake and alert. As we moved from position to position along the perimeter, I looked out into the darkness, wondering if an attack would ever actually come.

Never before had I been so conscious of the location of the thumb and index finger on my right hand. My index finger stayed right on top of the trigger housing, the thin metal strip that kept the trigger from being pulled accidentally, and my thumb was resting near the safety. While it was on, occasionally I would touch it with my thumb just to make sure I knew its exact location. There could be no hesitation in moving it to a firing position quickly.

If anything happens, I'm going to have to return fire immediately, I thought, along with a hundred other things that flashed through my mind during the very long night. Often the thoughts were disquieting, but all a usual part of the first-night experience on a combat assignment.

Just as I had decided that there wasn't going to be any need to return fire because nothing was going to happen (a mistake in itself), the entire north side of the hill erupted in gunfire. As I was on the south side, I jumped up and immediately started to run directly across the center of the hill. On my way, I encountered both sergeants and the Vietnamese sergeant in charge of the unit we were advising. As we met near the center of our perimeter, the sound of exploding grenades echoed up the hill.

"What's going on?" I yelled.

"I don't know, LT. Somebody must see something. Let's go take a look," one of the sergeants yelled back.

As we approached the northern perimeter, the streaking bright-red glow of tracer rounds could be seen blazing down the hill out into an open field and gunfire crackled all around us. The unique blooping sound of M-79 grenade launchers could also be heard along the perimeter.

The strange thing was that there didn't appear to be any incoming fire. I couldn't detect any muzzle flashes, which one would see from enemy weapons. At night, they would be distinctive and bright, but as I continued to look for what was drawing the fire of our Vietnamese soldiers, I saw nothing.

With the ear-piercing gunfire continuing, I yelled again, "Do either of you see anything?"

"No!" from one sergeant.

"No, nothing!" from the other sergeant.

"Do we have flares?" I asked.

"Yes!" came a reply from one of the sergeants.

"Have them fire flares!" one of the Americans yelled to the Vietnamese sergeant.

"Yeah, okay, okay," he responded. Then he started yelling in Vietnamese.

In seconds, the sky was filled with flares, and the landscape was lit nearly as bright as day.

When it could clearly be seen that no enemy unit was assaulting our position, the gunfire ceased and everything fell silent. Even though things grew quiet once more, my ears were still ringing from the sound of all the gunfire.

"What do you think these guys were shooting at?" I queried.

Once more turning to the Vietnamese unit commander, one of the American sergeants posed the question to him.

After speaking to several of the men along the perimeter, we learned that one or two of the men had seen movement and had opened fire. When they opened fire, others around them also opened fire, believing we were under attack—not an uncommon occurrence in any combat arena.

Only one question remained. What movement had they seen? We would discover the answer the next morning.

✦ ✦ ✦

With calm restored, I walked back to my position on the south side of the hill. Along the way, I had a comforting thought: *I'm going to be okay here.*

Even though our frenzied flurry of activity had apparently amounted to nothing, during the frantic scramble I realized something very important, but only to me: During the incident, I had reacted exactly as trained, to go to the source of the action and attempt to assess the situation. In other words, see what was happening in order to figure out what to do about it.

Settling back into my position and once again staring out into the night, I watched a flare fired from Hon Tre Island. Its bright pinkish-orange glow reflected and glittered in the small ripples on the South China Sea. As the flare hit the water and extinguished, I once again began to consider what had just happened and had another realization that was both comforting and reassuring. In the course of simply doing my job, I hadn't experienced any of the fear that had been so intense earlier in the night, perhaps simply because there wasn't time for it.

Everything had started happening so quickly that I hadn't had time to imagine what might happen next. There was only enough time to do something about what was actually happening. Everything considered, I was beginning to feel strangely comfortable in my new surroundings.

✦ ✦ ✦

After the one brief burst of excitement, a seemingly endless night wore on and on, during which time I made other discoveries. I found that spending time in the dark with the American and Vietnamese soldiers made it possible for me to detect subtle differences in their scents, in their colognes, after-shave lotions, and body soaps. American troops had been told not to wear any colognes and after-shave lotions for exactly that reason: If we could smell them, so could the enemy. Also, I detected differences between the body odors of American and Vietnamese troops. Neither odor was necessarily offensive, but they were different. I found myself wondering if the enemy would have yet another distinctive smell.

✦ ✦ ✦

Finally, my sensory extravaganza and the night came to an end. The glow of the morning light brought definition to the murky forms and figures on the hilltop. Threatening shapes that had resembled enemy soldiers in the darkness turned out to be nothing more than the twisted pickets of an old wooden fence. The danger of a real attack on our position had apparently passed.

When the bright morning sun had fully illuminated the hill, I walked back over to the north side to see if anything was there to be discovered. By the time I arrived, the Vietnamese soldiers had already found the bodies of the "enemy." Only, they weren't enemy soldiers; they were huge pigs. Sometime during the night, the pigs had wandered away from a nearby farmer's enclosure. The Vietnamese soldiers in fact had seen movement. Through the underbrush and at night, the pigs were mistaken as incoming VC or NVA.

In the interest of good community relations with the farmer and the village, we paid the farmer for the pigs that had been killed. Later, I was told that he was so happy with the settlement that he wanted to know if we wanted to shoot some more of his pigs.

✦ ✦ ✦

While there had been no combat, I thought that my first night had been exceptional, but the truly exceptional part of my trip to Buddha Hill was yet to come.

Just before we left the hill, the two sergeants walked up beside me.

"An interesting first night for you, wasn't it, LT?" one of them asked.

"That it was," I replied.

The two men, still clad in their camouflage face paint, could have also served as models for a Special Forces recruiting poster. Their appearance gave the impression that they had been hardened and made insensitive by their training and experiences as career soldiers. As we looked out over the village at the base of the hill, the war paint was virtually washed away as their true nature was unmasked. It became clear that they were actually very sensitive men.

"You know, LT," one of them said, "we've been up here a couple of nights now. And, every morning as we've watched the sunrise, we've felt as though we've been, I don't know, maybe guardians for the city and the families in the villages down there."

After a brief pause, the other sergeant added, "We've decided we like the feeling. It's a good feeling and a good reason to be on the hill."

It had been a very long, exhausting night for me. Knowing that the VC and NVA could have renewed their recent attacks at any time during the night had kept me at the pinnacle of alertness every second all night long. I was mentally drained and physically tired, but the feelings so openly expressed to me by the two seasoned soldiers were both surprising and, quite frankly, inspiring to me. The experience gave lift to my morning. I felt very good knowing that I was joining a team with men who felt as these two did.

I felt better still when by buddy Phalen walked up looking as tired as I felt. The four of us loaded our gear into the jeep, and we headed back to Trung Dung. Looking back as we drove away from the hill, I was certain that ghosts and guardians had both been present on Buddha Hill that night.

CHAPTER 5

Angels in Camouflage

IT WAS A LITTLE past midday. I don't remember whether it was a weekday or the weekend. I had been in-country for almost a month, and the day of the week didn't seem important anymore. I was now accustomed to the unexpected as routine. The war, rather than the time or day of the week, dictated the flow of work.

Paul Koch, my intelligence sergeant, and I had been working on a report for Fifth Group Headquarters for most of the morning. We were taking a break for lunch and were walking to the teamhouse across the assembly area in the center of the camp. The sky was overcast, which usually meant it could pour at any second, but it didn't look or feel humid enough for rain. We were about halfway to the teamhouse when we heard an explosion in the near distance and felt the ground tremor.

"What the hell was that?" Sergeant Koch asked.

"I don't know, but it wasn't thunder and it wasn't an impact from the ROKs. We would have heard the guns first."

ROKs was what we called the Republic of Korea troops, one of our allies during the Vietnam War. Their base was just north of the Song Cai River, which ran along the north side of Dien Khanh village. The Song Cai served as a boundary between our AO and theirs.

Occasionally, the ROKs provided artillery support for our operations. But their camp was northwest of us, and this explosion sounded as though it had come from the southeast. If the ROKs had been the source of the explosion, we would have heard their guns fire, and then heard the shells when they passed over the camp. Because we had heard neither, I felt sure it wasn't the Koreans firing.

When Sergeant Koch and I sat down for lunch in the teamhouse, we could hear the radios in the radio room buzzing with chatter. The radio room was immediately adjacent to the area where we ate, so we tried to listen to the activity.

"Who's in there?" I asked, trying to determine who was on duty in the radio room.

"It's me, sir," answered a familiar voice.

"Is that you, Miller?"

"Yes. It's me, LT."

"So, what's going on?"

"I don't know, sir, but there is someone on almost all of the U.S. frequencies. Everyone from Nha Trang to Soui Dau heard the explosion, but no one knows what it was."

"I'm going to go check with the Vietnamese," I said. "Let me know if you hear anything."

"Will do, sir."

✦ ✦ ✦

Lunch could wait. I walked over to the Vietnamese radio room across the compound to see what they had heard. When I arrived, they were already mobilizing. Vietnamese soldiers were running this way and that, gathering their combat gear as jeeps and trucks pulled up to carry them out.

I asked one of the Vietnamese sergeants what had happened, and he responded in broken English.

"Oh, Trung Uy, the VC ambush the train. They blow up the train that come from Cam Ranh Bay. We go after the VC now. You will come with us?"

Trung Uy (pronounced "trung wee") were the Vietnamese words for "first lieutenant." Most of the Vietnamese either called me "Trung Uy" or 'Trung Uy Ross."

"Yes, I go too. I need my M-16 and radioman. You wait for me, okay?"

"Okay, we wait. You go quick. We must *didi* to catch VC."

Didi meant to "hurry" in Vietnamese. I was learning.

✦ ✦ ✦

On the way back across the compound with my rifle and web gear that held my ammunition pouches, grenades, knife, 45 caliber pistol, and medical supplies. I saw Ahat (pronounced "ah-ott"), one of our Montagnard radiomen/bodyguards and yelled to him.

"Ahat, VC! . . . We *didi!*"

Knowing exactly what that meant, he immediately came running.

I ran toward one of the trucks, which were already beginning to roll out. Looking back over my shoulder, I could see Ahat with his radio and carbine right behind me. When he saw me looking to see where he was, he grinned widely, as if pleased that he had reached so quickly.

✦ ✦ ✦

The Special Forces often used Montagnards as radiomen, bodyguards, and trail watchers because of their loyalty and dependability. The Montagnards, who had also fought with the French when they were in Vietnam, were a tribal people who often lived in remote areas throughout the country. Frequently referred to by Americans simply as "Yards," the Montagnards were looked down upon by the Vietnamese. A minority group, they were considered inferior because of their primitive lifestyle. Vietnamese called them *moi,* which meant savages. In many ways they were very primitive; often they had only their traditional crossbows with which to hunt food and defend themselves. Obviously, so poorly armed, they were no match for the VC or NVA, who either by force or intimidation would press the Montagnards into servitude. But to the Americans who clothed, fed, and offered medical care to them, the Montagnards were fiercely loyal. After training from SF advisors, they proved to be equally fierce soldiers.

Typically, two or more of our SF team members would go out on a mission serving as advisors to a squad, platoon, or company-size Vietnamese force. American and Vietnamese officers at Trung Dung agreed that as much as 15 percent of the Vietnamese troops in camp could be VC sympathizers, so the Montagnards were used in the dual roll of radiomen and bodyguards. During the day and at night they took turns standing watch over their American advisors, if and when they slept.

Despite the primitive nature of the tribesmen, SF advisors and the Montagnards they trained developed many warm relationships as they shared a little of their respective cultures with each other. It was not unusual for an SF advisor to be taken as an honorary member of the Rhade or one of the other Montagnard tribes. The induction ceremony could be elaborate, taking as long as two hours, or it could be as simple as giving the honoree a carved metal bracelet, which symbolically bound him to the tribe. Such a bracelet given to me remains one of my proudest possessions.

While they were clearly primitive, the Montagnards seemed to me to be an attractive, gentle people with many fine qualities. They had dark brown skin, straight black hair, and larger, rounder eyes than other Vietnamese. They looked somewhat Polynesian to me, though with darker skin. The Montagnards and their consistently demonstrated loyalty to Special Forces soldiers was appreciated by the men of A-502, and eventually reciprocated. A-502 would one day launch a bold rescue mission in an attempt to free the inhabitants of an entire Montagnard mountain village.

✦ ✦ ✦

Ahat, who I used as a radioman and guard whenever possible, was young, about eighteen or nineteen. At twenty-two, I wasn't much older than he was. I came to treat him as a younger brother and thought of him as a friend. He possessed all the qualities he had been hired for and more. He was loyal and dependable, and he took his role as my protector very seriously.

Because the Vietnamese troops treated the Montagnards as inferiors, no love was lost between the two groups. In addition, because of the ever-present suspicion about VC sympathizers residing among the South Vietnamese troops, Ahat watched the Vietnamese troops as closely as he watched the jungle for the enemy whenever we were out on a mission.

On one particular patrol we had stopped and set up camp for the night. It was almost dark when a Vietnamese soldier who was on patrol with us spotted a piece of fruit hanging from a tree. He had taken his knife out and was moving toward the tree to cut it down. Ahat saw his knife come out and had no idea of the soldier's intention. When he saw him moving in my direction, he didn't wait to find out what his intentions were. He jumped out of the semi-darkness and jammed his carbine up into the soldier's ribcage. After an interpreter convinced him that the soldier wasn't trying to kill me, Ahat stepped aside so the soldier could cut down the fruit. Not surprisingly, the soldier had momentarily lost his appetite and put his knife away.

After that incident, the soldier always stayed far away from me whenever Ahat was around. Ahat would laugh and point when he saw the soldier taking the long way around us.

So on this day, just as every other, I knew I could count on Ahat to be close at hand. We threw our gear on the back of the truck and jumped on. The trucks roared out of the gate and down the road toward the section of the railroad that the VC had blown up.

When we reached the site of the explosion, we found a number of cars that had been derailed. The train had been carrying several different types of ammunition that had been shipped into Cam Ranh Bay for distribution around the country. Mortar rounds and grenade-launcher rounds had been blown out of one of the derailed cars and were strewn about. Both types of rounds become armed after traveling a certain distance from the firing tube or barrel. Because these had all been blown out of the train with much the same force as if they had been fired from a tube, we had no way to know which, if any, were already armed. We treated the area as if it were a minefield.

A Vietnamese soldier who saw me stepping gingerly through the area was amused at my cautious movements and started to laugh. He was obviously unaware of the danger involved in handling the explosives scattered all around us.

He bent down and picked up a large mortar round and held it out in my direction.

"You want, Trung Uy?"

"No, I don't want. You keep it. You go boom!"

Without warning, he began running toward me with the round. I could see that he was just clowning around, trying to scare me, because he was laughing as he ran. The situation changed quickly when Ahat and I leveled our rifles at him. His laughter stopped abruptly, and he froze in his tracks.

I asked an interpreter, who was also standing nearby, to explain to the soldier how dangerous the mortar round he was holding could be and that it could explode at any second.

The words had barely passed the interpreter's lips when the soldier, now very frightened himself, turned and threw the round toward an open part of the rice paddy in which we were standing. The round was heavy and didn't go very far.

Everyone close enough to the situation to realize what was going on hit the ground, trying to get as low as we could before the anticipated explosion. But because we were in a rice paddy, we all hit water and mud rather than dirt.

Holding my breath, with my face in the mud at the bottom of a Southeast Asian rice paddy, I counted to five to be sure the round had more than enough time to impact and explode. Luckily for everyone, it splashed and simply sank to the bottom of the muddy paddy.

As we stood up, we were dripping wet and muddy, with pieces of grass and rice plants hanging all over us. The sight of soldiers covered with mud and weeds was a ridiculous one, and someone started to laugh. The laughter became contagious.

As the laughter subsided, I was struck by both the absurdity and the more serious aspect of the incident. There I was, halfway around the world from my home, standing in water and muck almost up to my knees, and my life could have been lost because of a stupid accident, an accident caused by one of the very people I had come so far to help.

SF advisors had to deal with this type of incident and situation all too frequently. We laughed about it that time, but other incidents weren't funny at all. Some ended in tragedy.

✦ ✦ ✦

Everyone's mood changed quickly when someone noticed incoming rifle fire hitting in the water around us. The fire was only sporadic, but it only takes one bullet in the right place to kill. We took cover behind a paddy dike and tried to determine the source of the incoming fire, which appeared to be coming from a hilltop on the other side of the train tracks.

We had responded to the explosion of the train so quickly that the VC hadn't had a chance to carry much, if anything, away from the site. Apparently, when they saw us coming into the area the VC had returned to the safety of the mountains. Some of them had taken up positions on a nearby hilltop and evidently were trying to kill a few of us or chase us far enough away from the train so that they could regain access to the spoils.

In addition to the incoming fire, we had another problem. The only cover was on their side of the tracks, and our only choice of movement in any direction would take us across the open paddy.

I motioned to Ahat to bring me the radio. He ran the short distance between us and splashed down beside me. Taking the handset from the radio, I called the ROKs to see if they could provide artillery support. Unfortunately, they were already on a fire mission in support of one of their own units and couldn't help. The mortar tubes at camp were too small and too far away to help, and I was concerned that the guns in Nha Trang might be on the wrong side of the mountain. We were in a tight spot.

The VC were still taking potshots at us, which prevented us from moving without exposing ourselves to the possibility of more intense fire. I decided to call "Trip Hammer," the artillery battery in Nha Trang and asked them to fire a few rounds in our direction, to see how close they could come. Because a mountain stood between the battery's location and our position, when they fired the rounds impacted far beyond the VC location. The angle of fire was not good. The artillery battery wasn't able to help us either.

We weren't about to leave the train and its cargo to the VC. Our only other immediate alternative was to make an assault across the tracks and through the wreckage to the other side of the railroad bed, where we could set up defensive positions until reinforcements came. However, with all of the live ammunition lying around the wreckage, none of us really wanted to make that move, especially while we were receiving incoming fire.

As I looked around, I could see that we were in a large area of open paddies. Any reinforcements coming in to back us up would also be easy targets for the VC, who from their hilltop perch had a bird's-eye view of the entire valley floor. Fortunately, we weren't going to have to make an assault or wait for reinforcements.

I had moved down the dike to determine the best path for a possible assault when Ahat called to me. "Zero Two, Zero Two." That was his way of letting me know someone was calling me on the radio.

I motioned for him to remain and made my way back to where he was sitting with the radio.

"This is Zero Two, go ahead. Over."

"Zero Two, this is Artful Thunder. I think I've got good news for you," came the obviously pleased response from the person on the other end of the radio.

That other person was one of the artillery officers from the FDC (fire direction center) at SF headquarters in Nha Trang. He had been monitoring the transmissions between the artillery battery and our unit.

"We've just located a flight of two Marine F-4s and advised them of your situation. They've offered to help. Do you want them? Over."

"Absolutely! How do we contact them? Over."

"We're giving them your frequency and call sign on another radio right now. They will be contacting you shortly. Their call sign is Red Dog. Over."

"Roger, thanks for the help."

"No problem. Good luck, Zero Two. Artful Thunder, out."

Within just a minute or two the F-4s checked in.

"Bunkhouse Zero Two, Bunkhouse Zero Two . . . this is Red Dog Leader, Red Dog Leader. Over."

"Roger, Red Dog Leader, this is Bunkhouse Zero Two. Go ahead. Over."

"Ahh, Roger, Zero Two. Understand you have a problem. How can we be of assistance? Over."

"Red Dog Leader, this is Zero Two. We have incoming fire from VC located on a small hilltop just south of our position. We'd like to discourage them. Over."

"Roger. Understand. We can do that."

"Good. Do you have my location, Leader? Over."

"Roger, Zero Two. Fire Control passed it to us. We should be over your location shortly. We are going to have to punch through the cloud cover somewhere. We'll check in with you when we think we're over you. You'll need to direct us from that point. Over."

"Roger, Red Dog. Will do. Zero Two, standing by. Out."

✦ ✦ ✦

Only a couple of minutes had passed when we could hear the sound of jet engines in the distance. They were coming toward us, but were still somewhere above the clouds.

This experience was my first in directing an air strike, and I wanted to make sure to avoid friendly casualties on the ground or in the air. The hilltop where the VC were located was flanked and backed by higher mountains. I was concerned about the two incoming pilots and how they would be able to approach the target, deliver ordinance, and regain altitude before smashing into one of the taller mountains.

As I would soon discover, there was no need for concern. We were about to witness an amazing flying demonstration by two incredibly skilled pilots.

"Bunkhouse Zero Two, this is Red Dog Leader. Over."

"Roger, Red Dog. Go!"

"Ahhh, Roger, Zero Two. We should be over your position just about—" There was a long pause and then, "—now! Over."

Almost simultaneously, there was a booming roar of jet engines as the two camouflaged jets burst through the clouds almost directly overhead. They were on an east-to-west heading, which would take them up the valley toward our camp.

"Roger, Leader! You came through right on top of us. Over."

"Roger, Zero Two. You say our target is to the south? Over."

"Roger, Leader."

"Ahhhh . . . Okay Zero Two, we're gonna make a turn to the north and pass back over you, headed toward your target. I'd like you to pop some smoke and direct us from your position. Over."

"Roger, Leader."

After tossing a smoke grenade up on the railroad bed, I prepared to give directions to the hilltop. Then I remembered the magazine of all tracer rounds I had been carrying around for about two weeks. I had loaded the tracers one day before a night ambush. My plan was to use it to mark a potential target for air support we were to have available that night. But since it hadn't been used, the magazine was still in one of my ammo pouches. Marked with red tape, it stood out clearly when I opened the pouch.

Pulling the regular magazine out, I shoved the one with tracers up into my rifle and waited for the two F-4s to return.

When the jets began their turn to the south, I called Red Dog.

"Red Dog, Zero Two. We've got smoke out and are prepared to mark the direction of your target. Over."

"Roger, Zero Two. We have yellow smoke. Over."

"Roger, Red Dog. That's us. Over."

"How are you marking our target? Over."

"Your target will be clear. It will be the hilltop at the end of our pointer. Over."

"Roger. Understand . . . at the end of your pointer?"

"Roger, Red Dog. And, watch the mountains on the south side of your target."

"Roger. Thank you. Get ready to mark. We're coming in."

Just before the two jets passed over my head, I pointed my M-16 at the hilltop and squeezed the trigger. It looked like a long red neon pointer. I held the trigger down until every round was gone.

Laughing into his microphone, "That's clear enough! We have your target, Zero Two," Red Dog said as they passed directly overhead.

Immediately, their 20-mm cannons began to roar. As they did, dust, dirt, bark, and branches on the hilltop were blown into the air. They were right on target.

We could hear gunfire coming from the hilltop, but there was no sign of rounds hitting anywhere around us.

The VC must be firing at the F-4s, I thought.

After making their pass on the target, both of the two jets appeared to narrowly miss hitting the top of the mountain on the far side of the hill. Even Ahat thought they had just missed it.

"Very close, Trung Uy," he said as we watched the jets pulling up.

This is crazy, I thought. *One of those guys is going to get killed trying to help us.* They needed to end the mission.

"Red Dog Leader, this is Zero Two. Abort your mission! That helped. We're getting ready to move across the tracks. Over."

The signal was given for the unit to get ready to go.

"No, stay where you are, Zero Two. We're going to clear the deck for you. We're okay. We just needed to get the lay of the land. Over."

"Roger, it's your call. We just want you to get back to the deck. Over."

"Roger. Thank you. Keep your heads down," was Red Dog's response as they screamed back overhead, en route to another pass.

What followed was an extraordinary display of aviation skill and commitment to men on the ground who depended on them. The two jets made pass after pass, firing their cannons and dropping bombs. Each time, they came in low and pulled up steeply just in time to miss the mountaintops beyond the target. Watching the two pilots work was nothing short of electrifying. Their flying reminded me of the air shows put on by the Blue Angels back home in Pensacola, only in this context the show was considerably more exciting.

The bombs the pilots dropped had fins on them that popped open as they cleared the plane's wing. The fins created drag and slowed their forward movement so they appeared to drop almost straight down. The accuracy with which the two pilots hit the hilltop time and time again made me believe they could drop their bombs down into a narrow well if that was their mission.

With apparent disregard for the danger he and his wingman faced with every pass, Red Dog Leader asked about our status as they began another one of their runs toward the hilltop.

Even before they made their final pass, the gunfire from the hilltop had ceased, and we were able to move up onto the railroad tracks to secure the area. I was looking inside one of the damaged cars when Red Dog called again.

"Bunkhouse Zero Two, this is Red Dog Leader. Over."

As I took the radio handset, I looked around above the horizon to see where they were. The two jets were coming out of a slow turn to our north and were headed straight for us again.

"Roger, Leader. Go ahead. Over."

"Roger, Zero Two. Ahh, I think we've eliminated your problem, and I'll bet they've been appropriately discouraged. But we're making one more pass just for a look-see. Over."

"Roger, Leader. We have no incoming, and we're up on the tracks now. Over."

We had moved up the tracks some distance to check all the cars, so the planes were almost directly over us when they made their pass at a very low altitude.

"Roger, Zero Two. I've got ya. I assume that was you and your radioman on the tracks. Over."

"Roger, that was us."

"Good to see ya! We rarely ever see the people we're flying for."

"Roger, understand. Well, we were very glad to see you. You two saved lives down here. We're glad you were around. Zero Two—out."

The two jets, one behind the other, passed low over the hilltop that was now smoking and virtually bald. Each pulled up steeply as he had on earlier runs, then rolled out to the west.

They had made their attack runs individually, but now they circled from the west and headed back to the east, the direction from which they had originally come. They reunited and were flying down the valley together. It was truly stirring to watch.

It is difficult to express the passion of my feelings as I stood there and watched the two jets approach our position. *There is something missing,* I thought, as they flew low through the valley toward us. *Where's the American flag, rippling behind them? Where's the symphony orchestra echoing through the valley with them? Where's "The Star-Spangled Banner"?*

Obviously, there was patriotic pride and great admiration for the two pilots who had unhesitatingly flown on our behalf. We had all watched as they carried out their mission, exposing themselves to ground fire and the possibility of fiery crash into the mountains, not just once or twice, but over and over again. As they came closer, I considered the reality that only a matter of time would pass before the two pilots were again called upon to exercise their courage and skill on behalf of another unit in trouble.

As they drew near, I squeezed the button on my radio handset.

"Red Dog, Zero Two, over."

"Leader. Go ahead, Zero Two."

As Red Dog Leader responded, the jets were passing just north of us, and very low. They appeared to be at eye level, and as they passed by us both pilots had raised a hand inside their cockpits.

"Take care of yourselves," I said.

"Roger, we will. You may need us again."

There was a short pause.

"Zero Two, Red Dog flight is headed home. Out."

With that as their last transmission, the two jets pulled up and disappeared back into the clouds almost as quickly as they had appeared. It occurred to me, as they vanished into the heavens, that they were like angels—two camouflaged angels, going back above the clouds to wait for another call for help.

I had already experienced bad days in Vietnam—days void of any warm, emotional feelings—and I was sure there would be more to come. This day, though, had ended well. I felt good and savored the feeling.

Turning to walk back down the railroad tracks, I chuckled to myself and wondered what the two marine pilots would think if they knew that they had been thought of as angels.

CHAPTER 6

In the Hands
of the Unseen

NOT FAR FROM THE place where the supply train that ran between Nha Trang and Cam Ranh Bay had been blown up a month or so earlier lay a village we suspected to be a safe haven for the VC. In fact, we suspected that the VC who had attacked the train might have used the village as a staging area for the attack. The decision was made to set up an ambush at a point between the village and the mountains. Our strategy was that a successful ambush might discourage the VC from using the village as a location from which to launch deeper penetrations into our AO.

My friend, First Lieutenant Bill Phalen, was scheduled for ambush duty the night of the village mission. Sequence for ambush duty was typically determined by a rotation schedule, and it was Bill's turn. He would serve as the senior U.S. advisor to his Vietnamese counterpart and a platoon-size unit (twenty-five to thirty-five men) from CIDG Company 555. A CIDG company was made up of part-time Vietnamese soldiers who might also work other daytime jobs in nearby villages when the unit wasn't scheduled for a mission. The really unique aspect about Company 555 was that its Vietnamese commander had been a Viet Cong soldier who decided to reveal his previous role and change alliances. The role reversal always bothered me, but Bill and Ahn, the ex-VC company commander, had apparently forged a very strong relationship. Even though Bill would always take at least one other American advisor with him when the patrol went out, I was always concerned about his safety.

As mentioned earlier, Bill and I met at Fort Bragg. We had gone through Special Forces training together and had been together since arriving in Vietnam. Bill was a low-key person who had been an enlisted man in the service prior to requesting OCS and winning his Special Forces assignment. He knew the service and wasn't easily ruffled.

Bill and his wife, Lisa, had been very kind to me when we were stationed at Fort Bragg. They lived off-post and on a number of occasions had invited me to dinner at their home. Other times, the three of us just went out for dinner after a long, hard day of training. Those times were a welcomed diversion from the rigors of military training, and I enjoyed the brief time I had shared with them. When Bill's call for help came the night of the ambush, a hellish barrage was uncorked in an aggressive and desperate attempt to save his life, but because I couldn't reach him in time, others would have to deliver the firepower that would attempt to save my friend.

✦ ✦ ✦

I had been asleep for about two or three hours on the night I will never forget when our radioman, SPC4 (Specialist Fourth Class) James Miller, burst into my room.

"Lieutenant Ross! Wake up! Wake up! Lieutenant Phalen is in contact!"

Instantly awakened by Miller's loud intrusion, I responded, "Let's go!" exploding from my bed.

On my feet but still not fully awake, I bounced off the walls of the hallway on my way to the radio room.

"Where is he?" I asked, trying to focus my eyes on the map in the bright light of the radio room.

I knew where the original ambush site was located, but I wasn't sure whether or not they had moved from that position.

Miller put his finger on the map.

"He's right there, sir."

"Fine, give me the handset."

I tried to reach Bill to check his status.

"Blue Bandit Zero Six, Blue Bandit Zero Six, this is Bunkhouse Zero Two, Zero Two. Over."

When the radio remained silent and there was no response, I tried again.

"Blue Bandit Zero Six, Blue Bandit Zero Six, this is Bunkhouse Zero Two, Zero Two. Over."

Miller and I just looked at each other while the radio continued to remain silent.

"You know," I said, "they're not that far away. Go to the door and see what you can hear."

Unless there was heavy rain, we could almost always hear from camp how intense a firefight was.

Miller came running back to the radio room.

"It sounds like a hell of a fight out there, LT."

"Okay, get the rest of the team up and make sure the Vietnamese are getting reinforcements ready to roll."

I tried again to make radio contact with my friend, whom I knew might have already been down and hurt . . . or worse. Knowing the fighting might be fierce and loud, my call was louder this time. "Blue Bandit Zero Six, Blue Bandit Zero Six, this is Bunkhouse Zero Two, Zero Two. Over!"

Finally, the first response came. At first there was no voice, just the sound of gunfire. Someone had squeezed the button on the handset but hadn't said—or wasn't able to say—anything.

The possibilities of what might be going on out there raced through my mind. *Is he hurt and unable to talk? Has an enemy soldier picked up the radio?*

Then came the familiar sound of Bill's voice. Instantly upon hearing it, I knew his situation was extremely serious. Over the sound of hammering gunfire, his voice was calm and unemotional.

"Tom, we're not going to make it outta here."

As he spoke, the speakers pounded with the background sound of exploding rockets and grenades. The ear-piercing clatter of gunfire filled any void between the sound of rockets and grenades.

Bill was a skilled, confident military man, but when his response came in the clear, using my name and no call signs, I knew he was in serious trouble. I was sure he believed what he had just said. He expected to be killed.

"Bill, reinforcements are on the way," I tried to reassure my friend.

"They won't make it, Tom. We've ambushed a whole damn company [perhaps 75 to 150 men], and they are going to roll right over us. In five minutes, there won't be anyone left to reinforce."

With Bill advising a unit of no more than 35 men and the enemy company having 75 to 100 or more, Bill's unit was vastly outnumbered.

"All right, all right!" I said. "Have you moved since you set up?"

"No, we're still here. But, they're all over the place and may be trying to surround us."

"Okay, stay near your radio and listen for me to call back."

I drew an X over Bill's position and then drew lines on three sides around him, essentially drawing a box around his position with one side open. Then I asked one of the other team members who had joined me in the radio room to help plot the three line positions. Artillery would be fired along these three sets of coordinates. Hopefully, a wall of fire would separate Bill from his enemy.

"Give them to me in this order," I said, pointing to the sequence we would use.

While he was writing down the line positions, I picked up one of the other radio handsets and set the frequency to the Korean artillery battery.

"White Horse, White Horse, this is Bunkhouse, Bunkhouse. Over."

The response of the Korean voice was quick and professional. "Roger, Bunkhouse, this is White Horse. Over."

We often entertained Colonel Chang, the commander of the ROK unit to our north, and some of his key officers at Trung Dung. As a result, I became close to Captain Lee who was the Korean operations officer. While very different culturally, we enjoyed an excellent military and personal relationship. There was no doubt the ROKs would help unless they were already firing a mission for one of their own units or someone else.

"White Horse, we have a fire mission. We have a unit in contact and need your assistance. Over."

"Roger, Bunkhouse. We will help. At what coordinates do you want us to fire? Over?"

"Wait one, White Horse."

I asked for the first set of coordinates, checked the map quickly to confirm them, and squeezed the handset.

"White Horse, Bunkhouse. Use these coordinates," I said, and immediately gave them to him. "Wait for my command to fire. Then, fire all rounds HE (high explosive). Over."

"Roger, Bunkhouse. You don't want smoke first? Over?"

"No, we have no time. Over."

"Roger, we are ready. We wait for your command. Over."

"Roger, White Horse. Bunkhouse—out."

Normally, smoke rounds are fired first as marking rounds, to ensure that the high-explosive rounds don't kill friendly troops in case the coordinates were reported incorrectly. As I had told the Korean radioman, though, we had no time for taking that precaution. Our men might all be killed even before we fired.

Picking up the handset from a third radio and, while one of the other team members set the frequency, I called the artillery battery in Nha Trang. When they answered, I repeated the same directions given to the ROKs, using the second set of coordinates. Again, they questioned us when the high-explosives portion of the fire mission was requested.

"Bunkhouse, this is Trip Hammer. Are you sure you don't want a marking round?"

"Trip Hammer, this is Bunkhouse. No smoke, HE first rounds. Wait for my command to fire. Out."

"Roger, understood. Trip Hammer is standing by. Out."

Then, quickly changing the frequency to reach the big guns in Ninh Hoa, several miles away, fire mission directions were given, using the third and final set of coordinates.

As with the other two artillery units, they questioned the request for HE rounds first. The HE confirmation with these guns was critical and more important. They were firing 175-mm shells from miles away, and any one of them could kill or injure many of our own troops if they went off target.

The direction to Ninh Hoa was confirmed. All guns were now ready to fire.

I called Bill to tell him what was about to happen. Because time was so short, much of our communication was abbreviated.

"Blue Bandit Zero Six, Blue Bandit Zero Six, Bunkhouse. Over."

"Go, Two."

Heavy gunfire and explosions could again be heard in the background when Bill responded.

"Bill, we've built a wall of artillery around you and are ready to fire. Over."

"Roger, Fire!" he yelled.

"Bill, there's no smoke."

"Roger, understand, no smoke. Fire!"

"Roger. Bill, after impact, run north and into the village. Give me a mark every two hundred meters, and we'll follow you. Get down! Over!"

"Roger, understand! We're down! Fire the damn things!"

At that point, I was holding handsets in both hands. I dropped the one Bill was on and picked up another one, on which one artillery battery was waiting. All sets of guns were waiting, and two handsets were now open.

As I moved them close to my mouth, I looked at the X over Bill's position on the map and into both handsets gave the command to fire simultaneously.

"This is Bunkhouse. Fire! Fire! Fire!"

Then, quickly, Miller, who had returned to the radio room, rolled the frequency dial around to the third set of guns and the "Fire! Fire! Fire!" command was given once more.

I could do nothing more now. I had made marks on a map with a grease pencil and reported them to the artillery batteries just as I had been trained to do. The difficult part of the fire mission fell to men at the various batteries who would take the coordinates we had given them and translate that information into firing settings for their artillery pieces, which they had done. All three artillery batteries were pouring ordinance into the inky-black night sky. All we could do was to wait and hope to hear Bill's mark after he began to move.

When the artillery rounds began to impact, we could hear them in the radio room. As the big ones impacted, they boomed like thunder. I prayed they had been on target.

While the first rounds were still impacting, each of the artillery batteries were called and given directions for shifting their next volley of rounds. When we received Bill's mark, they would shift fire to cover his disengagement and withdrawal as he and his unit made their way to the village.

While we waited to hear from Bill, Miller told me the trucks with reinforcements were on their way. Those of us gathered around the radio wanted to believe they were going to make it in time to help.

Time dragged painfully as we waited for Bill to call with the signal indicating he had been able to disengage and move two hundred meters north. I wondered if the call would even come.

Maybe I've killed him, I thought. *How ironic and terrible it would be if he has been killed by a friend, rather than by the enemy.*

As the sound of impacting artillery rounds continued to thunder in the distance, Miller, who I'm sure didn't want to make anyone feel worse, voiced his concern.

"LT, that's an awful lot of ordinance hitting the ground out there. Do you think he's still there?"

He had simply verbalized what we were all thinking.

Then, a short while later, without any reason to believe it would happen, I felt the call would come. Even in the face of Miller's concern, I believed Bill could move his men out if he were given just half a chance. Quietly, I started to urge him on.

"Come on, Bill . . . come on. Call! I know you're out there somewhere."

I rubbed my forehead, looked at my watch, folded my arms, and leaned back against the radio room wall.

Then, finally, the call came!

"Bunkhouse, this is Blue Bandit! MARK! MARK! MARK!"

Without a moment's delay, the order was given to the three sets of guns that were providing Bill's lifesaving wall of protection.

"Shift and fire!" to the ROKs.

"Shift and fire!" to the Nha Trang guns.

"Shift and fire!" to the Ninh Hoa guns.

Then, without knowing anything about the emergency situation to which they had been asked to respond, and without being able to see their target, the gunners at three artillery batteries once again lit the black Vietnamese sky with huge muzzle flashes. More high-explosive rounds were on their way to shield Bill and his men from enemy pursuit.

After giving command to the guns, I again urged Bill and his unit on.

"Run, damn it, run!"

✦ ✦ ✦

The contributions of the men who manned the artillery batteries in Vietnam have often been taken for granted or simply overlooked. The men who pulled the lanyard dispatching what could be lifesaving artillery rounds often spent long and boring hours or even days at remote fire bases waiting for a fire mission. When ground troops received support from jets dropping bombs and firing 20-mm cannons or helicopters launching rockets and firing .50-caliber machine guns, you could almost always hear and see your support. Often, though, artillery rounds fired by unseen hands would arrive from so far away that you couldn't even hear them being fired. Nor would you see the faces of those who had fired them illuminated in the dark by the muzzle flash of their artillery pieces.

Men who served in the artillery had a tremendous responsibility. After days of inactivity, a call for help transmitted over a crackling radio could require them to respond within seconds. When they ran to man their guns, it could be mid-afternoon or the middle of the night, under a hot, scorching sun or in cold, drenching rain. Their mission was to send life-protecting artillery fire on its way to a distant target that they would probably never see. They might not ever know the outcome of the battle, or whether their efforts had helped at all.

The men of the forward firebases, on the other hand, might have welcomed more frequent breaks in the action. These artillery units were in highly active parts of the country and were given equally active missions. They were charged with disrupting enemy movement and supporting field units on combat patrol, those that were out constantly seeking enemy contact. When they did make contact, the artillery battery would either aid in the attack or assist in defending the field unit.

Action at the forward firebases could be fierce and last for days. The artillery units often came under attack themselves during both day and night, even while they were firing in support of the field units who were counting on them to deliver. And they did deliver, continuing to do so unless or until an enemy hit silenced their own guns. These men who stood in support of others were extremely brave.

I once visited a field artillery unit that had been set up near Trung Dung. Early in my tour, the purpose of my visit was to become used to the sound of loud explosions. I thought that if I became accustomed to it, the sound would be less distracting in the field if we ever came under attack. I felt if I could keep my composure and focus in that situation, then I would surely have a better chance to survive and do the job I needed to do when the time came.

I'll never forget the look on the young artillery sergeant's face when I told him why I had come to his camp.

"You want to do what, sir?"

"I really want to go up next to the guns while they're firing."

Then I explained the reason for my strange request.

"Well, lieutenant . . . you're welcome to go help yourself to all the sound you want. But, here, take these earplugs. You'll need 'em."

"No, that's the point," I said. "I want to hear the real sound."

"Okay, sir. Go ahead," he said, shaking his head as I walked toward the guns.

It was very dry that day. Every time the guns were fired, the earth rumbled and dust rose up from the ground and boiled in shockwaves that surrounded each gun. The first few times, I flinched as if hit when they fired. By later in the day, I had become accustomed to the sound. (The logic of the exercise made sense to me, but it probably wasn't the smartest thing I've ever done. To this day, I experience ringing in my ears and often punctuate conversations with a frequent "What did you say?")

In spite of my current situation, the experience served me well later on in my tour, and also gave me the opportunity to meet a great group of men, young soldiers who were still improving their skills as well as older and seasoned men who were teaching them their art. They took pride in the idea that when a unit needed help, they could reach out to a distant battlefield and provide their explosive ordinance, which often meant the difference between life and death for the combat unit they were supporting. Their effort was always urgent and focused, even though they might never see the battlefield or know the outcome. For that reason, I always tried to make it a point to call or visit each of the artillery batteries, to thank them and tell them exactly what they had done and how they had helped in our efforts.

✦ ✦ ✦

Bill was still in danger, but we were encouraged that his unit had moved the first two hundred meters successfully, and hopeful that they would make the next mark. So, the guns were called with new shift directions in anticipation of Bill's signal to fire again. Then, once again, we waited for his next call.

As we were waiting, Lieutenant Colonel Baer, an air force FAC (Forward Air Controller) who had heard what was happening from his base in Nha Trang, had gotten his 0-1 Bird Dog observation plane airborne. He checked in with an offer to help.

Colonel Baer had more or less adopted, or been adopted by, our unit. Our small runway had been built by the Seabees with the assistance of the 864th Engineer Battalion and was only about twelve hundred feet long. Major Lee and Major Nguyen Quang Ngoc, the Vietnamese camp commander, named the airstrip "Baer Field" in honor of the colonel who was the first pilot to land on it.

Colonel Baer, Captain Bill Boyd and two other FACs flew many missions for A-502 both before and during my time in Vietnam. Just before I left the country, word was circulated that one of the other two FACs had been reported missing after failing to return from a mission far west of the camp.

The FAC's primary job was to direct artillery fire or close air support, which is fire provided by other more heavily armed aircraft, from a key vantage point in the air above the action. They also flew observation missions to seek out and report any detected enemy ground activities. That job was often more dangerous, because it required flying low and slow which, of course, presented a tantalizing target of opportunity for the enemy, which perhaps is what had happened to the missing pilot. I never discovered his fate, but I always hoped he had somehow survived. When American prisoners of war were released after the war, my hope is that he was among them.

Having a FAC available in support of a mission was helpful because he could fly directly over any ground activity and see where the artillery rounds or bombs were impacting in relation to both enemy and friendly troops. After observing the impact, he could then adjust fire as necessary. However, at night, as in this case, even the FAC was likely to have difficulty determining who was where, especially with both friendly and enemy units on the move.

While he might not be able to see much by the light of hand-fired illumination flares, knowing he was up there was nice, just in case.

"Bunkhouse Zero Two, this is Walt Three Zero. Over."

With Bill due to signal at any second, I wanted to keep the frequency clear. My response to Walt Three Zero was brief.

"Roger, Walt Three Zero. This is Zero Two. Try to determine Blue Bandit's location and stand by. Out."

When the word "over" is used on the radio, a response is expected. When the word "out" is used, it means the transmission is complete and no response is required. It was a good thing our communication was short, because just as the button on the handset was released, Bill's signal came.

"Bunkhouse, this is Blue Bandit! MARK! MARK! MARK!"

Once more, the guns were called with the direction "Shift and fire!" As before, battery gunners sent rounds of various sizes streaking on their way to a point between Bill and his pursuers.

For the first time since the situation had begun, we all began to relax a little.

They're going to make it, I thought. Miller and others who had gathered around the radio room were also confident that Bill and his unit had successfully disengaged.

"They're going to make it!" could be heard from more than one person.

After the second set of shifted fire hit the ground, Colonel Baer called back. Knowing the situation, his transmission was brief.

"Zero Two, Walt Three Zero. Assuming they're on the north side of your fire, I have them, over."

"Great! How does our fire look?"

"It looks fine if those are your guys running in north of it."

"Roger, please stick with them. We may need you. Out."

"Roger—out."

Now a third set of shift directions were given to the guns and, one more time, we waited to hear from our team member, who was very literally running for his life.

After a couple more "Marks!" and shifts of fire, Bill and his unit finally made it into the village. When he called to say they were there, cheers of "All right!" "Yes!" and "Okay!" responses went up from the small group collected around the radio. Smiles of relief filled the room.

Bill and his unit had reached cover from which they could more effectively defend against the much larger unit they had ambushed. Now they waited, and we waited, to see if the attack would continue.

While we waited, the reinforcing unit called to say they were offloading from trucks and would soon be approaching Bill's position from the rear. We made sure he had heard the transmission, so he and his men wouldn't open fire on them.

When the artillery finally fell silent, there was no gunfire to be heard. The night was once again quiet. Time passed, and the enemy unit had evidently chosen to break the contact. Bill and his men wouldn't need to defend against anyone. The artillery batteries had discouraged the VC from continuing the battle: they had apparently turned and headed back into the Dong Bo Mountains.

However, the night was far from over. Responding to the impact of the final set of artillery rounds, Colonel Baer called in with a message that ensured there would be no more sleep for me that night.

"Zero Two, Walt Three Zero. Over."

"Roger, Walt Three Zero. Go ahead."

"Zero Two, I think one of those last rounds hit inside the village."

"No! Are you sure?" I asked, my stomach turning as I considered the possibility.

I couldn't believe what I had just heard. But, the fire had been moved so quickly. . . .

Maybe I made a mistake, I thought.

Because I knew there were families with children living in the village, I began to ache with the fear of what I might have done. The accidental killing of adult villagers caught in the middle of this war was upsetting enough, but the thought of children being hurt or killed flushed me with nausea.

"Zero Two, this is Walt Three Zero. Yeah, I'm afraid so. I was turning and didn't have a real good angle on it, but it looks to me like it must have hit inside the village. I've got smoke rising from inside the village perimeter. Over."

"Roger, Walt Three Zero. I knew we were getting close, but I thought sure I stayed far enough away not to hit the village."

Colonel Baer sensed the distress in my voice. "Ah . . . Zero Two. It's really dark out here. Most of the flares are gone. Your unit is in the village and they're okay. I could be wrong about the artillery. I'll come back out at first light and take a closer look. Over."

He was trying to make me feel better about the situation until we could be sure exactly what had happened, and I knew it. But with the night still very dark, neither of us could do anything at that point.

"Roger, Walt. Thank you much, I would appreciate that. I'm going to see what our ground unit can find out, but I'll be right here with the radio at first light. Over."

"Roger. See ya in the morning, Zero Two. Walt Three Zero—out."

Putting the handset down, I told Miller he could find me outside. I asked him to let me know when Bill and the reinforcements linked up. However, my joy over Bill's escape was now tempered by the anguish of the terrible mistake I had apparently made. My friend and his unit were safe, but if my direction of the artillery had accidentally killed innocent children in the process of saving him, I wasn't going to be able to feel the full joy of his survival.

Outside, I walked a small, slow loop around the compound, then stopped, leaned up against a fence post, and looked out across the dark night sky. Off in the distance, the last flickering of one of the flares that had illuminated the battlefield was barely visible. As I watched it drift down over the village, I wondered about the families below it and hoped that they were all safe. In my mind, I pictured the faces of some of the children with whom I only had a passing, but warm, friendship.

From time to time, I would borrow one of the motorcycles in camp and ride out through some of the villages near the camp. It was a way for me to relax and at the same time familiarize myself with the area around the camp. While out on some of those rides, I had encountered children in or near their villages. After they had seen me a few times, they would return my wave as I passed by. Theirs were the faces I pictured now in my mind's eye.

This isn't what I came here for, I thought.

Children weren't supposed to be involved in war, only enemy soldiers, but sometimes it happened. I was now learning in a very personal way that children are unfortunately all too often involved as innocent and direct victims of war.

For a while, I struggled in an unsuccessful attempt to rationalize what might have happened.

This is a war . . . these things happen . . . my friend is safe . . . but none of it worked. It didn't make any difference to me why or how the village had been shelled. If it had in fact been hit, I knew I was responsible. If the worst had happened, I would carry with me for the rest of my life that terrible and sickening tragedy.

The euphoria I felt only a few moments before when Bill and his men reached safety was gone—replaced with feelings I'd never experienced before and didn't care to experience ever again.

This turn of events was totally unexpected and caught me completely by surprise, the kind of mistake I never expected to make. I honestly loved being a Special Forces officer and tried not just to be good, but to be exceptional at my job. No one could have been tougher on me than I was on myself for possibly making such a horrifically stupid mistake.

During the entire episode, I had known exactly where the village was located, since that was where Bill was headed. I had watched the movement of fire as it neared the village to be sure it wasn't hit.

I know it wasn't hit, I thought. *But, then, what was the smoke Walt Three Zero had seen?*

"Lieutenant Ross, the reinforcements have linked up with Lieutenant Phalen." In the quiet of the night Miller's voice boomed from the doorway, refocusing my attention on the here and now.

"What?"

"The reinforcements have linked up with Lieutenant Phalen."

"Great. Thank you, Miller."

"Yes, sir. Everything turned out fine."

I didn't say anything else, but followed Miller back into the team-house. Returning to the map in the radio room, I retraced one last time all that had happened. All over the clear Plexiglas, numbers written in grease pencil covered the map.

All of the numbers looked good, and I had checked each set myself before calling them into the guns.

Could I have repeated the last set of coordinates wrong when I called them in? I wondered. I didn't know. Whatever had happened, it was too late to change things now. In a couple of hours, daylight would arrive and I would know with certainty.

I told Miller I would see him in the morning and walked down the hallway to my room.

Back in my bunk, my eyes closed and I tried to sleep, but that wasn't going to happen. I knew I would be haunted by ghosts of restlessness until I had heard Colonel Baer's morning report. Rolling over to face the wall next to my bunk, I stared at the strange shapes formed by the camp lights shining through the bamboo curtains. With nothing to do but wait until daylight, my mind flooded with countless, endless, troubling thoughts.

During that long night, the images that filled my head were often garbled and disjointed, a jumbled collection of my life's experiences. Because the possibility of having shelled the village made me feel so terrible, my mind searched for good thoughts of better times. For a while that tactic helped distract me from the horrific situation I now faced. Unfortunately, the good thoughts never lasted very long, always replaced with images of a smoking crater inside the village.

Just before daylight, I sat up and rotated to a sitting position on the edge of my bunk. As morning approached, my fears remained unabated. Closing my eyes, I could see the village children lined up like pickets on a fence. They were waving and smiling as I passed.

I suppose those visions of the children and the motorcycle rides that had introduced us had caused me to recall the day another small group of Vietnamese waved to me.

◆ ◆ ◆

The encounter occurred on a trail to one of the villages near the base of the Dong Bo Mountains. I had never ridden that far from camp before, but the bright, beautiful day made me feel as if I was back on my old dirt bike riding through the piney woods of Northwest Florida—with a difference. I rode wearing my green beret, an olive green T-shirt, a pair of camouflaged cut-off shorts, jungle boots, and a .45-caliber pistol strapped to my side— a real military fashion plate. Regardless of my appearance, the wind and sun felt good on my face as I raced along the trails. Feeling as though I had left the war back at Trung Dung, I enjoyed the beauty and pastoral serenity of the Asian countryside. Time and location was unimportant, but it soon became evident that I had driven much too fast and had definitely gone much too far from Trung Dung.

As I came to a sharp turn in the trail, I slowed just enough to navigate the curve and once again began to accelerate. Upon rounding the turn, I was surprised by what at first appeared to be a group of Vietnamese farmers. They were all squatted in a circle and a couple of them had sticks in their hands. I waved, hoping not to scare them and to let them know I saw them on the side of the trail. As I drove closer, they stood up. Clearly something was strange about the situation. The men were all similarly dressed in greenish faded khaki clothing that I had seen before—on the bodies of dead VC/NVA soldiers.

The hair on the back of my neck stood upright, telling me all was not right. Just then, I noticed what appeared to be weapons leaning against a log near the men who were now standing at the edge of the trail. Because the weapons were on the far side of the log, and because I was moving by so quickly, I didn't have time to see what they were. Whether carbines or AK-47s didn't make much difference anyway. Because of the quickness of our encounter and my speed, neither the group nor I could do much except to acknowledge each other's presence. I smiled and waved again as I rode past within an arm's length of the small assembly. None of them returned my smile, but two gave me a half wave, perhaps a reflex response, while another one kicked sand across whatever they had scratched in the dirt. It was obvious he didn't want me to see whatever it was that they had drawn. After passing the men, I accelerated even more and disappeared around the next turn in the trail. Without ever looking back, I left the area as quickly as I could.

The group might have been village militia and could simply have been surprised by the appearance of an American where none should have been. But, to this day, because of the way they were dressed and because of the way they looked at me, I am absolutely convinced that the men were VC on a daylight recon patrol.

I had momentarily allowed myself to become disconnected from the war and had gone where I shouldn't have been, an error in judgment that could have meant my life. While we knew that VC routinely infiltrated the city of Nha Trang, the village of Dien Khanh, and the other outlying villages, such action typically occurred at night. I didn't expect to see them on such a bright sunny day, but I think they were shocked to see me.

When I returned to camp that afternoon, I went to see Giao (pronounced "yow"), a Vietnamese sergeant who frequently displayed a sixth sense about where to set up ambushes. I mentioned the incident to him and asked if he could check it out.

To quote one of our team members, Sergeant Giao was a "fearless son-of-a-bitch." When he led his combat recon platoon out on patrol or night ambush, his unit rarely returned without enemy bodies. He knew the entire Nha Trang valley as well, or better, than some team members knew their own hometowns. I also suspected that he had his own well-developed network of informants. His choices of ambush sites were too productive just to be lucky guesses.

When I told him about my experience he said, "Yeah, sure. I check it out, Trung Uy." Then, frowning, "That not a good place for you to be. You need stay away from there," he cautioned.

Less than a week later, after an ambush near the site of my bike ride, Giao and his unit returned with the bodies of four VC. Were they four of the men I encountered? I'll never know.

Weeks passed before I said anything to anyone else about the incident on the trail, other than to my interpreter, who found the story extremely amusing. I didn't want Major Lee to find out and was afraid that everyone else would think I was just dog stupid, although a dog would likely have been smart enough to avoid a dangerous situation. Ironically enough, after sharing a few bottles of beer with him one Saturday afternoon, Major Lee would be the only other person to whom I ever told the story. His response, "Goddamn it, Ross! Don't do that again! I don't want to have to write a letter to your family."

While he was appropriately firm, Lee wasn't as angry as I had expected him to be. In fact, I thought he was as amused by the tale as the interpreter had been—maybe because of the beer. Whatever the case, he never mentioned the incident again and neither did I. While I continued to take motorcycle rides, I never went that far away again.

✦ ✦ ✦

The luminous dial on my watch indicated that first light was imminent. Recollection of the episode with the men on the trail, which even I found amusing, had only briefly distracted me from my growing anguish. As every other time that night, I was forced to return to the present and to face a reality that was in no way amusing. Sleep wasn't possible, so I decided to get up and wait out what was left of the night.

The radio room shift had changed and Miller's replacement, Sergeant Jean Lavaud, was on duty when I walked in to look at the map one more time.

"Good morning," I said.

"Good morning, LT. That was sure one heck of a scramble last night, wasn't it?"

"It sure was. I just hope I didn't scramble the village. You haven't heard from Walt Three Zero yet, have you?"

"No, sir, not yet."

"Okay, I'm going outside. Come get me when he calls."

"Will do, sir."

Outside, I found the post that had supported me in my distress earlier in the night. Leaning against it once more, I watched for the first glimmer of morning. On the eastern horizon, sky met ground with a faint, thin, gold glow. As the light along the horizon widened and grew brighter, I wondered how really bright the morning would be for me. With my friend's life spared, I felt the sky should have been ablaze and the morning a glorious one. Instead, that morning dawned with me leaning against a post, waiting anxiously to find out how much damage I had done.

My God, how will I ever explain this to my family and friends back home? I thought. I was deeply troubled over the possibility of actually having to tell them I had been involved in killing innocent people.

What will I say? What will I tell them? And, Dear God, how can I tell my mother I killed children. I didn't know, but just the thought was horrifying and physically upsetting. If true, the incident would haunt me forever.

Finally, Sergeant Lavaud called to me.

"Lieutenant Ross, Walt Three Zero just called to say he was airborne."

I went to the radio room where it had all started the night before and made a call to Colonel Baer.

"Walt Three Zero, this is Bunkhouse Zero Two. Over."

"Roger, Zero Two. This is Walt Three Zero. How are ya this morning?"

"Tired. Where are you?"

I made no attempt to hide my anxiousness.

Sensing the importance of his report, Colonel Baer gave me his location and began to narrate his flight for me.

"I'm close, Zero Two. I'm only about five klicks (kilometers) east of the village now. I'll tell you what I see."

"Roger, thank you, Three Zero."

There was a short pause as he approached the ambush site and then turned north toward the village.

"Well, I'm headed toward the village and can see where the artillery rounds probably impacted first. I'll follow them in."

There was another pause that was uncomfortably. Then he was back again.

"Zero Two, I'm coming up on the village now. We'll know in a minute."

Then, he started to count slowly, "One . . . two . . . three . . . four."

He was counting the impact craters created by the artillery rounds. There was another long pause that made brief seconds seem like long minutes. My insides turned, churned, and twisted in anticipation of his pending observation.

Then, finally, the torment of waiting for a report ended.

"Zero Two, Walt Three Zero reports NO . . . I repeat, NO friendly damage. Over."

You could tell in his voice that Colonel Baer was as glad to make his report as I was to hear it.

While this moment may have been as close as I ever came to tears while in Vietnam, my response was brief and unemotional.

"Roger, Walt Three Zero . . . understand, no damage."

I put the handset down and didn't move for a minute so I could let Colonel Baer's report echo around inside my head. Then, I turned my head slowly and smiled at Lavaud, who was sitting at his station next to the radios. He met my smile with one of his own and two thumbs up.

My outward response to Walt Three Zero's report was subdued, but my inner response was more dramatic. I felt my spirit soar, as though it had burst out through the top of my head and up through the ceiling of the radio room. A feeling of incredible relief poured over my body like a hot refreshing shower, a feeling of genuine redemption and peace.

After several minutes, I reached out and picked up the handset to thank Walt Three Zero.

"Walt Three Zero, this is Zero Two. Over."

"Roger, Zero Two. Go ahead."

"Roger, Walt Three Zero. Thank you for your report and thank you for getting out so early to make it. Over."

"No problem, Zero Two. I didn't think you would get much sleep last night."

"Well, you're right about that. Not a wink."

"Ahhh, Zero Two, wait one . . . okay, now I know what I saw last night. Yea, that's it. Zero Two, there's a flare chute hung up in the trees, right smack in the center of the housing cluster. It must have started a fire down there."

"Roger, Walt Three Zero. I was sure you had seen something. Over."

"Roger, Zero Two. I'm sorry I called it wrong last night."

"Forget it. You were reporting what you saw. Believe me, I'm glad you were wrong. You made it right this morning. Over."

"That's a roger, Zero Two. I'm glad I could. Walt Three Zero is returning to base. Out."

I placed the handset down on the countertop and pushed it over to Lavaud.

"Sergeant Lavaud, I'm going outside to enjoy the sunrise."

"Enjoy it, LT. It looks like it's going to be a nice one."

"Sergeant, I can guarantee it."

Just about the time I stepped outside, the trucks began to arrive bringing back to camp the reinforcements and the ambush team. I walked along the column as it rolled in, looking for Bill inside the front and back of each truck. Finally, near the back of the column, there he was, sitting in the passenger's side of one of the trucks.

We made eye contact as I crossed in front of the truck to his side. I jumped up on the running board of the truck as it rolled to a slow stop.

"Have a rough night, did ya?" I asked with a half grin on my face.

As my grin grew bigger, he started shaking his head and hesitated only momentarily before responding. "Yes, I damn sure did! And I don't ever want another one like it, thank you."

With that, he pushed me off the side of the truck as he opened his door. Then, bouncing down from the truck, he looked me eye to eye.

"I thought it was all over," he said.

"It is now," I said, and added, "It's good to see you."

"It's good to see you too," he responded as he put his hand out and we shook hands. A great deal was communicated in that handshake. Nothing more was said, or needed to be said.

The terrible experience Bill had been through showed on his face. I suggested that he go clean up and get some sleep. He nodded his head in agreement, picked up his gear, and headed for the teamhouse. Turning, I continued down the column past the last of the trucks.

With my friend back in camp and the village intact, I could now savor the new morning and the glistening sunrise. There was no doubt in my mind that the joy found in this day was owed to artillerymen whose faces might never be seen, but whose presence was known and felt in the power and protection they had dispatched with surgical precision. Deeply grateful to them for the difference they made in the events of the past eight hours, I took a deep breath to fill my lungs with the fresh morning air, took one last look at the sun as it continued to rise over the east wall, then went to get some much-needed sleep of my own.

CHAPTER 7

Are We Who We Were?

THE THIN, HOT STRIP of light made it feel as though a laser beam had pierced the bamboo blinds and was cutting its way through my eyelids as I tried to sleep. Rolling over in my bed deflected the beam of sunlight away from my eyes, but not away from the wall. With one eye opened, I lay and watched the thin line of light move, almost imperceptibly, down the wall toward the floor. The sun was getting higher and the hour was growing later. There would be no more sleep, and I had a lot to do that day anyway.

I had been on ambush the night before with a visiting observer from the British Embassy in Saigon, Lieutenant Colonel Peter Varnwell. Fifth Group Headquarters had sent him to A-502 early the day before. He had arrived with instructions that he was to be briefed on past, current, and future operations. We were also instructed to extend him every courtesy and show him whatever he wanted to see.

The responsibility of escorting Colonel Varnwell was passed to me, and I was very glad for the assignment. The colonel, who had arrived in his tiger fatigues ready for business, was a very pleasant man who displayed a lively interest in everything he was shown.

The day began with a tour of Trung Dung and introduction to several of our team members. Next we went on an air observation mission so he could see the extent of our area of operation.

After lunch, we went to My Loc, our westernmost outpost, a very small camp manned by only three or four U.S. advisors and less than a company of Vietnamese troops. Referred to as the Rock Pile by team members, My Loc was strategically located on a small hill that wasn't much more than a pile of rocks. However, a commanding view of the western approach to the Nha Trang valley made it valuable real estate.

First Lieutenant Bob Ochsner, the senior American advisor at My Loc, briefed Colonel Varnwell on the outpost's mission. Bob, who had become a friend, had also been one of the tactical officers (staff officer) for my OCS company at Fort Benning. While his assignment in Vietnam was quite different from his Stateside training role, Bob's briefing was typically professional as he explained the remote outpost's key role of providing early warning for Trung Dung and Nha Trang.

When we left My Loc, Colonel Varnwell observed that the men who manned this outpost were "extremely vulnerable and dangerously in the middle of nowhere." His observation was an accurate one. My Loc was miles west of Trung Dung; beyond it was virtually nothing but uninhabited villages, flatland, and jungle. The only other thing out there was the enemy, who used the area as an infiltration route and who could easily approach undetected to within meters of the tiny outpost. Then, with similar ease, they could overrun the hill or shell it with mortars, which they did from time to time. I often wondered how Bob and his men were able to sleep. The truth was that they didn't sleep much, and when they did it was on a rotation basis. The rest of their time was spent reinforcing the hill's defensive positions to give themselves a fighting chance to survive a major attack.

Within days of our visit, the small team at My Loc would become engaged in a heavy firefight not to defend themselves, but to assist and protect others.

By late afternoon, Colonel Varnwell and I had developed a friendly relationship. I enjoyed answering his many stimulating, and sometimes probing questions. We had been told that he would only be with us for the day, so I was disappointed to know he would be leaving soon. However, on the way back from My Loc he decided to change his schedule and asked if he could stay the night. He said that he would very much like to go on one of the ambushes we had described to him.

I was concerned about his safety, but we had been told to show him every courtesy. While going on an ambush wasn't my idea of extending a courtesy, I told him that if that were his desire we would certainly accommodate him.

After an early dinner, the colonel was outfitted for ambush. Just before we left for the site, he produced a large red handkerchief that he tied around his neck. He said he didn't want us to lose him or shoot him.

Our ambush was uneventful, but one of the other units near the base of the Dong Bo Mountains made contact with an enemy element in the vicinity of my earlier motorcycle incident. A firefight ensued, and the battle filled the radio with chatter and the night sky with illumination flares. We prepared to move and reinforce the unit. Colonel Varnwell was eager to get into the fray, but just as we started to move out, the unit advisor called to say that the enemy had disengaged and had retreated across the railroad tracks back into the mountains. Even though we hadn't been involved in any action that night, enough had happened to hold the colonel's interest.

On the walk back in from the ambush, Colonel Varnwell's questioning became more personal and more intellectually probing. He wanted to know about some of my personal opinions and concerns about the Vietnam War. By the time of his visit, I had been in-country long enough to change old opinions and form new ones. I certainly didn't have the same optimistic outlook with which I had arrived. While wanting to be honest with my new acquaintance, I reasonably candid but still guarded with my responses.

As we made our way back to Trung Dung, one of Varnwell's first questions was a global one.

"As a member of the U.S. military, how do you feel about the progress of the war?" the colonel asked.

"It is my opinion that we (the American fighting men) are in a situation that is growing more and more untenable, " I said.

"What do you mean?" he asked.

I explained my response by saying that because this war had become so extremely controversial, it was causing pain in the smallest, most patriotic hometowns in the United States. With some sadness, I told Varnwell a distressing story that my mother had shared with me in a recent letter. During a trip to her local grocery store, my mother encountered a friend who told her about her son's return from Vietnam. The young soldier arrived on the West Coast and was walking through the airport on his way to a connecting flight. About midway through the terminal, an antiwar activist walked up to him and spit on his uniform.

"It's no secret. We're losing the support of the American public," I said, "and this war will be very difficult, if not impossible, to win without them."

My expression of the challenge we faced was delivered in a tone of frustration. Many negative things had happened since arriving in Vietnam, beginning with Tet. Noting the significant events that concerned me, I shared them with the colonel.

"Certainly these things must be evident to you, even in England. Reporters in the U.S. now discuss them openly on television network news reports," I said.

The Tet Offensive, simply by its occurrence, demonstrated to the world that the VC and NVA weren't as beaten as we all had been led to believe. They obviously had the men, equipment, and will to launch well-planned surprise attacks all over South Vietnam, virtually simultaneously. That realization fueled and significantly increased antiwar sentiment in the United States. Everyone was beginning to realize the war could drag on indefinitely.

1968 was a tragic year for the United States. Tet was only the first in a number of negative historical events to cause great pain in our country. In April, Dr. Martin Luther King Jr., was killed by an assassin's bullet. I once passed within a few feet of him in Atlanta's Hartsfield Airport while traveling to a duty assignment. The recognition commanded by Dr. King's mere presence as he walked through the terminal was impressive. When we received news of the tragedy at Trung Dung, there was little doubt in my mind that his death would be a significant loss, not just for the black community who had placed so much hope in his efforts, but for our entire country. I was a little surprised by my own feelings of loss, perhaps because I had seen him and witnessed his effect on those around him. Unquestionably, he was a remarkable man.

Another assassin struck in June, killing Robert Kennedy in a hotel kitchen. News of his assassination was met at A-502 with near disbelief, a second Kennedy assassinated. I can remember one of our team members saying, "What in hell is going on back home?"

Finally, rioting took place at the Democratic Convention in Chicago. We had an old television in the teamhouse, and we were watching a reasonably clear black-and-white picture broadcast by the Armed Forces Network. I watched coverage of the convention in open disbelief as pictures of young Americans waving enemy flags appeared on the television screen.

"The United States is in a tragic state of affairs," I said to Varnwell. "We're tearing ourselves apart as a republic."

"How do you and the other men deal with it?" he asked. "It must affect your team's morale," the colonel probed.

"I'm sure they're disappointed by things happening bank in the States, but these men are well-trained professionals and deal with everything by simply doing their jobs as well as they can every day. I have come to know them very well, and what I can tell you with complete confidence is that they will fight until the day they are called home, regardless of their personal feelings about the politics of this war."

To lighten conversion and partially in jest, I asked Varnwell if the British were planning to become involved and help us with the war. In a dry British accent, he assured me that the possibility was "quite unlikely. I'm here simply as an observer," he said, quickly posing another question.

"Speaking of Tet, how do you feel about Cronkite's remarks?" he asked.

✦ ✦ ✦

He was referring to a personal commentary by Walter Cronkite that was presented in late February on his CBS television evening news program. The report was in response to his Vietnam visit, which took place shortly after the Tet Offensive. In the commentary, Cronkite, probably one of the most respected news reporters in the U.S., expressed his doubts about the worthiness of our presence in Vietnam and our ability to win the war. He said he felt we were "mired in stalemate."

✦ ✦ ✦

"As you know, there is no impenetrable wall that keeps information from reaching troops in the field. There are many ways for news to reach even the most remote areas of a combat arena. Yes, we heard about Cronkite's remarks and were disheartened by them. But, as I said, we'll be here until someone calls us home."

Colonel Varnwell's questions were thought provoking, and they gave me pause for thought over the next several days. We had spoken as officers and as professionals, and I had shared my honest, personal feelings about the war with him. While we had also discussed the ways we had seen war change men, I was reluctant to share my deepest feelings and concerns: the way I feared the war had changed me.

It was still very early in the morning when we finally reached camp. I invited Colonel Varnwell to stay for breakfast, but he said he needed to return for other visits and meetings that had been scheduled for him in Nha Trang. After arranging a ride back to the city for him, I skipped breakfast myself and sought my bunk and a couple of hours of sleep, which were just about all I had gotten before the sun's late-morning laserlike rays woke me.

✦ ✦ ✦

"Good morning, Trung Uy," Pop said when I walked out into the team room.

Pop was our Vietnamese cook. He was a small man with large skills when it came to preparing meals for the team. His culinary repertoire had been created when he learned to cook for the French while they were in Vietnam. Pop was a warm, kind, and soft-spoken man whose cooking skills were only surpassed by his caring manner and the charm of his humble demeanor. Even though he was paid as a civilian employee, Pop had adopted the team and treated all of us as if we were his own sons. In turn, the team had adopted him and cared about him as if he were a close family member.

I was still rubbing my eyes and trying to remember everything I had to do that day.

"You want some breakfast?" Pop asked.

"No, not right now, Pop. I think I'll check on something first. Thanks, though. I'll eat a little later."

"Okay, Trung Uy."

Knowing that one of our other ambushes had contact with an enemy unit the night before, I knew there might be intelligence work that needed to be done early in the day, certainly before the sun rose too much higher in the sky and the day grew really hot. I walked over to the intelligence shack to see if Sergeant Koch and Bau, one of our interpreters, were there yet. When I reached the shack, both were already at work, waiting for me.

"Do we need to go to the river?" I asked.

"Yes, they got three last night. We should go now, before the sun is on them too long," Sergeant Koch said.

"Yeah, I know. Okay, let's go ahead and go now."

✦ ✦ ✦

Whenever there was a contact in which VC were killed, common practice was for the camp's Vietnamese units to take the bodies down to the river near Dien Khanh village. There, the bodies would be lined up on the riverbank. Because many of the VC had grown up in local villages, their bodies were left along the river to be claimed by family members. Members of the camp's Vietnamese intelligence unit would be positioned somewhere along the river to make an effort to determine the family names of those claiming bodies, given that those families were also likely to be VC sympathizers and supporters. Any bodies that weren't claimed by sundown were buried.

I had been with our Vietnamese intelligence counterparts before while they searched the bodies for maps and any other information they could find. Normally, that unpleasant task was theirs, but this morning the job would be mine.

Colonel Chang, commander of the Koreans' White Horse Division, was seeking approval for an operation into the Dong Bo Mountains. He had recently sent his operations officer, Captain Lee, to asked that A-502 provide him with our most current information on any enemy activity in or near the mountains. Because the ambush the night before involved an enemy unit that had probably come from the mountains, I would personally conduct the search.

When we reached the river, the bodies were laid out on display. They had already been lying in the sun for a while, so they were bloated—blown up like huge rubber balloons. The sight, even though I had seen it too many times before, was still a disgusting one. The bodies, riddled with bullet holes, bore testament to the battle that had cost them their lives.

The skull on one of the bodies had been shattered by the impact of the killing bullet. The skin that once covered the skull, including the face, now lay on the ground like a deflated volleyball. The skull of one of the other bodies retained its form, but was cracked open like an egg, and the brain was exposed to the morning sun, which was already becoming hot. Swarms of flies were gathering while others already present were crawling in and out of the eyes, nose, ears, and mouth of the three bodies. The sight was an extremely repulsive one.

I clearly understood the purpose and the intelligence value of placing the bodies by the river. Even though we were at war, it just didn't seem right that a human body, even a foe's, should be exposed to such abuse and disrespect.

As I gazed across the morbid sight, I thought, *Well, I might as well get this over with.*

As I approached the bodies to do what needed to be done, a foul smell was already rising from the corpses. The odor grew worse as I bent down over the first body. Knowing I wouldn't be able to hold my breath for the entire time it would take to complete the search, I took only very shallow breaths, hoping to avoid the foul smell, which unfortunately didn't help much. The stench of death was much too strong.

As I began to search the dead soldier's pockets for information, the body was so bloated that the worn khaki uniform had been drawn extremely tight around it. Even in death the body resisted my intrusion. As I was going through the shirt pockets, I noticed a chain hanging around the corpse's neck. Pulling the chain out from under the man's shirt, it slid between my fingers until a medallion popped out and rested in the palm of my hand. It was a religious medal, very similar to one my grandmother had given me.

Probably Catholic, I thought.

I told a nearby guard who had been posted to keep onlookers away to make sure the medal stayed exactly where it was until the family claimed the body or until it was buried. Continuing my search, I checked the rest of the soldier's pockets, but found nothing. While checking the pockets of the next body, I found the picture of a young woman. *Girlfriend? Wife? Sister?* I wondered.

Whoever the young woman was, she didn't know what I knew at that moment: The young man who was carrying her picture wouldn't be coming home. I imagined her grief when she was given the news.

God, I thought, looking at the faded picture, *this body could easily be mine, and someone could be going through my pockets, finding pictures of my family.* Discarding the thought, I continued to search the soldier's pockets for intelligence information.

With no conception of it at the time, I realized later the great irony in those events. The army for which this soldier had fought and given his life would, in the end, be victorious. However, even with the eventual outcome of the war, on this day his death would likely result in a similar fate for still more of his comrades.

In the next pocket searched, I found a small folded piece of paper: a crudely drawn but clearly detailed map with Vietnamese writing on it. Potentially valuable, it appeared to be a map that may have guided the three soldiers to the village where they had been killed. The body searches were created to recover this type of intelligence. I put the map in my pocket in order to deliver it to the Vietnamese intelligence officers when we returned to camp.

A search of the third body revealed nothing. With the task complete, Bau, Sergeant Koch, and I headed back to Trung Dung.

During the short ride to camp, I thought about what I had just done, realizing that, as gruesome as the task was, it wasn't affecting me as intensely as it had in the beginning. In fact, such distasteful duty had become all too routine for me. After washing up and changing my clothes, I was able to sit down and eat breakfast.

As I sat at the table and ate the scrambled eggs Pop had prepared for me, I reconsidered some of Colonel Varnwell's questions regarding the war. While I had expressed opinions honestly, I hadn't even mentioned one of the thoughts that began to occupy me: my concern that many of us may have been forever changed by service in Vietnam, and not in a good way.

When we returned home, would we be the same people we were before service to our country? Surely, we were all being changed in some manner by our experiences. I was saddened to think that I might be so hardened by those experiences that a girlfriend's touch, my mother's voice, or my sister's smile might not mean as much to me as they once had.

✦ ✦ ✦

When I finally did return to the United States, I discovered something truly extraordinary. My wartime experiences had not affected me as negatively as I feared they had. On the contrary, I had a much greater appreciation for life, its beauty, and its gentle accompaniments. My father's handshake and spontaneous bear hug when he saw me for the first time, my mother's kiss on the cheek, and my sister's smile meant more to me than they ever had before, not less.

However, many of those people who served in Vietnam weren't as fortunate as I was, and they were never the same. Some of them returned with their lives, but with portions of their bodies or their essence left behind in Southeast Asia.

Because of things they saw or did, some Vietnam veterans remain saddled with immense guilt and anguish regarding their roles during the war. Others still wake up at night with cold sweats, having relived the nightmare of a wartime experience. They have each had to bear the weight and psychological pain of their burden, essentially alone.

As true as any statement that can be made about the Vietnam War is the fact that almost everyone I met in Vietnam was trying to be a good American, a good soldier—a patriot who simply wanted to serve his or her country. As time passes and their numbers thin, some of those men and women who served with honor and dedication may still be trying to be who they were before they went to Southeast Asia.

CHAPTER 8

The Beast

NOT EVERYTHING THAT HAPPENED in Vietnam was bad. Numerous opportunities were available to laugh and to find inspiration in the American spirit, even though we were all very far away from home.

✦ ✦ ✦

Over a period of several weeks, I noticed that Sergeants Mitchell Stewart and Louis Trujillo, two of A-502's team members, would disappear from the camp for hours. I also noticed that sometimes when they returned, they were covered with dust or mud, depending on the weather. Their appearance caused me to believe that they had been on a somewhat extended journey. If they had been involved in some type of military operation, I would have known about it. Even though their behavior was peculiar, I didn't say anything about it to anyone because they were both very good men. However, despite their excellent military records, I did keep an eye on them, because I knew they were up to something.

Finally, after one of their particularly long outings, my curiosity got the best of me. I caught up with them as they were walking to our motor pool. "Where have you guys been?" I asked.

Then, tauntingly, I let them know that I knew something was going on. "I know you two are up to no good. I just don't know what it is yet."

Looking at each other, both men grinned widely. I was obviously right, but the duo was only willing to offer a perfectly meaningless explanation. "We've been scouting, LT," Sergeant Stewart said.

"You're gonna like it, sir," Sergeant Trujillo added. "It's a surprise for the team."

"You don't want to know more than that, LT," Sergeant Stewart quipped.

That usually meant either that it was NCO business, something commissioned officers weren't to be concerned with, or that it was something that could get someone, possibly even everyone, into trouble. Either way, I respected their suggestion that I not become involved. But I couldn't resist asking, as I turned to walk away, "We're not going to have to come somewhere to get you two outta jail, are we?"

They both laughed and, almost simultaneously, said, "We hope not!"

After that day, I didn't pay much attention to their forays to who-knows-where, until one day when they pulled into camp with what I came to call "the Beast." They dragged it in behind a truck and claimed it was an old armored fighting vehicle that had been used by the French.

"What are you going to do with that thing?" I asked.

"We're going to fix it up and use it," Sergeant Stewart said. "We have some special things to put on it. That's where we've been going and what we've been working on."

As they began to work on their project the next day, everyone in camp became interested. Both Americans and Vietnamese would stop to watch as the two sergeants worked on the Beast, which more closely resembled a rusted-out war relic than anything that would ever see battle. It was in desperate need of serious repairs, from its tires to its hatch.

As the days rolled by, the two men worked on it in their spare time at all hours of the day and night. Often, late at night, it was not unusual to see the glow of a torch coming from inside the belly of the Beast or to see sparks flying from welding on its thick outer hide.

I remember the great excitement on the day they finally got it to run. With Sergeant Trujillo at the controls and Sergeant Stewart on the ground in front of him, Trujillo turned the ignition switch. The deep churning sound of the starter could be heard from within this huge mechanical monstrosity as it struggled to live. Then, after several seconds of trying, the Beast came to life! Belching thick black smoke, followed by a loud "Boom!" its heart began to beat as the diesel engine roared.

After Stewart and Trujillo got the Beast's engine running, they turned their attention to fine-tuning it and replacing or repairing damaged or missing pieces and parts. Their resourcefulness was amazing: If they couldn't find or repair an important part, they would make a new one. Though the focus of their pride was much larger than a watch, their work was as precise as that of a master Swiss watchmaker.

When all of the mechanical malfunctions on the Beast had been corrected, Stewart and Trujillo set in on its cosmetic appearance. When they sprayed the inside battleship gray, I suspected that one of their excursions might have taken them to the navy facility in Nha Trang. No one had any idea where they had found the paint or the air compressor they were using, and nobody was asking.

When the time came to paint the outside of the Beast, they demonstrated that they were not only excellent craftsmen, they were artists. Their pallet consisted of two or three shades of green, a reddish brown, gray, and midnight black. With their small array of paint they began creating an interesting camouflage pattern. When they were finished, the work looked as though it had been done in a California custom body shop. The Beast was beautiful!

Just before what Stewart and Trujillo called the "official unveiling," another flurry of secretive work took place. The two sergeants erected a fabric wall around the vehicle's top turret. When anyone asked, "What are you doing now?" their reply was always an elusive, "Oh, just some finishing touches."

The two sergeants had selected the day of one of our big camp formations, a formal gathering of both U.S. and Vietnamese troops during which a number of citations and medals were to be presented, as the proper time for their official unveiling. When they drove the Beast out into the camp square, it was impressive, shining as if it had just come off an assembly line.

The two men who had given the Beast a second chance to serve were dressed in crisp, freshly starched fatigues. Their green berets smartly set atop their heads, they had gone a little Hollywood with the addition of flowing ascots to their uniforms. One was in the driver's position, with only his neck and head protruding from the lower portion of the Beast. The other stood waist high in the main turret, positioned behind a .50-caliber machine gun. They were both clearly very proud of their creation. Perched on top of their fighting vehicle, they looked a great deal like proud vintage tank men. I am sure that General George S. Patton, himself a veteran of mobile tank warfare, would have been proud to have men of such ingenuity in one of his columns.

Everything on the Beast looked new, from its headlights to the auxiliary gas cans on the back deck. It even had an imitation leather-grained cover made of vinyl for the machine gun, which pointed forward. A small flap made of the same material covered a strange, small protrusion on the rear side of the turret. When one of the team members asked what the flap covered, Sergeant Stewart said somewhat mysteriously, "We'll show you . . . later."

After the formation had been dismissed, the Beast was returned to a restricted area in the motor pool. Then Major Ngoc, Major Lee, and the American advisors were invited to attend a special demonstration.

Stewart and Trujillo took turns talking about what they had done to the fully restored and improved armored vehicle. When they began describing details of work they had done on the turret, one of the men pointed out the .50-caliber machine gun. He said it had replaced a smaller-caliber gun originally installed on the vehicle.

While it was good to have an armored vehicle with a mounted .50-caliber, one might have expected more of a vehicle that resembled a tank and appeared as though it might have had a small cannon mounted on it at one time. But no one would have said or done anything to show disappointment in the Beast; the two sergeants were obviously bursting with pride in their creation. As would soon become apparent, it was a good thing that no disparaging remarks were made.

Demonstrating the ability of the electrically operated turret to rotate as smoothly as the day it was made, Sergeant Stewart quickly spun the .50-caliber to the rear. He then commented, "You may think the fifty is our main gun, and that's exactly what we want everyone to think. But, as you will see, it isn't."

Sergeant Trujillo then began unlacing the flap. When it was lifted, everyone was shocked at the sight. The two resourceful sergeants had removed the damaged cannon the French had originally installed and replaced it with an electric minigun.

With a function and design based on that of the more famous Gatling gun, the minigun fired 7.62-mm ammunition, and its rotating multiple barrels made it capable of pouring out six thousand rounds per minute. It could literally cut a tree in half.

With the Beast and its fire-breathing minigun, Stewart and Trujillo had essentially made themselves a rolling two-man army. Everyone attending their demonstration was appropriately impressed, but also very curious as to how they had acquired such a formidable piece of weaponry, because such weapons were very strictly controlled. When asked where and how they gotten it, the two men would only say they had traded for it, "the same way we got the armored vehicle." Because of the firepower of the minigun and the improved mobility the vehicle brought to the camp, no one was about to press them for a more detailed response.

The only question I never asked them, but really wondered about, is a chicken-and-egg-type query. *Did they find the armored vehicle first and need a gun for it? Or did they find the gun first and need something to put it on?* Whichever the case, they had shown impressive creativity and demonstrated typical Special Forces resourcefulness. The Beast would prove invaluable not only in defending the camp but in serving as a means of rapid reinforcement for many of our ambush locations.

The only opportunity I had to see the men and the Beast in action came on their first emergency response, which occurred late one night, only a couple of weeks after they had made the Beast operational.

Major Lee, First Lieutenant Lane, and Sergeant Major Vasquez had been on the outskirts of Nha Trang City working on a construction project at one of our outposts. When work ran longer than expected, it was sometime after dark before the three men were able to start back to camp. Recognizing the potential danger of being on the long, narrow road after dark, they were moving fast on their way back to Trung Dung when the worst happened. An explosive burst of automatic weapons fire erupted as the jeep drove into an ambush.

As soon as their urgent call for support came in, the usual alerts for reinforcements were quickly passed along. No one was ready before Stewart and Trujillo. Within minutes, the Beast was rumbling at the teamhouse door.

I had just taken off my fatigues and was standing clad only in my undershorts and T-shirt when I heard the commotion and learned what had happened. Then I saw the Beast roar up from its berth in the motor pool. I ran out and yelled for them to wait for me. Then, as fast as I could, I ran back to my room, jammed my feet in my boots, grabbed my web gear and M-16, and ran out the back door.

Climbing up over the side of the Beast, I yelled, "Go!"

With other team members hanging on for dear life, Sergeant Trujillo poured full power to the Beast, which lunged forward as we raced toward and through the camp gates. We were quickly through the arch in the Citadel's massive wall and charging down the road toward Nha Trang. In fewer than five minutes, Stewart and Trujillo had a response team well on the way to the location of the ambush.

As we roared down the road, Sergeant Stewart rolled the turret around, uncovered the minigun and prepared it for firing. It took about ten minutes to reach the location where the ambush had taken place. We found the jeep in which Lee, Lane, and Vasquez had been riding. It was sitting abandoned in the middle of the road. It was parked sideways, with its lights on and the engine still running, testifying to the quickness with which its occupants had left it. When we saw several bullet holes across the jeep's windshield, we were sure one or more of the three must have been hit. But where were they?

Those of us who were riding on the Beast jumped to the ground and fanned out on both sides of the road around the empty jeep. We called out the names of its missing occupants, hoping for a quick answer to our calls. Moving along the north side of the road, still only in my shorts, T-shirt, and boots, I glanced over at the Beast. The lights of the abandoned jeep illuminated the rumbling Beast, which sat surrounded in its own rising exhaust. The sight it created was a fearsome one. The turret of the silhouetted monster rotated in search of a target or challenge, but found neither. If the ambushers were still in the area, they were staying quiet and hidden.

In barely a minute or two, our calls to the missing trio were answered. They had taken cover near a small village hut on the south side of the road and, remarkably, all three were uninjured.

Would that have been the case had Trujillo and Stewart not arrived so quickly with reinforcements and such an imposing vehicle? If they hadn't arrived so quickly, would the three men have been pursued and killed by those who had initiated the ambush? We'll never know, but it was obvious that Lee, Lane, and Vasquez were glad the response to their call had been so swift.

The two sergeants were feeling pretty good about their response to the emergency, and they had every right to do so. When they rolled around to escort the jeep back to camp, I saw Stewart, who was in the turret, pat the Beast on its side, as if it were a loyal mount. When he yelled, "Let's go!" to his companion in the driver's position down front, the Beast once again lunged forward and headed back up the road in the direction from which it had come. The only things Trujillo and Stewart were missing at that moment were masks and silver bullets.

Knowing them, if they'd had masks, they certainly would have worn them, and they could have made silver bullets.

Clearly, the thought may sound somewhat melodramatic, but one meeting with Sergeants Mitchell Stewart and Louis Trujillo would confirm their worthiness. They were good friends and good men. Their indomitable spirit and the pride they took in doing their jobs and doing them well were characteristic not just for these men of the Green Beret, but for many others with whom I would have the good fortune to meet and serve.

CHAPTER 9

Flight into Darkness

IT WAS SHORTLY AFTER sunrise. A bright yellow Vietnamese sun had risen from the deep blue depths of the South China Sea and was pouring bright first light over Trung Dung's east wall. The warm morning air was still, and the sound of barking dogs in the surrounding village was perceptible over the background drone of the camp's one-hundred-kilowatt generator. Already up for about an hour, I had been preparing for the arrival of the combat orientation class.

With preparations complete for the COC group's presentation, I walked up to the top of the south wall and watched as the sun illuminated the tropical foliage along the far side of the moat. It contained more shades of green than could be mixed on an artist's pallet. The irony of the gentle beauty that filled this war-torn country never ceased to amaze me.

While this day had started quietly enough for me, I sat atop the massive Citadel wall and knew that somewhere else in South Vietnam a fellow soldier was very likely fighting for his life. For many, when the sun rose it was not on the soft pastel colors of a tranquil village scene. Rather, it was on a battlefield where the smell of gunpowder and magnesium from burnt illumination flares still lingered, mixed with the growing stench of death—made worse as the rising sun reached and heated the bodies of both friend and foe killed during the night. For those who survived the battles, sunrise often prompted a prayer or simply a hope that they would make it through the new day and following night to the next sunrise.

✦ ✦ ✦

The combat orientation class would be arriving very soon. Our job at A-502 was to give these men every opportunity not just to make it to the next sunrise, but to make it to the end of their tour and home. Even though statistics were probably heavily weighted against everyone in this class going home alive or without serious injury, we would share every important lesson we had learned with the intention of lessening any statistical odds against them. Unaware of a looming battle with the statistics of war, I continued to watch the morning illumination of Dien Khanh village.

Before any hint of the next sunrise, members of the soon-to-arrive COC group would find themselves in a fight for their lives. Ironically, a lesson I learned only days after my arrival at Trung Dung would encourage a daring helicopter crew to launch a midnight mission to save one of those lives.

✦ ✦ ✦

The lesson learned months earlier would lead to an encounter with a group of aviators once referred to as "God's Own Lunatics." The long-past day began with an intelligence briefing from my S2 sergeant, SFC (Sergeant First Class) Paul Koch. It was only my third day at Trung Dung, and we were in the S2 office where he was reviewing maps and pointing out suspected enemy locations. As Sergeant Koch reviewed the maps, I found the notion extraordinary that A-502 was responsible for such a vast and heavily populated area.

Because of our large TAOR (Team Area of Responsibility) and TAOI (Team Area of Influence), 502's normal staffing had been increased to give it greater capabilities in the achievement of its various missions. Much of the increased staffing in 1968 had occurred because of requests in each of Major Lee's monthly reports to Fifth Group Headquarters. As a result of those repeated requests, my position of S2/S3 (Intelligence/Operations) had been created to help meet Lee's needs. Sergeant Koch was doing his best to break me in quickly to the S2 portion of my assignment and was teaching me some of the many things I needed to know, but I was about to learn a great deal more.

Special Forces soldiers, as well as those in every other special operations unit in the U.S. military, are trained to expect the unexpected and to learn from it when it occurs. This philosophy is not unlike one first taught to me as a youth by the Boy Scouts of America. The simple philosophy, which had been carried into adulthood and amplified by Special Forces training, was embodied in the scout motto of "Be Prepared!" Within the hour, I would be reminded of the importance of that motto.

A failure to prepare was about to result in a major flap over a combat assault mission gone awry and consequently aborted. Major Lee would involve me in the mission as an observer and, as such, I would only be dusted with fallout from the incident. Despite its failure, the mission afforded me the opportunity to learn a great deal very early in my tour. What I learned would prepare me for the many challenges ahead, particularly the COC group's visit.

Sergeant Koch, a mild-mannered man who had soft features and wore glasses, looked more like an accountant than a Special Forces soldier, but he knew his job and was very committed to it. He was still familiarizing me with the maps when Major Lee stuck his head in the door. "Are you coming up to speed, Lieutenant Ross?" he asked.

"Yes, sir, I am."

"Good," he said. "There's a helicopter assault mission going out this morning to attack a suspected enemy location. I'm going as the senior U.S. advisor, and it'll be a good mission for you to begin learning our

AO. Gather your gear and meet me at the airstrip ASAP. Oh, make sure you bring a map."

"Yes, sir. I'll get my things and be right there."

Lee was waiting for me when I reached the airstrip.

"Let's go," he said as I ran toward the waiting helicopters.

The choppers were ready to go. Their blades were already spinning in anticipation of an imminent liftoff.

"I want you to ride out with us. After we're on the ground, stay on site until the insertion is complete. Then I want you to be ready to come back with the choppers to pick us up. Is that clear?"

"Yes, sir. Clear."

Lee and I jumped on the lead chopper and were almost immediately airborne.

"Watch where we're going, Ross," Lee yelled over the roar of the helicopter's engine and churning blades.

"Since I don't know how long we'll be on the ground, when we're ready to get out I don't want any screw-ups. I want to make damn sure somebody knows where to find us. You may need to come in a hurry, and I don't want to take any chances of anyone getting lost. No screw-ups! Are you with me?"

"Yes, sir, understand. We'll find you."

"Good. I don't want you to have to hunt for us, so make damn sure you know exactly where you are when we get out. I'll give you our pickup location from the drop-off point."

"I've gotcha, sir. Don't worry, we'll be there."

During our flight toward the drop-off point, Major Lee pointed out terrain features that would serve as landmarks on the way back. As he did, I marked my plastic-covered map with a grease pencil. But as the line my pencil created grew longer and we continued to fly further out over terrain that was totally unfamiliar to me, I became a little concerned about the responsibility with which I had been charged.

I had only been at 502 for two full days and barely had time to familiarize myself with the area by looking at the maps on the wall in the S2 office. I had only been away from camp during my two trips to Buddha Hill, which was in the opposite direction from where we were now headed.

What if the unit gets into trouble and we really do need to get to them quickly? Will I be able to find them? Surely the pilots will know the way back, but the responsibility has been given to me. That isn't Fort Bragg or Fort Benning down there, I thought to myself.

Then it occurred to me that second-guessing myself had been left on the runway in Nha Trang only days earlier. Any doubts about my ability had to be set aside, and dependence on anyone other than myself couldn't be considered. This type of situation was exactly what Special Forces was about and exactly what its members were trained to do. So, in Lee's own words, I would have to make damn sure I knew exactly where he and the unit were dropped off.

As the flight continued in a westerly direction, I looked back occasionally to remember the route we had taken. Once again I marked my map as we passed over a distinguishing terrain feature, but then things got strange. We began snaking back and forth over one particular part of the AO. Then, when our pattern of flight became more circular, it appeared to me that something was wrong or someone was lost. I quit tracing our route on my map when lines began to intersect and the ground beneath us became familiar even to me.

When it was obvious that the drop-off point couldn't be located, Major Lee became furious.

"Take us back!" he commanded into the small microphone on the headset that he was using to communicate with the pilot. With that directive the pilot turned back to the east, and we headed toward Trung Dung.

Whoever was guiding the mission was unable to find the drop-off point. At the time, it was unclear to me who was responsible for the mix-up. However, I later learned that the problem lay with one of the Vietnamese team leaders who was to have guided the unit to the drop-off point. That man was fortunate to be riding in another helicopter. Having worked with Major Lee back at Fort Bragg, I knew he liked a precision operation, and clearly he considered this one a complete failure.

My first encounter with then-Captain Lee took place back at Fort Bragg, when he was the leader of one of my Special Forces training classes. Lee was a man of many fine qualities, but like other leaders he was short on patience and didn't like excuses. He wouldn't tell you how to do your job, but he expected it done right; if he were displeased, he wouldn't hesitate to share his dissatisfaction about whatever had occurred. Even if you didn't know him, you could look at his face and know that he was extremely displeased with circumstances. I had little doubt that the current situation upset him greatly. Lee had a scowl on his face and sat nearly motionless most of the way back to camp, moving only occasionally to shake his head in disgust. I was sure someone was going to catch the devil for this debacle.

When we stepped out of the helicopter back at camp, Lee looked at me very deliberately and issued a stern warning.

"Ross, don't ever let this happen under your direction."

His message was clear. No misunderstanding was possible.

✦ ✦ ✦

Later that afternoon, with Lee's warning in mind, I asked Sergeant Koch to request a helicopter to take me on observation missions over our AO during the next few days.

"Will do, sir," he said. "This will give you a chance to meet the 281st helicopter guys. They fly most of our support," he said.

"Yes, I know that unit," I told him. "I saw their place the other day when I arrived," remembering their "Intruders" insignia at the Nha Trang Air Base.

Starting that afternoon, a ship from the 281st AHC (Attack Helicopter Company) began flying me over villages, jungle, rice paddies, and flatland, through river valleys and around and over mountains. After spending so much time being flown east, west, north, and south in the UH-1 (Huey) helicopter with the call sign "Rat Pack," I started to feel a part of the pack myself. The pilots were extremely patient and perfectly willing to take me anywhere I wanted to go. Because of their total willingness to help, by the end of the third day of flying I knew every river, hill, and valley in our AO. My hope was that all the time and effort, not to mention my bouts with airsickness, would one day prove their value. Little did I know that day had just dawned.

✦ ✦ ✦

With the COC group expected through the gate at any minute, I walked down off the wall and went to gather my presentation notes. As 502's S2/S3, one of my jobs was to plan and coordinate missions for the COC individuals, Special Forces personnel who were new arrivals to Vietnam. Fifth Group Headquarters had instituted the combat training program known as the combat orientation class. It was designed to familiarize incoming Special Forces soldiers with the country before they were assigned to an established unit. Simply put, the class gave them the opportunity to become acclimated to the war. Because Tet had interrupted training, my own class was given informally in two nights on Buddha Hill.

After completing the basic course in Nha Trang, the new troops were sent out in trucks from headquarters and would generally spend three days working out of Trung Dung. After an in-camp orientation, the troops were given a combat assignment and mission with a combat patrol, ambush, or combination of each. A South Vietnamese unit and seasoned A-502 team members would accompany each of the units.

While presenting the COC briefing had become routine for me, the importance of its purpose and message was always critical. The class had been created to give every Special Forces soldier the best chance possible to return home alive. As this class began it was no different, but before ending it would become unlike any other. What was yet to happen had never happened before.

"They're here, LT," Sergeant Koch shouted from the quadrangle in the center of the camp. "They just came through the gate."

"On my way," I replied, gathering my presentation material.

The idea of a combat familiarization period was an excellent one. As I had discovered, Vietnam was very different from training sites back in the States. Besides being a real war zone, the country had its own distinct sights, sounds, and smells. The three days that the new men spent at Trung Dung allowed a brief period of adjustment. They were able to work with other men who were already adapted to the Vietnam arena. They were also given the opportunity to experience some of the new and unfamiliar things they had only been told about before they would be thrust into their various demanding Special Forces roles.

Before each of the out-of-camp orientation missions, I would present a briefing. It was usually a standard military operations briefing, along with some do's and don'ts for the new men. Then one of the advisors accompanying the group would provide specific details about the mission. A question-and-answer session normally closed the in-camp portion of the orientation. Of all the groups that passed through Trung Dung in all my time there, one group and one individual were to forever stand out in my mind. That group and that individual had just arrived.

As with previous groups, the members of this one were milling around outside in the briefing area after arriving. Some of the men were standing and some sitting when I stepped in front of them to introduce myself. While the program had a formal outline and provided critically important information, my greeting was warm and informal, as was the briefing. The briefing was presented as if I was sharing important information with someone I already knew. This briefing wasn't one where anyone needed to be bored or put to sleep.

If we needed to stop and talk about something during the presentation, we stopped and talked. I had many questions of my own upon arriving in Vietnam, and I wanted every one of these men to leave

Trung Dung feeling his own questions had been answered. I personally wanted every chance to make it back home to the southern
United States, and I knew our job was to give these men every chance
also to make it back to wherever they called home.

As with every other group briefed, I found myself looking at their
faces and into their eyes. Often, I wondered what had brought them
to Vietnam.

During the briefing, our primary role as Special Forces advisors
was always emphasized—we were there to advise. The group was
reminded that we were not sent to Vietnam to perform John
Wayne–type heroics. Despite the courageous nature of these men and
even though courageous deeds frequently occurred out of necessity,
being heroes wasn't in the job description. We were to provide our
military expertise, instruction, and guidance on the use of various
types of weapons, tactics, equipment, and so on.

Because this group's first mission was a night ambush in an area
where recent enemy activity had been reported, particular points were
stressed. Even though thoroughly taught back at Bragg, one piece of
information emphasized was the importance of the manner in which
a night ambush was initiated.

"We know that all of you are aware of this, but it's important enough
to be restated since your mission will be a night ambush. If you are the
first to see an enemy unit approaching tonight, pass the word so the
ambush can be triggered simultaneously along the line," I said. "You
should not individually initiate the ambush unless absolutely necessary.
Only open fire if you have no choice. If they surprise you and are on
top of you . . . of course, take 'em out! Otherwise, hold your fire."

There was little doubt that each of these men knew the obvious reason for not being the first to open fire at night. When fired, a weapon
causes a muzzle flash, a conspicuous and easily seen flash of fire. At
night, a muzzle flash is highly visible, equivalent to setting up a target
directly in front of your body and indicating your exact location to
incoming enemy soldiers.

The point was an important one to make for the new men on their first tour of duty, so it was emphasized.

"So, remember, whatever else you do tonight, don't be the first to open fire unless absolutely necessary to protect yourself or your unit. By waiting less than a second or so, you give yourself the chance to go home in twelve months."

Generally, the group grew very quiet after that line and appeared thoughtful.

Typically at this point, one or both of the accompanying A-502 advisors were introduced to the group. Today, it was Lieutenant Bill Phalen. He was the Dien Khanh team leader, and two members of his Blue Bandit unit were going with the COC group. Bill knew both the area and the type of operation very well, so he presented the field portion of the briefing.

When Bill's briefing was complete and after every question had been answered, time came to prepare for the group's ambush mission. During the preparation and organizing of equipment, I had a chance to visit with several of the men. One officer, a young first lieutenant like myself, was also from the South. Dale Reich was warm and very friendly, with bright red hair. He said he was from Atlanta. As we talked I learned he had attended the University of the South in Sewanee, Tennessee. After graduating from college and entering the service, he volunteered for Special Forces and, like so many others, duty in Vietnam.

While Reich applied black and green camouflage to his face and hands, we talked about what had brought us to this meeting place and even a little about our families. Dale had a wife whom he spoke about with great warmth and affection. He said she was pregnant with their first child, and he was very excited about the prospect of becoming a father.

As we continued to talk, I noticed that he appeared to enjoy camouflaging his face. Earlier, he mentioned playing football in high school and college, so maybe the camouflage rouge reminded him of game preparation and the smudge of black that many players put under their eyes to reduce glare. One thing was certain: He still had the competitive spirit of a football player waiting to get out onto the field and was anxious to get the night ambush under way.

Just before going to confirm that final ambush locations had been selected and to make sure that the Vietnamese troops were getting ready, I slapped Reich on the back and asked if he remembered everything we had discussed during the briefing.

"You got all this stuff, right?"

"Yeah, yeah," he said with a grin. "I'm ready. How long before we go?"

"About an hour."

"Are you going with us?"

"No. We use a rotation schedule, and tonight isn't my night. Two of Lieutenant Phalen's men are going with you. But, who knows? If you guys get into trouble, you may see me."

He laughed as we shook hands. I wished Reich good luck, and we agreed to visit again when he returned from the mission, not knowing that our paths would, in fact, cross again later that night.

When the group was ready, everyone went through an equipment check. Phalen's Blue Bandit team members then directed the men onto trucks that would take them to a drop-off point near the ambush site. As the trucks started pulling out, I gave them all the thumbs-up sign as they passed. Many smiled or waved and returned the positive gesture.

Another great group of guys, I thought as they disappeared into a huge ball of boiling dust stirred up by the trucks. To the man, they had all been enthusiastic and eager to assume their rolls as advisors. Some were even returning for a second tour.

When they reached the drop-off point, the group would leave the trucks behind and walk to the ambush site. As usual, their ambush location, along with others out that night, would be plotted on the map in our radio room after they were in position. We plotted ambush locations on the map so that we knew where everyone was located. In the event that an enemy unit did walk into one of the ambushes and they became engaged in a firefight, we could support the unit with illumination, mortars, or artillery, or could send help in the form of reinforcements or air support.

On my way to bed at about 11:00 that night, I checked in the radio room to see what was happening. SPC4 James Miller was on night duty, sitting in his familiar surroundings where he was so capable. He was chewing gum and reading a book when I walked into the small room that was only about five feet by ten feet.

"How's it going, Miller? Any action?"

"No, sir. It's all quiet on the western front. Sergeant Bardsley and Sergeant Key are out on ambush tonight. I heard Sergeant Bardsley on the radio asking somebody where he was, but that's about it. Really, it's a pretty boring night, sir."

"Good. Let's hope it stays that way. I'm really tired. Okay, I'll see ya in the morning."

"Sleep well, LT."

My visit to the radio room hadn't given Miller or me any reason to expect that his boring shift or my sound sleep would be shattered in less than two hours. With no inkling of what was to come, I left the radio room and headed for my bunk.

After getting into bed, I fell right to sleep. Then, just before one in the morning, with little more than an hour of sleep, Miller exploded into my room.

"Lieutenant Ross! Lieutenant Ross! The new guys are in contact!"

His words meant that their ambush had been successful, and they were in a firefight with an enemy unit.

"Okay, okay! Let's go!"

I jumped out of bed and made my way toward the radio room, still half asleep.

"Any casualties?" I asked.

"I don't know, sir. It just started, but it sounds like a big one. I do know My Loc is firing mortars and illumination for them."

"Good!"

My Loc was just north of where the unit had set up the ambush.

I grabbed the radio handset and called the unit. It took two or three calls to them before any response was heard, which likely meant that they were in a serious fight and had no time to talk.

"We'll wait for them," I said to Miller. "They'll call when they need us."

Then we just stood helplessly and looked at the X and coordinates written on our wall map that represented the unit's location.

It seemed like ten minutes, but less than a minute had passed when we received the next transmission from one of our advisors with the unit.

"Bunkhouse, Bunkhouse, this is Blue Bandit, Blue Bandit! Over!"

Heavy gunfire could be heard in the background as the unit's radioman made his urgent call.

"Roger, Blue Bandit. This is Bunkhouse. Go ahead. Over," I immediately answered.

"Bunkhouse, this Blue Bandit! We're in heavy contact! Over!"

"Roger, Roger, Blue Bandit. Understand! Can you give us a Sit Rep? Over."

A Sit Rep is a situation report that would tell us what had happened as well as what was happening now with the unit in contact. Once we had the Sit Rep, we would know what alternatives existed with regard to providing support.

"Bunkhouse, this Blue Bandit! We've ambushed a major unit! Fire is coming in from everywhere! Over!"

"Roger, Blue Bandit. Are you still at your set-up coordinates? Over."

"Roger, Bunkhouse! We haven't moved! Over!" Each of his communications was urgent, with the sound of gunfire and exploding munitions in the background.

"How far out is the enemy? Over," I asked.

"Damn close! Inside thirty yards!" came the reply.

✦ ✦ ✦

Later, we would discover that the point element of the enemy unit had been much closer than thirty yards and seemingly popped up from nowhere. The group following the point unit was now firing and advancing! Intelligence gathered later would also confirm that they faced no ragtag unit. Two of the enemy KIA (killed in action) were high-ranking officials from a local VC unit. They were dressed in black pajamas and were leading an NVA unit through the area. The NVA unit was suspected to be from a small base several kilometers west of the ambush site, a base that we would later visit.

✦ ✦ ✦

"Roger, Blue Bandit. Understand. Reinforcements are getting ready and will be on standby. The ROK's artillery battery is being alerted for a possible fire mission. Over." I wanted to reassure the unit that reinforcements were getting ready if needed and to let them know artillery support was available immediately. The Koreans were just on the north side of the river and had once occupied My Loc outpost. They knew it well and could quickly bring their artillery pieces into action.

"Blue Bandit, Bunkhouse. Do you have casualties? Over."

"Bunkhouse, this is Blue Bandit! Standby one!"

"Roger, Blue Bandit. Bunkhouse is standing by. Out."

✦ ✦ ✦

The first moments in a combat firefight can be absolutely chaotic. It would be difficult enough for the unit in contact to determine what was happening around them if only one army was involved. In this case, there were two: our American COC orientation group and our Vietnamese troops, both firing on the VC/NVA unit they had ambushed.

Both of the units involved in this firefight were communicating information back to their respective radio rooms. We were talking to our Trung Dung advisors with the COC unit while the Vietnamese radio room, only about twenty-five yards away, was communicating with their unit. Information gathered from both radio rooms would be used to coordinate an overall support plan.

In the case of our current situation, while we were on standby waiting for Blue Bandit to respond with information on casualties, we were receiving confirmation from the Vietnamese radio room that their Vietnamese troops at My Loc were firing heavy mortar rounds on enemy positions.

✦ ✦ ✦

Then came news we didn't want to hear.

"Bunkhouse, Bunkhouse, this is Blue Bandit, Blue Bandit! Over!"

The sound of heavy gunfire and exploding mortar and artillery rounds continued in the background every time Blue Bandit called or answered. It sounded as if it must be an extremely fierce battle.

"Roger, Blue Bandit. This is Bunkhouse. Go ahead. Over."

"Bunkhouse, it's crazy out here! We know we have men down, but we don't know how many or their condition! Over!"

"Roger, Blue Bandit. Understand. We've just been told that My Loc is firing mortars. So, you should feel some relief soon. Over."

"Roger, Bunkhouse! I can hear them hitting now! Over!"

"Roger, Blue Bandit. We have alerted reinforcements and they will be ready soon if you need them. Over."

"Roger, Bunkhouse! Understand! Blue Bandit, out!"

From the urgency in our team member's voice and the reverberations of the battle in the background, the COC group members were obviously in a fight for their lives.

With loud sounds in the radio room and the roar of the trucks pulling up in case reinforcements were needed, everyone in the teamhouse was now awake. A few had gathered around the radio room to listen, while others were gearing up for the potential call to reinforce.

After a few minutes, we received a calmer, but still urgent call.

"Bunkhouse, Bunkhouse, this is Blue Bandit, Blue Bandit. Over."

"Roger, Blue Bandit. Go ahead."

"Roger, Bunkhouse. It's settled down a little out here. The Rock Pile [My Loc's call sign] mortars have had some effect, so the incoming is only sporadic now. I've got a casualty report for you. Over."

"Roger, go. Over."

"This is Blue Bandit. We have at least three Vietnamese WIA (wounded in action), and one American KIA. Over."

The radio room fell silent with the news of a KIA. Everyone in and near the radio room was stunned.

My God, I thought, *we've lost an American.*

If true, this would have been the first American killed out of Trung Dung since I arrived, and no one in a COC group had ever been killed while at A-502. The thought sickened me. It was a truly nauseating experience that was felt in the pit of my stomach. I looked at Miller, who had a grim expression on his face and was shaking his head mournfully. He and everyone else who was gathered around the radio room appeared shocked.

After hesitating for a moment or two in disbelief, I gathered my thoughts.

Wait a minute, I thought.

I remembered that the medic with the unit was one of the new men. Once again pushing the "press to talk" switch on the radio handset, I placed a call to Blue Bandit.

"Blue Bandit, this is Bunkhouse. Over."

"Roger, Bunkhouse. I'm here. Over."

"Blue Bandit, do something for me. Your medic is one of the new guys. Have him go back and check the man reported KIA. Have the medic make sure he's KIA. Over."

"Roger, Bunkhouse. Will do. Out."

My hope was that perhaps in all the chaos of the thunderous gunfire and impacting mortar rounds, a terrible mistake might have been made. Under the circumstances, the new medic could have been wrong unless the wounds were catastrophic. We didn't know who the downed man was and didn't care. But if he was still alive, none of us wanted him out there on the ground with what might be the last of his life dripping into foreign soil.

A few minutes later, we received a reply.

"Bunkhouse, this is Blue Bandit. Over."

"Go, Blue Bandit."

"Bunkhouse, the medic says he's gone. Over."

The downed man would have been only the third American lost out of A-502 since the team was formed in 1964. Standing motionless there in the radio room, I thought for a moment about what I had just been told and what my response would be.

Then, speaking in a monotone from an almost statuelike position, I gave a direction to Miller.

"Get the Dust Off frequency on the other radio."

Dust Off was the call sign for the helicopter medical evacuation unit. They were the ambulances in Vietnam.

"LT, they won't come. Our unit is still in contact. When a unit is in contact, they aren't allowed to make a pickup."

Miller had been in-country longer than I had, and I was sure he knew what he was talking about. But the effort needed to be made.

"Go ahead and get the frequency. Let's talk to them and see what they say. If that guy is still alive out there he needs to be picked up *now*. He may be dead, but they're going to have to prove it to us."

"Yes, sir."

Miller adjusted the frequency on the radio and began calling.

"Dust Off, Dust Off, this is Bunkhouse, Bunkhouse. Over."

Almost immediately, Miller had a response.

"Roger, Bunkhouse. This is Dust Off. Go ahead."

"Good luck, LT," Miller said as he gave me the handset.

"Roger, Dust Off. This is Bunkhouse Zero Two. We've got at least four men down, and one of them is an American. We need a pickup ASAP. Over."

Bunkhouse was our team call sign, and Zero Two was my individual call sign, the Zero Two identifying me as A-502's S2 officer. So, the Dust Off radioman knew he was talking to an officer.

"Roger, Zero Two. Understand you need a pickup. Is your unit still in contact? Over," the radioman asked.

"Roger, it is." I wasn't going to lie to them, although I was pretty much prepared to do whatever it would take to get them flying.

"Okay, Zero Two. I am alerting a crew right now. Call me back when your unit is no longer in contact and they'll take off. Over."

"Roger, Dust Off. But one of these guys will be dead by then. He may be dead now."

"Roger. I understand, Zero Two, and I'm sorry, but we're not permitted to go in if the unit is still in contact. Our crew is getting ready right now. They're firing their ship up and will be prepared to launch as soon as contact is broken. We'll get your men out. Over."

Clearly the man on the other end of the radio wanted to help, but he was simply following his unit's procedure. Even so, I felt somebody had to do something, and we didn't feel we could wait for the contact to end. So, I tried again.

"Dust Off, this is Zero Two. Over."

"Go ahead, Zero Two. You've got me. Over."

"Roger, Dust Off. What if we have our man carried out, far enough away from the contact site for your crew to be safe? Will they go? Over."

"Zero Two, Dust Off. There are still other problems, Zero Two. We'd send them now, but it's dark out there and things get scrambled during a contact. Our crew might fly into an ambush themselves. We could lose our chopper and crew if we're not sure exactly where to sit down. Over."

I was quiet for a minute or two and then it occurred to me: *Now is when Major Lee's warning and the days spent flying back and forth over the AO will be put to good use.*

"Dust Off, Zero Two. I know exactly where they are. Your chopper will have to fly right over our camp to make the pickup. Your crew could stop and pick me up. Will your crew go if I go as a guide and show them the way? Over."

Now the quiet shifted to the other end of the radio. After a brief period of silence came the sound of a different voice on the radio.

Later, I was told that the voice heard next was that of the Dust Off pilot who was to fly the mission. He was standing near the radio and had been listening to the exchange of transmissions between his radioman and me while his copilot powered up their ship.

"Zero Two, this is Dust Off. You're sure you know exactly where your men will be for a pickup. Is that affirmative? Over."

"Roger, exactly!" I emphasized.

"Okay, Zero Two, get out on your landing pad and turn on the lights. We're coming your way."

"Roger. Thank you. I'm going out the door now. Out."

Because of the situation, the pilot and his crew were not obligated to fly the mission we requested until conditions became safe enough for them to attempt a rescue. But because another American was down and because a reasonable chance of finding him now existed, they were going to fly the mission anyway.

Just before leaving the radio room, I called Blue Bandit and told them to get their KIA and WIA ready for pickup by Dust Off and made sure they understood the need to be ready to move quickly when we arrived.

As I turned to leave, Bill Lane, the team's executive officer, who had also been roused by all the commotion, was standing at the door to the radio room.

"I'll handle the radios," he said, "and I'll coordinate the link-up if they call for reinforcements. Go get our men."

Because members of his unit were involved in the contact, Bill Phalen was standing at the radio room door fully outfitted. He was waiting to see if reinforcements were needed, but said he would run ahead of me to turn on the pad lights while I went for my gear. The helipad was located directly behind his Blue Bandit teamhouse.

When I reached the pad, Bill was standing in the center of the lighted square.

"Who do you think the KIA is?" he asked as I walked onto the pad.

"I don't know. But the odds are it's one of the new guys, and if that's the case, he's been in-country little more than a week or so. God, I hope he's hanging on."

We weren't on the pad long before we could hear the distant sound of the inbound helicopter. Then, as it was coming in over the pad, our lights illuminated the white square with the big red cross on its underbelly and nose. The whirling machine rested on the ground just long enough for me to jump aboard.

"I'm going back to the radio room. Good luck!" Bill shouted over the loud sound of the helicopter.

"Go! Thanks for the help."

With the engines still nearly at full power, the chopper quickly lifted up and returned to the pitch-black sky from which it had descended.

As we gained altitude over the camp, one of the crewmen handed me a headset. The earphones were barely positioned over my ears when the pilot began speaking.

"You want us to go west, is that correct?"

I pulled the microphone around in front of my mouth and answered, "Roger. I'm sure we'll see the illumination as soon as we gain enough altitude."

Then I quickly added, "Thank you for coming."

"Because of our flight regs [flight regulations], I couldn't order a crew to come," the pilot said, "so you've got volunteers. But I think they'll do."

"I'm sure they will," was my very sincere and grateful reply.

"What kind of terrain are we going to be landing in?" the pilot asked.

"It's all lowland rice paddy, but our guys know we're coming and they'll have the injured men on solid ground."

"Good, I don't feel like getting wet."

"That's not a problem. They're in a dry area," I responded.

"Even better," the pilot said.

It was always comforting to me to hear the humor or relaxed calm in the voices of the many helicopter crews with whom I flew, even in the some of the worst situations.

This trip would be my first flight in a helicopter at night. The only lights in the chopper were the red ones that illuminated the instrument panel. The reflected red light from the instruments gave an eerie glow to the front portion of the cabin where the pilot and copilot were located.

As quickly as we cleared the trees around Trung Dung, the illumination flares over the contact site could be seen flickering in the distance.

"Our guys are out there under those flares," I told the pilot.

"Roger, I see the flares."

After we passed over the populated villages around Trung Dung, I looked out the door toward the ground. Everything looked black, with no lights visible beneath us. With no moon that night, everything was much darker than I had expected. As we cut through the thick, humid, black sky, I strained to see landmarks below. The effort was useless. I couldn't see a thing.

Guided only by the instruments and the distant flares, the pilot and his copilot navigated confidently through what appeared to me to be more like nothingness than sky.

As we neared the contact site, the flares became brighter. We could see occasional tracer rounds streaking randomly across the ground.

Aided by the light emanating from the flares, I began to see terrain features.

"Okay," I said to the pilot. "Our unit will be located about a hundred yards out on the southeastern side of the lighted area."

"Roger," the pilot responded.

"Did you get that?" he asked his copilot.

"Roger, the friendlies are about a hundred yards out from the light on the southeast side," the copilot repeated.

At about that point, I contacted the ground unit and told them we were near and needed a LZ (landing zone) marked. The unit acknowledged our request and said they would be ready.

With everything prepared for Dust Off's arrival, the pilot began to make his approach for the pickup. The pitch of the engines changed as we started down. Then that the experience of the pilot and his crew became apparent.

"Keep an eye out for flare chutes" was the pilot's first direction to his crew as we neared the ambush site.

The parachute and canister from a burned-out flare could bring the helicopter down as quickly as enemy gunfire if they became caught in the rotor blades.

As if synchronized and practiced, the responses of "Clear right" and "Clear left" came from the each of the two door gunners.

"Damn! I still see muzzle flashes," the pilot said. "You guys keep your eyes open and report. We're gonna drop down and go in as low as we can.

"Zero Two, are there any obstacles we should be looking for?"

"Only the trees, between here and the pickup point," I said. "The land is flat except for the paddy dikes. But there's a small hill to the northwest. That's where the illumination and fire support is coming from. If you stay on this line you'll be fine."

"Roger, that's good."

Through the cockpit windows I could see trees ahead silhouetted by the familiar pinkish-orange glow of the illumination flares. Some of the trees appeared to be higher than we were. But, as we closed on each set of silhouettes, the pilot would either fly over them or around them. If the skids hit a treetop, the mission would end quickly and abruptly.

The experience was like flying through an obstacle course. The only sound aboard the chopper as it zigged and zagged toward the hastily prepared LZ was the occasional message of well-being, "Clear right" and "Clear left," from the door gunners to the pilot.

As we neared the pickup point, the two door gunners who had been searching the sky for airborne debris swung their guns forward to meet the danger, which was not far ahead.

I watched one of them as he scanned the ground for hazards. With flares as a very limited source of light, only parts of his face were visible as he moved his head. Oil forced to the surface of his skin by the heat and humidity of the night caused the visible parts of his face to shine slightly. In spite of the restricted light, I could tell he was young. The apparent lack of fear in his face was surprising. In fact, he looked as calm as the pilot did and appeared composed as he went about the responsibility of protecting his side of our helicopter. He was so focused on what he was doing that I don't think he knew he was being observed.

My own heart pounded in anticipation of what the next few minutes would bring, but as I watched the actions and listened to unexcited exchanges between the pilot and crew, I felt confident that a better flight team couldn't have been drawn. With no more air support than the two M-60 machine guns on board and uncertain ground support, these men had dared to take to a very dark night sky.

I moved to the door and looked toward our proposed landing site, which was now outlined by only four red specs created by filtered flashlights aimed in our direction. The team with the injured men was exactly where they said they would be, but with confirmation necessary the pilot radioed the unit.

"Blue Bandit, this is Dust Off in bound. Over."

"Roger, Dust Off. This is Blue Bandit. Go ahead."

"Roger, this is Dust Off. Describe your LZ. Over."

"Dust Off, we have four reds pointed right at you. Over."

"Roger. Get ready. We're coming in for your men."

With the extinction of almost all of the flares, everything suddenly became considerably darker again. Our outpost had quit firing illumination to cover our landing. So, besides the stars, the only light in the sky was the occasional flicker of a dying flare.

We had become engulfed in almost total darkness when the pilot cleared the last set of trees and began maneuvering to put the chopper down inside the area outlined by the red flashlights. At that point, the contact had substantially reduced in ferocity, but we were close now enough to the ground to still hear occasional gunfire and see intermittent tracer rounds and muzzle flashes.

As we dropped toward the ground, I wondered how the pilot could see. I couldn't see anything clearly, and he hadn't turned on any landing lights yet. The ground wasn't far beneath us because the flashlights weren't much lower than eye level. I braced for the impact that was surely coming. But within the last few feet before touchdown, the pilot turned his lights on for just an instant. Then he settled the chopper onto the narrow paddy dike as gently as if it had been high noon.

As soon as the skids touched the ground, the men from our unit immediately rushed to the chopper and began loading the wounded. As one man was being lifted up onto the chopper, the medic recognized me and shouted to be heard over the noise of the chopper's engine and blades, "This is the KIA, sir."

"Okay, I've got him," I answered, pulling him further into the chopper.

While the others were getting the rest of the wounded aboard, I knelt beside the man the medic had reported as KIA.

With my red filtered flashlight, I searched for wounds. The circular patch of red light from my flashlight skimmed over his legs, torso, and arms, and onto his face. When the red glow of light illuminated his face, I was stunned by what I saw. It was Dale Reich. His eyes were closed and his face was pale. I immediately reached for his neck to feel for a pulse.

However, upon placing my fingertips on his neck in search of the pulse I hoped could be found, I feared the medic had been correct. His body had an uncommon chill, and in spite of my hope for any sign of life, no pulse could be felt.

The medic had been watching me check Reich for pulse.

"I'm sorry, sir," he said. "I wish I could have done something for him. I wanted to give you a different report."

"I know. It wasn't your fault. I'm sure you did everything you could."

As one of the wounded was lifted onto the chopper, someone yelled, "Watch this one, LT. He's VC!"

The man appeared lifeless and obviously near death, so he didn't appear to be much of a threat, but there was something remarkable in what the men of the American COC group had done. After finding him down in the dry rice paddy bed, they carried the wounded enemy soldier to the chopper and put him on board so that he could receive medical treatment. Many others would simply have left him to die. While I could easily argue both sides of their actions, I know they did the right thing.

"That's everybody!" one of the other team members shouted, letting us know that all of the wounded had been loaded.

I passed the word to the pilot.

"That's it. We're clear to go."

"Roger, power's coming up," he responded.

With the increase in engine power came the familiar "Clear right" and "Clear left" from the door gunners to let the pilot know that once he had enough power he could lift off.

As we lifted off the paddy dike and rose above tree level, the pilot rotated the chopper and headed back in the direction from which we had approached.

With all evidence to the contrary, I clung to the hope that Reich might still be grasping to a thread of life. Pressing the radio switch on my headset, I asked the pilot to get us to the hospital as fast as he could.

"I'm going as fast as and as straight as I can. We're radioing ahead now for an emergency crew to be on the hospital pad when we arrive," he said.

The flight seemed long and slow, but when we arrived at the hospital Reich was the first one taken off. He was quickly wheeled inside on a gurney. We hurriedly began moving the other wounded off the chopper and into the emergency room.

We had just finished helping the last of the men inside when a medical corpsman walked up to me.

"Who should I speak to about the American lieutenant you brought in?"

"Me," I said.

"I'm sorry, lieutenant. He didn't make it. He was gone before we got him inside. I wish there was something we could have done."

For a moment, I said nothing and only nodded in understanding. Then I thanked him for coming out with the information and watched as he turned and went back into the hospital to help with the others. When the doors swung shut and closed behind him, I turned and walked back through the semi-darkness toward the waiting helicopter.

Only hours had passed since Lieutenant Dale Reich and I had talked. Now he was gone. He was the first American I knew who had been killed. The death of other Americans was something I expected to witness and had tried to mentally prepare for. But now it wasn't imagined; it was a reality. That night, I discovered that even though I wore a combat uniform and expected to see it, the death of a fellow American wasn't going to be something I could simply shrug off.

When I reached the Dust Off chopper, the pilot was restarting the engines so they could return to base. He knew Reich had died, as he overheard the corpsman give me the news. I walked up to his window to thank them for making the effort.

"Get in," he said. "We'll take you back out to your camp."

"Are you sure you have time?"

"Yeah. I just checked, and it seems to be quiet everywhere else tonight. It's not that far anyway. Get in."

"Okay. Thank you. I'd like to get back out there."

After we had taken off and were headed back to Trung Dung, I put the headset on and adjusted the microphone. I knew the whole crew could hear me, so I spoke to them collectively.

"I want to thank all of you for what you did tonight. I know none of you had to come."

"We tried," the pilot said. "We wanted him to make it. We believed you thought there might be a chance. That was one of the reasons we came."

The rest of the flight back to camp was silent. After we reached Trung Dung and began to settle in on the pad, I reached up to take my headset off. Just before I did, I squeezed the microphone button one last time.

"I'm really proud to have flown with you guys. Thanks for showing up."

With that, I pulled the headset off, handed it to one of the door gunners, and jumped down onto the pad. Then, walking to the pilot's window, I shook his hand and thanked him one last time.

"If you need us again," he boomed loud enough to be heard over his engines, "call. You've got our number."

"I will. You guys take care of yourselves."

Then I backed away from the chopper as it powered up for lift-off. A wave of appreciation was my final offering as the chopper rose above me and ascended back into the dark sky. It only took a minute for it to disappear in the east, where there was still no hint of the yellow morning sun that would soon be rising.

A thank-you was all I had given to the crew of the Dust Off helicopter. It seemed such an insignificant thing to say after they had risked their own lives trying to save another. Somehow, though, I suspected that was probably all they wanted or expected.

Later that morning, after the sun found its way into the sky and illuminated another day in Vietnam, we held a debriefing. While conditions were exactly as they had been on the previous day, this day didn't seem as clear or as bright. But as the debriefing unfolded, at least a clear understanding of what happened would emerge.

During a recap of events surrounding the previous night, we learned from one of the men who had been near him that Dale Reich triggered the ambush. Reich and the rest of the unit were lying in hidden positions behind a dry paddy dike where they could observe some of the many trails running through the area near My Loc. These trails were routinely used as infiltration routes for enemy units approaching from the west.

Listening to the account of events, I had to wonder about Reich's reason for being the first to fire on the enemy patrol, especially given that it was one of the things emphasized and discussed thoroughly during the pre-mission briefing.

Surely, he hadn't forgotten, I thought. Then, I wondered, *Was he so gung-ho on his first combat mission that he was compelled to ignore the cautions about the danger of being the first to fire? Or had he felt that he may have been the only person to see the approaching danger and, unable to pass the word undetected, acted to protect the men with him?*

As it turned out, and it was no surprise to me when it did, the latter was the case. According to one of the other men near Reich, no one saw the enemy until after he opened fire.

"They were just there," the man said. "They came out of the darkness near the edge of the paddy and were on top of us before we knew it. If the lieutenant hadn't opened fire, they would probably have walked right into the middle of our unit."

Then he quickly added, with passion in his voice, "He was responsible for saving many of us around him!"

Other Americans confirmed that Reich, who was lying behind the paddy dike, had evidently noticed the men in the point element when they emerged from the darkness. It is likely that no one noticed them because of the black pajamas they were wearing. This was normal attire for VC and certainly made them nearly invisible at night. With no time to warn his unit, Dale Reich did what was obviously instinctive for him: He took the lead. He immediately engaged the enemy unit with his M-16 at what was reported to be nearly point-blank range. As a result of his action, Reich instantaneously drew the wrath of the enemy response as he and members of the VC point unit exchanged fire.

Having seen his muzzle flash, the VC poured their return fire directly into Reich's position, wounding him immediately. He had taken a stand on the battlefield, just as he must have done many times on the football field as captain of his high school team. Unfortunately, this one had cost him his life. Still, his quick action and selfless act gave his COC teammates time to react and the opportunity to survive.

Alerted to the approaching danger by Reich's opening burst of fire, other COC team members and the South Vietnamese joined in the fight, which quickly grew fierce and resulted in a heavy exchange of mixed weapons fire between the opposing units.

Sergeant Bob Hines, another member of the COC class, was a tall man whose handlebar mustache gave him a swaggering vintage look. He seemed an extremely steady man who was not easily excited. On the night of the ambush, Hines was carrying an M-79 grenade launcher along with three bandoliers of grenade rounds he was given when the class members were armed for the mission. Each bandolier contained six high-explosive rounds. Testifying to the intensity of the ensuing battle, Hines emptied all three bandoliers in the first few minutes of the exchange.

In addition to Sergeant Hines and our A-502 advisors, twenty to twenty-five other Americans and a similar number of our South Vietnamese soldiers composed the friendly force. Considering the rate of fire exchanged with the enemy unit, it isn't difficult to imagine how loud the initial moments of the encounter must have been. We witnessed some of those moments back at Trung Dung when our radio speakers pounded with the sound of the battle.

Despite the ferocity of the fight, the new men of the COC group and their veteran Vietnamese troops held their ground as the battle continued. Finally, with supporting mortar fire from My Loc, artillery from the ROKs, and Spooky's illumination flares, the unit was able to cause the enemy to retreat in disarray. The new men, who became combat veterans that night, had represented themselves well. They never called for reinforcements and moved forward to sweep the entire area. While this night would offer the first combat action for most of the Americans, because of the initial advantage given to them by Lieutenant Reich, they would win the battle.

Because of Sergeant Hines's conduct throughout the encounter with the enemy unit, one of our team advisors with the group suggested to Major Lee that we recruit him for A-502. As a result, Lee called Fifth Group and Hines became an A-502 teammate. He was assigned to an open slot at our Binh Tan outpost.

Later in the day, the Vietnamese confirmed what we heard from the Americans who had been near Reich. One of the old Vietnamese sergeants told me that he was certain that he and many of his men would have been killed or wounded if the American lieutenant had not opened fire. Because the night was so dark, none of the Vietnamese had detected the VC unit until seeing their muzzle flashes when they returned fire on Reich's position.

His family and those who knew him were very likely not surprised by his selfless action. Despite the briefness of my encounter with Merrill Dale Reich Jr., I will always remember his eagerness to serve and the courage with which he faced it. Neither am I likely to forget the courage and bravery of the evacuation helicopter pilots and crew who tried to save him. Their deeds are indelibly etched in my memory.

CHAPTER 10

Powder-Blue Surprise

WHERE IS IT? The tip of my index finger traced the thin, narrowly divided elevation lines on the map.

Where is it? It has got to be big, and it has got to be right in here somewhere.

Putting another spoonful in my mouth of whatever delicious thing Pop had cooked for lunch, I continued to slide my finger slowly across the map.

The object of my search, while halfheartedly picking at my food, was an enemy base camp that was located somewhere in the now familiar Dong Bo Mountains. The mountains were located south-southeast of camp and were surrounded by flat lands on the north, west, and south, with the South China Sea on the east. While they stood majestically over the city of Nha Trang, their history was infamous. Several South Vietnamese units searching for the enemy base camp had been run out of the mountains on a number of occasions. The base camp had a long, mysterious history, and many stories were told about the small but notorious mountain range.

According to one of the stories, the French discovered the heavily fortified position during a patrol into the mountains when they occupied Vietnam. The story also spoke of artillery pieces and large numbers of troops that would emerge from well-camouflaged caves. The position had obviously existed for some time, and headquarters was pressuring us to knock it out of action.

Sergeant Koch and I spent days mapping each of the locations where other allied units had previously made contact with enemy forces. The frequency and location of those enemy encounters in one particular area suggested the Viet Cong stronghold must be somewhere nearby. They obviously were trying to protect something; why not a base camp? The area of greatest activity was along the eastern face of the mountains overlooking the entire city of Nha Trang. It would be an excellent place to construct a base camp from which activity all along the coastline could be observed—a natural. But was it? When sighted and pursued, the VC simply seemed to dissolve into the mountains. They were also able to vanish with equal ease in widely separated areas, which was an indication that tunnels and hiding places must exist throughout the mountain range.

While continuing to search the map, which was spread on the table like a Sunday newspaper, people were coming and going for lunch. I could hear others around me talking. Because we were one of the closest A-Teams to Fifth Group Headquarters, we often had visitors and provided briefings for high-ranking officials. Activity in the teamhouse at lunchtime was not unusual.

"We'll seat you here next to Lieutenant Ross," I vaguely heard someone say.

I was so engrossed in my search for the legendary enemy base camp that I didn't look up. Picking up another spoonful of perfectly cooked fried rice and moving it slowly in the general direction of my mouth, I detected a strange smell. I sniffed the rice, but it seemed fine. Putting it in my mouth, I wondered if Pop, who acquired his culinary skills from the French, had discovered some exotic new spice. The rice, with its blend of vegetables and meat, tasted fine. In fact, it tasted delicious as usual. But, as I reached for the iced tea pitcher, the aroma persisted.

Can't be, I thought, *but it smells like perfume.*

My tea glass was almost full when I finally noticed the person who had been seated at the table with me. For a moment, I was stunned and couldn't quite believe what

I was seeing.

"Your tea," my table guest said.

"What?"

"Your tea glass. It's full now."

"Oh, geez. I'm sorry," I said, quickly reaching for some napkins.

My glass had been filled and tea overflowed onto the table when I was momentarily distracted by my unexpected table guest, a beautiful young woman in a powder-blue uniform.

For a quickened heartbeat or two, my mind simply went blank as I looked at her. She had eyes that sparkled, and her hair shined like satin as it traced the gentle shape of her very pretty face.

Where has she come from, and what is she doing here? I wondered.

Shortly, I regained enough composure to speak coherently. "Hello. Welcome to A-502. Who are you, and where did you come from?" I asked.

"Well, hello, Lieutenant Ross," she said with a chuckling, bright warm smile.

"My name is Molly, and I came from the Red Cross. I wondered if you were going to speak to me."

As with too many of the people I encountered so briefly, she is but a distant memory, but I remember clearly how warmly her presence affected me—as though a little part of home had mysteriously materialized before me.

I had been in Vietnam long enough to miss the sweet fragrance and round eyes of an American woman. Then, suddenly and inexplicably, a captivating example of American womanhood sat easily within arm's reach. In her striped powder-blue uniform, she was an unexpected and very pleasant surprise. It was difficult not to reach out and touch her, just to make sure she was real.

She hadn't been there long when the old, crookedly hung kitchen door creaked open. Pop poked his head out, as he often did to make sure all was well in his tiny dining room.

When he saw we had a visitor, he hurried through the door. He smiled widely at me and wiped his hands on the apron tied snugly around his waist.

"Hello," he said, as he approached the table.

He offered a humble bow to our visitor.

"Can I bring lunch for this lady, Trung Uy?" he asked politely.

Pop's gentle manner and warm Asian features ingratiated him with the many visitors to A-502. As would every other member of the team, I would have adopted him and brought him back to the States if I thought his wife and family would let him go. Pop was more than cared for by our team; he was loved.

I looked to Molly for her response to Pop's invitation and hoped—no, I prayed, if you can pray that fast—that it would be yes. She nodded and returned Pop's warm, disarming smile.

"I would love to have lunch. Thank you for asking."

Just the sound of her silky voice made my spine tingle.

Pop disappeared back into the kitchen and quickly returned with a plate of food that he had decorated with lettuce leaves, small vegetable pieces, and a flower. I have no idea where he found the flower, but he proudly placed his creation on the table in front of our guest.

"It looks delicious, and it's beautiful. Thank you very much."

Pop's chest appeared a little more puffed as he once again disappeared into the kitchen.

My heart rate settled back to normal as we ate lunch and continued to become acquainted. We found many different things to talk and laugh about. She bubbled as she spoke and was obviously very good at what she did. We shared information about our backgrounds, interests, and families. For a while, I could have been back in the States with one of the hometown college girls.

It had become apparent during lunch that there was much more to this woman than met the eye. Not just attractive, she was intelligent and articulate, and beyond her pretty smile and delicate appearance was her unmistakable dedication to a mission.

✦ ✦ ✦

Dedication to a mission sounds like a quality you expect a soldier to possess, but as I came to know my luncheon guest—and later some of the other Red Cross volunteers who came to visit our camp—I found that they were indeed very much like soldiers.

Just as some of the men in military service, the Red Cross volunteers had been recruited out of college to serve their country. A bachelor's degree was required for service in a unique volunteer organization that was referred to only by its initials SRAO, which stood for Supplemental Recreational Activities Overseas, a title created for its members by Red Cross's Board of Governors.

The unit had first been organized for service in World War II. Its mission was to bring comfort and diversion from the monotony and tragedy of that war to the troops who had been sent to fight. The female volunteers shared news from the Unites States; organized recreational activities and games; and, when possible, they served hot coffee and pastries or other refreshments, even in forward or remote combat areas. But, among the most important things they did was to reestablish the humanity and civility of home while providing a patient ear and an understanding heart.

After World War II, SRAO was reorganized for service in Korea, and then again for Vietnam. In all three wars, simply because of their presence in combat zones, it was not unusual for their volunteers to come under enemy fire. As a result, as with soldiers in combat zones, some SRAO members died as a consequence of their decision to serve.

While their service somewhat paralleled that of their male military counterparts, at least one important difference existed between the women and the men they hoped to help. Even though they both worked together in a combat zone, the women were unarmed. Rather than weapons, they carried smiles, tenderness, compassion, and tremendous moral support to military servicemen and women in various parts of the world during extremely trying times.

✦ ✦ ✦

When we finished lunch, Molly and other SRAO members spent time visiting with surprised team members whom had come to eat. When word spread through the camp of the presence of American women, the small dining area became a bit more crowded than usual.

Later in the afternoon, I invited Molly outside to show her the camp and introduce her to some of the other men. As we walked, I asked a question I hadn't asked during lunch. "What brought you here and why did you come to Vietnam?"

"Oh, I don't know . . . lots of things, I suppose," she said.

She kicked at an old shell casing that was lying on the ground with one of her black leather shoes. It slid and bounced long in front of us.

"Probably some of the same things that brought you and the other men here, I suppose. It became very important to me that I do something to help. I didn't want to simply stay at home and watch it all happen without becoming involved in some way."

The idea that a woman would want to become involved in a war was something I had never given much thought to, but found very interesting. It wasn't a chauvinistic matter or a question of courage. My own mother was a woman who would have fought physically to protect her family, but I am reasonably certain it was the unconscionable thought of seeing a woman down and seriously injured on a battlefield that had prevented me from considering women involved at all.

After spending time with Molly and others like her, my feelings changed. I discovered that, besides courage and skill, they also had a strong devotion to duty and country. You could hear it in their voices or learn it by just being around them as they did their jobs.

Sometime after meeting Molly, I encountered another "Red Cross Girl," as they were frequently called. Her name was Ann. I posed to her a question similar to the one I asked Molly. "What was your reason for choosing service in Vietnam?"

She didn't hesitate. "A close friend joined the service and went to Vietnam as a medic. He said it was because he wanted to make a contribution. He was in the Special Forces, too."

Her tone was warm and caring as she spoke of him. "He provided primary care and gave inoculations to people who lived in outlying villages. He felt he was doing something very worthwhile," she said, then hesitated for a moment. "When I thought about what he was doing, I wasn't able to think of a reason why a woman couldn't go do something worthwhile as well. So, I started looking for ways to get to Vietnam."

It was easy to hear passion and resolution in Ann's voice as she spoke about her desire to serve. For her, there was no question about whether or not she was going. Her only dilemma was how she would get there.

Passion and resolution seemed to have been a part of every Red Cross volunteer's personal traits, because they had also been evident in Molly during her to visit Trung Dung. Something else was also noticeable about her. She appeared very comfortable and at home as we meandered around the camp, probably because she had done it so many times before. Her interest in anything we had to say seemed genuine. Every time someone showed her or told her something about A-502, even if she had heard it twice before, she acted as though she was hearing it for the first time.

Occasionally, as Molly and I continued our tour of Trung Dung, I would look down at the partially refolded map I had carried with me, then back at her. I wanted to see if she would still be there when I looked up again. And, of course, she was.

It was interesting and fun to watch the reactions of team members when we would stop to visit. The surprise I had experienced when first meeting her was also apparent in the eyes of others who were unaware that Red Cross girls existed. The most common responses after introducing her were, "Where did you find her?" or "How did she get here?" or "Where did you come from?" Each time, she would laugh in response to the question. Then she offered an explanation of her presence and warmly shared her time.

One thing was sure: When you looked into the faces gathered around her, they didn't really care where Molly had come from or how she'd arrived there. They were just glad that she made the trip.

Molly had been brought to the camp with a couple of other girls. Unfortunately, the time came far too quickly when she and the others had to leave. Back at the teamhouse, a small group of appreciative men gathered to say good-bye when the girls got into their jeeps for the return trip to Nha Trang where they were stationed.

Even though their visit had been brief, evidence that it had not been insignificant lingered for some time after they had gone. Off and on during the rest of the day and evening, someone would find a way to work mention of the girls into conversation. That went on for days, maybe longer.

◆ ◆ ◆

Such was my first encounter with the women of the Red Cross and their organization, but after that day, I had several other opportunities to learn the importance of their work.

Occasionally, when in Nha Trang for a briefing or supplies, I tried to find time to stop by the Red Cross facility. Donuts, cookies, punch, and coffee were always available in abundance. Also in abundance were the men who sought a few minutes of attention from one of the SRAO staff members.

As warm and understanding as they were, at least one thing would cause some of the girls to raise an eyebrow. Besides being called "Red Cross Girl," they were often referred to by the affectionate nickname of "Donut Dolly," which to them was not a favored one.

One of the girls, Jean, told me they only served donuts if they were available in a unit's mess hall. She said she didn't care for the name even though she knew a few of the girls thought the nickname was cute. Jean said she didn't care for it because she felt her education and efforts deserved a more responsible nickname and didn't hesitate to vocalize her discontent.

"If they're going to call us anything besides the names we have pinned on our uniforms, I wish they would just stick to 'Red Cross Girl,'" she said.

Despite the too-frequent use of the disfavored nickname or the rare sexist remark made by a serviceman who hadn't thought before making it, the SRAO volunteers went about their jobs with a remarkable attitude and spirit. Most of them were far more than the image suggested by the "Donut Dolly" nickname. Some were actually quite daring.

In addition to working out of assigned facilities in cities around Vietnam, they would also visit remote camps and firebases that were accessible only by helicopter.

Ann, the woman from whom I learned the most about Red Cross's SRAO volunteers, was one who pushed the limits of where she could go safely. On one particular occasion, her daring and dedication almost cost her life.

Only after being pressed for details, Ann shared her experience. She was on board a C-130 aircraft flying in the II Corps region of Vietnam, the same corps area where A-502 was located. She was headed toward LZ Baldy with a unit of troops. "We had just past north of An Khe when enemy gunfire began to rip through the thin metal skin of the plane," she said.

In telling her story, something else had obviously captured her attention as much as the continuing bursts of enemy ground fire that ricocheted through the C-130. "Two Second CAV (Cavalry) soldiers, who were also passengers, made their way to where I was sitting," she said.

"They wanted to know if I was okay. We had spoken earlier, so they knew that I only had two weeks left on my tour. Since I was supposed to be going home soon, they told me I was too short to be flying around out there. The concern they showed for my safety was extremely touching. It was my job to make them forget about the war, but there they were, right at my side, trying to make me forget about what was happening."

These courageous young women clearly remembered the difficult and unpleasant times. But, more vividly, they remembered the men, their faces, and how they tried to make the girls themselves comfortable during their visits. During one particular visit, Ann said she and the girls found that the troops had painted the latrine pink and hung curtains in it. "We were quite taken by their gesture and couldn't imagine where they had found pink paint," she said.

In discussing with Ann the role of the Red Cross SRAO volunteers, I found that she had strong, even mixed, feelings about her service in Vietnam, and still does. As of this writing, she continues as an active member of the American Red Cross. When talking to her about Vietnam and her memories, it becomes quite apparent how much she cared about her time in Vietnam.

"I remember how young and unworldly some of them looked. I saw them carrying puppies or holding a child by the hand. You could see the Iowa in their faces. So many were not much more than boys, yet they were doing a man's job."

Because of her current position, Ann is not only a veteran of Vietnam, but also of many other campaigns against devastating natural disasters. Being experienced in emergency situations, she spoke articulately and unemotionally about her Asian experiences until she made one particular comment.

"I just wanted to make it all go away for them, but I couldn't." Her voice cracked almost imperceptibly, but it became noticeably softer. I didn't say anything and just let her talk.

"They had such wonderful senses of humor," she said. "They made us and each other laugh. But sometimes, when they came back from a mission or a patrol, you could see it in their faces. They had been through some terrible experience."

Ann paused, and when she did, I imagined she was seeing those faces once again. Then, she continued, "I couldn't imagine what they must have gone through. There were those who wanted to talk about it and those who didn't. So, we had to be very sensitive and respect their different needs. We would sit quietly and eat cold C-Ration ham and lima beans with them in case they decided, at some point, they wanted to talk. I felt helpless and wanted to make the look in their faces and the pain go away. I wanted to make them smile again. But, I couldn't. I just couldn't."

Ann's sensitivity and understanding are typical of the Red Cross volunteers I met while serving in Vietnam. They were a part of a small, eight-hundred-member female unit, but their contribution was a selfless and very important one.

Other women served in Vietnam whose service was equally important. When you consider the female nurses and administrative specialists, and the long list of other positions filled by women who cared and who served, this brief retrospection of their contributions doesn't begin to provide the recognition they deserve.

No story of Vietnam is complete if it does not include the women who served there. Their presence often provided an understanding ear and a warm or gentle reminder of home for many soldiers. There was, however, far more to women such as these. Charles Dickens recognized that fact long ago when writing in reference to bravery, "Nature often enshrines gallant and noble hearts in weak bosoms; oftenest, God bless her, in woman's breast."

CHAPTER 11

Friendly Fire

THE SWIRLING CLOUD OF stifling dust chased us across the old wooden planked bridge until it met a warm breeze that blew down through the wide riverbed. The breeze played above the river's surface and glistening ripples traced its path toward the South China Sea. Bridge planks vibrated rhythmically as our jeep rolled over them, and the breeze offered a momentary respite from the dust that it chased into the trees at river's edge.

The warm westerly breeze felt good for the short time it lasted. It disappeared when we bounced back down onto the road on the far side of the bridge where we reentered the tree line. With the breeze gone, the dust resumed its pursuit as the tread on the tires spun and regained their grip on the hard, sun-dried dirt road.

I rotated my map when we turned and began driving west along the road on the north side of the river. We followed the road for a few kilometers until we found the location on the map outlined with a circle from my grease pencil.

"There it is," I said, pointing to our destination. "Pull in over there."

After getting out of the jeep, we moved slowly. They hadn't seen us yet, and I didn't want them to be frightened when they finally noticed our presence. Some were standing, while others ran here and there. It had been some time since any of us had seen a sight like this, so, for a while, we just stood and watched.

Then, watching as one group tried to form into a line, I locked eyes with her and knew we had been seen. With her big almond eyes, she looked almost like Bambi and every bit as delicate.

This moment can't pass without a picture of her, I thought.

Raising my camera slowly, so not to scare her, I found her in the viewfinder and focused.

She's looks very delicate, I thought as the shutter snapped and I muttered, "I got her."

"Which one?" one of the other men asked.

"The little girl over there next to the one in the sun bonnet. The one looking this way."

With our presence at the small Vietnamese elementary school detected, we walked further up into the schoolyard. Still moving slowly so none of the children would be frightened, we smiled as we made our way to the chairs that had been prepared for our visit.

The school was in the Korean AO. As a part of their community action program, they had arranged to conduct a karate demonstration for the school children. Our invitation to the school came from Captain Lee, a Korean military counterpart, with whom I had just finished exchanging operations and intelligence information. As he was preparing to leave, Lee asked if I though any of the Americans would enjoy seeing their demonstration. While we had an operation going out that afternoon and still had preparations to make, I accepted his invitation and took a couple of other team members with me.

Because of the close scrutiny we received from the children, we suspected we might be the first Americans some of them had ever seen. Our round eyes may have appeared very strange and foreign to them. Even though we smiled and tried to greet them warmly in their own language, just as children anywhere, they were reluctant to return our greetings with any enthusiasm.

We took our seats in time for the demonstration. The children sat on the ground around us. We were all entertained as the Koreans broke boards and concrete blocks with their hands, elbows, feet, and heads. The children seemed particularly amazed at the feats of the Korean karate masters and applauded enthusiastically when the demonstration ended.

As we rose from our chairs, one of the teachers who spoke fluent English walked over to us and asked, "Would you care to see our school?"

In spite of our tight schedule, I told the young teacher we would be honored to visit her school.

"Oh, wonderful," she said. "Please come this way. I would like for you to see some of the things our children have done."

When we reached the small one-story building, the young female teacher showed us through some of the classrooms. She took great pride in the students' work, which was displayed on the walls of her classroom. As I looked at the papers around the room, it came to mind that it could have been a classroom at almost any school in America. There were numbers on some papers and letters on others that formed the basis of their language, all meticulously written by her student's small hands. There were also brightly colored pictures that depicted life in and around their small village community. Drawings of rice paddies weren't likely to appear in an American child's picture, but the clouds, trees, grass, and sun all looked the same.

When our brief tour finished, we thanked the proud young teacher for showing us the school and started back across the school-yard. We smiled and waved friendly good-byes as we walked. This time, unlike when we arrived, some of our smiles and waves were returned. Those few returned tiny smiles brought an unexpected gentleness to the morning and provided a pleasant start to the day as we headed back to camp to meet our own students who would be arriving soon.

✦ ✦ ✦

We arrived back at Trung Dung just as the trucks from Nha Trang were arriving with another combat orientation course group. After we parked the jeep, I went to the assembly area to greet everyone and outline the long-range patrol we would be conducting. After the usual pre-mission operations briefing, we began final preparations and equipment checks.

When everyone was ready, we climbed on the trucks that would take us to our drop-off point and departed. The group was not unlike the one that Lieutenant Dale Reich was with when he arrived at Trung Dung. This time, I would be along on the mission and, hopefully, we wouldn't experience a tragedy similar to the one that claimed Reich's life. But because tragedy haunts the battlefield, we would find ourselves attempting to elude it in an ironic twist of war. This infrequent occurrence would demonstrate that tragedy is not alone on the field of battle. Shrouded and waiting to claim an opportunity, tragedy is joined by the courage of those who would face it.

Upon reaching our drop-off point just west of My Loc outpost, we dismounted and immediately headed further west. With approximately one platoon of about thirty-five Americans and an equal number of CIDG soldiers at five-meter intervals, our column was nearly a quarter mile in length and wound along through the lowland terrain like a long, slow-moving train.

Every patrol included new experiences. You never knew what would happen next or what might be encountered along the way, and not everything was bad. Only on the trail a short while, we passed a small heard of red deer grazing in an open field. They nibbled on the new growth of plants in an area that had been burned during a fire created by exploding artillery shells. Our point unit guided us through a maze of craters opened by the impacting shells that started the blaze.

We walked for some time, threading our way west over and around small hills, along the dikes of overgrown rice paddies, and through the abandoned villages of those who once tended the paddies. As we passed a natural or man-made feature that would serve as a landmark, it was noted on my map and became an indicator of the path back to Trung Dung.

Toward the end of day, when our shadows became long and night began to fall, we stopped and made camp. Security was set out in a 360-degree circle around our position. Shifts were established with American and Vietnamese soldiers sharing security responsibilities. My position was established near the center of the circle to make it easy to reach any point on the circumference of our perimeter with equal speed if trouble developed.

When we stopped, my feet were hot and sweating. After stringing my hammock between two trees, I sat down in it and unlaced my boots. Normally, I would not have walked around without my boots, but, because the ground was dry and fairly clear of debris, I took them off and set them under the hammock. Since it was past dinnertime and lunch had somehow been overlooked, I pulled my pack over and took out one of the freeze-dried meals. It was rice and shrimp, which was one of my favorites.

After boiling water in my canteen cup over a small can of sterno, I dumped the rice and dry shrimp in and waited for everything to puff up. Everyone had their own method of improving the military cuisine to make meals more appealing. Mine was to season it with red pepper and soy sauce. Many of the Vietnamese and some of the Americans carried small cans of sardines, which they would eat with their rice. The smelly little fish weren't for me though.

While my dinner was absorbing water, I walked over to a small tree and cut my utensils, a pair of matched chopsticks. During earlier trips to the field, I watched some of the Vietnamese fashion theirs from a small, thin tree branch and had started doing the same just as a rapport builder. When I first started trying to use chopsticks, it took several awkward attempts to develop the art, particularly with rice. My unskilled attempts to feed myself amused the Vietnamese, who took pride in demonstrating the proper use of their ethnic tableware. Eventually, eating with sticks became as easy as eating with a fork or a spoon. A knife wasn't needed because meat and fish were already cut into bite-size pieces.

After learning to use chopsticks, the only challenge involved in eating food that had been prepared by one of the camp's Vietnamese cooks was to determine exactly what type of meat the small bite-size pieces were. Fish was never difficult to identify because it had a distinctively fishy aroma. Chicken and pork were other easy ones, chicken usually tasted like chicken, and pork usually cooked to a white color. The difficulty came in separating the red meats: beef from venison, monkey, or dog.

Separate from geographic differences, U.S. soldiers often found themselves in culturally unique surroundings where customs and cuisine could be very different from home. Meats that a soldier's mom or wife wouldn't think of preparing or even consider as food were occasionally found in a Vietnamese meal. I am thoroughly convinced that, at one of the camp's Saturday get-togethers, my own dog was a part of the menu.

If it had been a particularly hard week, the Vietnamese CIDG soldiers would be rewarded with an afternoon party-type affair to which the American advisors were always invited. Along with a special meal the parties often included local entertainment. This entertainment usually took the form of twanging strings from various musical instruments and an array of Vietnamese solo or group vocalists with varying degrees of talent.

A day or two prior to one of the Saturday parties, a small dog I had adopted disappeared. The small mixed-breed and I became fast friends after he wandered into the camp early one morning. He looked hungry, so I found some left-over scraps to feed him. He ate until he looked as though he might pop. I named him Frank after a crazy but lovable uncle who had seen me off at the Seattle/Tacoma airport when I left for Vietnam. Every night after our first meeting, Frank would sleep outside the door at the end of the teamhouse where my room was located, and every morning he would bounce around and bark when he saw me look through the bamboo blinds to check on him. Frank, nothing more than a scruffy little mutt, was good company and a very pleasant reminder of our family's dog, Bingo, back home.

Because he would occasionally wander off, I didn't think too much about it when Frank wasn't outside my window one morning. But when he wasn't back by dark, that was unusual. He had never been gone overnight before. When he still wasn't back the next night, I assumed he had found his way back to wherever he had come from. I imagined him back home with his Vietnamese family in one of the nearby villages. The next day at the camp party, though, another more disturbing conclusion was considered.

As we ate and listed to the high-pitched strings and voices of the village band, one of the CIDG soldiers asked an intriguing question, "Trung Uy . . . what are you eating?"

Looking down at the things on my plate, there were vegetables and what appeared to be beef in some thick, gooey steamed rice.

"I don't know. What am I eating?" I asked, knowing that I probably shouldn't have asked the question.

"What is the meat?" the questioner persisted.

It didn't require a high IQ to assume the meat wasn't going to be what it appeared to be, given that the question had been raised.

"Beef? Cow? I don't know. What is it?" I responded apathetically.

When my guess was met with laughter, little doubt remained that, whatever it was, it wasn't beef. But since the meat was sweet and tender, exactly what it was didn't make much difference. I assumed it was probably monkey, which made it a little less appetizing. But, since it tasted good, I continued to eat.

Snake eating had once been demonstrated during a Special Forces survival exercise at Fort Bragg and I had tasted it, so I was certain this wasn't snake. While my curiosity was growing about the identity of our entree, I wasn't about to let the Vietnamese see even the slightest sign of distress on my face.

When the question, "Trung Uy, what is the meat?" came again, I was sure it must be something strange like goat, horse, or cat. Turning to one of the Vietnamese sergeants, I asked, "Okay, Trung Si, what is it?"

He laughed a little and said, "Don't worry, Trung Uy, it is only deer meat." Then, speaking in Vietnamese to those sitting around me, he gave what sounded like a stern admonishment. The question didn't come up again until after the meal was finished.

The party was over and I was on my way back to the teamhouse when a couple of CIDG soldiers who appeared to have had one too many beers approached me. They were giggling when one asked, "Trung Uy, did you enjoy the food?"

"Yeah, it was number one." In Vietnam, everything was either "number one," which was the best. Or, it was "number ten," the worst. As was pretty much the case, there was little in-between.

"You like it . . . yeah?" They were still giggling between themselves like little girls.

"Sure, it was numba one." The word "number" often deteriorated and became "numba."

Persisting, the other one asked, "What was the meat?"

"I don't know. Trung Si said it was deer. Was it deer?"

"No, it wasn't deer meat." They had fallen to the ground and were, literally, rolling with laughter. They couldn't wait to tell me the identity of the mystery meat. "Oh, Trung Uy . . . it was dog!"

While I would like to think that he lived a full life with a village family, to this day, I'm reasonably sure the dog was Frank because he never came back.

✦ ✦ ✦

When my canteen cup became filled with puffed rice and rehydrated shrimp, it was time for the red pepper and soy sauce. After a long walk and no lunch, the concoction actually tasted very good, and because we had set up camp in an abandoned orchard, the meal was complemented by an unexpected treat for dessert.

Taking advantage of our presence in the overgrown orchard, I walked over and pulled something that resembled an orange from one of the trees. However, once peeled, it tasted more like a grapefruit. Whatever its botanical identity, it was sweet and it was fresh. I considered myself fortunate, knowing how much small things like a piece of fresh fruit meant to soldiers in the field.

As I dropped the last piece of fruit peel, something tickled my leg just below my knee. Thinking it was nothing more than my fatigues against my skin, I brushed at my pant leg. When the tickle persisted, I stood up. When I did, whatever was on my leg moved. At first, I thought it was probably a piece of weed that I had picked up while walking around without my boots, but then it started to crawl further up my leg.

That's no weed, I thought.

Easing myself back down onto my hammock slowly, I kept my leg straight so whatever was making its way up my leg wouldn't be disturbed. Then, just as it reached a place on my leg where the fabric rolled, I made a quick jabbing grab at it and squeezed very tight. Liquid from the crawler oozed onto my leg. Quickly, I jumped up and shook it out of my pants.

One of the old Vietnamese sergeants, who was sitting on a stump not far away, saw my dance and started to laugh until he saw what fell out of my pant leg. It was a large, dark-brown scorpion. As soon as he saw it hit the ground, his mood changed and he became serious immediately. He ran toward me and was speaking frantically in Vietnamese to the interpreter.

"No, no . . . it's okay. I'm okay." I tried to let him know that I hadn't been stung, but he continued to speak rapidly in Vietnamese to my interpreter and kept pointing at my leg.

"Trung Uy, he wants to know where this bug has bitten you."

Of course, he meant stung, but it had done neither.

"No, Light. Tell him I'm fine. It didn't sting me. I'm okay."

Light translated quickly and the old sergeant looked at me and asked, "Sure, Trung Uy?"

"Sure, Trung Si," I responded.

Satisfied I hadn't been stung by the scorpion, the old sergeant turned and walked over to where it had fallen out of my pants and crushed it under his boot and said, "Numba ten, Trung Uy . . . numba ten." Obviously, his way of telling me it was very bad.

Having grown up in Florida, scorpions were not unknown to me, but I'd never seen any as big as this one. It was almost six inches long.

After shaking my pants out thoroughly, I did the same with my boots and put them back on. While lacing them up, I thought *At least it wasn't a two-step or three-step snake.* They were extremely poisonous and they struck quickly. Their name was well deserved. If you were struck by one of them, depending on which one it was, you could expect to take two steps or three steps, then be immobilized and probably die. Never again did my boots come off my feet while in the field.

Aside from the enemy, scorpions and snakes were simply two more of the many perils soldiers had to contend with along the trail in Vietnam.

✦ ✦ ✦

The rest of the night was long but uneventful. After walking the perimeter, I would nap briefly and then walk it again. There was never much sleep for me while in the field, so I was always glad when morning finally dawned. The sun's first light filtered through the trees and spread golden shafts of light across our temporary campsite. From my hammock, each shaft appeared as though it was made of hundreds of soft golden threads. Despite its venomous inhabitants and the war within it, the jungle often appeared beautiful to me. Within hours though, the morning's ethereal beginning would be forgotten when we were forced to deal with an unexpected attack that ripped into the natural beauty of the jungle that surrounded us.

Reaching up and unhooking my radio handset from the hammock rope where it hung, I checked in with the radio room at Trung Dung to let them know we would soon be moving again. Within thirty minutes or so from our check-in, we were packed up and continued west in the general direction of the Cambodian border, which was far beyond our position.

We forded small creeks and streams and walked . . . and walked. In all that distance, we found no sign of recent enemy activity, other than occasional foot traps. The Viet Cong and North Vietnamese dipped sharpened sticks into human feces then placed them in the bottom of pitfall foot traps along trails. Known as "pungee sticks," these seemingly passive weapons could inflict serious infections and even death.

We were just about to stop for lunch when one of the members of the COC group ran up behind me.

"Lieutenant Ross, hold up, hold up." He was nearly out of breath from having run up the column to find me.

"What's the problem?" I asked.

"I think one of the men is having a heart attack," he said.

"What? Where is he?"

Pointing back down the trail, he said, "Back that way about a hundred meters or so."

"Okay, let's go check him out." I asked my Vietnamese counterpart to call the point unit and have them stop while we checked on our man.

When we reached him, he was sitting under a tree. He was an older man, a sergeant on his second or third tour in Vietnam. His breathing was labored, his face was pale and he was complaining of chest pains. Whatever his problem, it was obvious he couldn't continue with the patrol. Juan Sotello, one of A-502's team medics, was with us. After confirming that the man's condition could be grave, we requested a Dust Off medical evacuation chopper.

Fortunately, there was a clearing not far away that was large enough for the chopper to make a safe landing. We quickly reorganized the patrol to provide security around the clearing.

While we were moving the downed man to the opening, he apologized for being sick and said he thought he could continue after a short rest. Sotello assured him that there was no reason to apologize and told him he needed to go back to be examined.

While we were waiting for the medevac chopper to arrive, and since we were stopped anyway, members of the patrol were told to have lunch.

It took the chopper about twenty-five minutes to reach us. When it appeared over the trees, the pilot was directed to the secured LZ. In a matter of only minutes, he was in and out. As the chopper turned east with the ailing soldier, we packed up and once again headed west. Our objective was an area of trails the Vietnamese suspected were being used by enemy units moving up and down the country. The mission was planned after one of our Air Force FACs, Colonel Baer, reported seeing activity on the trails.

✦ ✦ ✦

We had been walking for at least two hours over, around, and across an unending assortment of hills, gullies, streams, and finally into denser jungle. We were a long way out, further than any of our units had ever been on foot. The further away from Trung Dung we got, the closer I watched the jungle.

Are the NVA out here today? If they are here, I hope we see them before they see us? I thought.

✦ ✦ ✦

Every soldier in the field had the experience. Hundreds, maybe thousands, of thoughts could flood your mind while you were on a long-range patrol or were posted out in the middle of nowhere on an ambush. On patrol, you didn't talk while you walked, chopped, crawled, climbed, or sloshed your way along in search of the often-elusive enemy. On ambush, you had to be still and very quiet, sometimes for many hours, as you simply waited for the enemy to walk into your position. Often you fought not only a yet unseen foe, but also the urge to sleep. While these weary blocks of time could become painfully boring, it was absolutely necessary to stay alert because your life might depend on it.

Whenever on a mission, no matter how dull or routine, I tried to keep my thoughts on military matters—exactly where we were and what we were doing. Sometimes, though, no matter how hard I tried, thoughts of my family and friends back home refused to be dismissed. At times, they would persist longer than I knew they should. Typically, that only occurred after a recent mail delivery when news from home was fresh. Since we had received mail the day we left Trung Dung, I occasionally fought the distraction of thoughts about home as the patrol continued to follow the long course marked on my map.

◆ ◆ ◆

It was late afternoon. We were a long day-and-a-half walk from camp when the quiet of our stealthful movement was broken by the flutter of a helicopter somewhere in the distance behind us. The cobwebs of weak concentration quickly cleared as the sound of the chopper moved closer. Occasionally, a burst of machine gun fire could be heard.

Probably from the chopper, I thought. *But, if it is the chopper firing, what are the gunners shooting at? Maybe they've spotted an enemy unit.*

As the sound of the chopper moved still closer and the gunfire continued, I could see some of the men in front of me looking back over their shoulders. I didn't blame them. It was beginning to sound very close, and the gunfire still burped intermittently. I turned around to take a look myself. It wasn't visible through the thick double canopy growth of jungle, but certainly sounded to be coming our way.

Motioning to Ahat, our Montagnard radioman who was walking behind me, I slung my rifle over my shoulder and took the radio handset from him.

Even though we had walked beyond the western border of our official AO, I first tried signaling the helicopter on A-502's frequency. My thought was that if the pilot had flown through our AO, or simply because he was near it, he would be monitoring our radio frequency and would recognize our call sign.

"This is Bunkhouse Zero Two to an unidentified helicopter in Bunkhouse's western AO. Over."

I waited for an answer, but nothing. There was no response.

Once again: "This is Bunkhouse Zero Two to the chopper firing in Bunkhouse's western AO. Over."

Still, there was no response.

Because it sounded to be firing in different places, I was uncertain about the chopper's target. It was unlikely that helicopter could be shooting at a hard target on the ground, because nothing in the jungle moved as fast as it was flying. The only thing that made sense was that its gunners were firing randomly in an attempt to draw fire. That was sometimes a tactic used to locate VC camps or hiding places. If return fire were received, an air strike would be called in to destroy the source of the ground fire. But, if that was the case and they were going to attempt such a mission so near our AO, we should have been notified.

Then, as with many things in war, what should have been was no longer of consequence. Machine-gun fire rained into the trees above us.

"Take cover! Take cover!" came the urgent yells in both English and Vietnamese up and down the patrol line. With the call being repeated in two languages by dozens of voices, everyone scrambled to get behind a tree opposite the incoming gunfire.

Maybe it's one of the 281st's choppers, I thought.

Reaching for the frequency knobs on the radio hanging across Ahat's back, I changed the frequency from ours to the 281st's.

"This is Bunkhouse Zero Two to any chopper in Bunkhouse's western AO. Over." But, again, the radio stayed silent. Then, much stronger and more aggravated, "This is Bunkhouse Zero Two to any chopper who can hear this transmission! Over!"

The chopper sounded like an American Huey. But, in case it was one of the older Vietnamese choppers, I yelled up the line for my Vietnamese counterpart to try and reach them on his radio.

The Vietnamese sergeant tried several times to reach anyone in the air or on the ground, but with no luck. We were so far away from camp his signal wasn't even reaching the Vietnamese radio room at Trung Dung. Then, I tried to reach our radio room, hoping they might know something about the chopper and have him called off. But, again there was no answer. I was only receiving a fuzzy unintelligible response from someone in the radio room trying to respond to my call.

For a few minutes, the gunfire stopped as the chopper moved off ahead of us, but then its engine pitch could be heard to change.

"It's coming back!" someone said.

What a terrible mistake, if they've seen us and think we're VC, I thought.

Once more, the chopper began to fire and was coming back in our direction. The sound of its blades pounded against the jungle canopy, causing vibrations that could be felt as well as heard. The sensation was like being on the inside of a huge base drum. The chopper flew over us on a course almost exactly parallel to ours. I could hear cursing as pieces of tree leaves shredded by incoming machine-gun rounds fell around us.

"Idiots," someone said. "They're going to kill one of us."

As the patrol's senior American advisor, the responsibility to do something began to weigh on me, but what was there to do? The only obvious thing was to keep everyone down or behind trees. I could have thrown a smoke grenade, which would have given the pilot a visual clue to our presence. However, because of our location, that would not have necessarily established us as Americans in his mind. There was one thing it would have done for sure. It would have alerted any NVA/VC units to our presence and exact location, which was the last thing we wanted to do.

When the sound of the chopper started to fade, we began to feel fairly certain that, at least, we hadn't been spotted or they would have pressed their attack.

The heat to do something is off, thank God, I thought, even though I wasn't quite sure what I would have done.

Apparently the close brush with one of our own support choppers had ended, but that wasn't the case at all. Just before the sound of the chopper slipped back into the inaudible distance, a subtle change in the pitch of its engine could be detected. Then the sound began to get louder. It was coming back again.

As our nemesis grew closer, it occurred to me that the chopper crew might have seen us on their last pass and just moved away to give the gunners an opportunity to reload. Looking around, I noticed a small clearing not too far away. I patted Ahat on the shoulder and motioned for him to take the radio off his back and give it to me. Then, after dropping my backpack, I donned the radio. Motioning for Ahat to stay put, I headed for the clearing.

Damn! This is crazy! I thought. But, something *had* to be done, and it was my responsibility to do that something.

Moving as quickly as possible, I ran through the undergrowth with vines and branches slapping me in the face nearly every meter of the way. My thought was that the wet jungle canopy might be interfering with our radio signals. Reaching the clearing might make it possible to establish radio contact.

My growing concern was that if the helicopter crew had seen us, they might start firing directly into our position—or worse, call in an air strike. If they couldn't be reached by radio, throwing a smoke grenade and trying to establish visual contact would be the only other option, short of trying to shoot the chopper down. Obviously, we weren't going to do that, even though the idea had been suggested.

Upon bursting into the open, I ran toward the center of the clearing and tried, as before, to contact the chopper by radio.

"This is Bunkhouse Zero Two, Bunkhouse Zero Two to an unidentified helicopter. Over."

Even though my call was repeated several times, there was still no answer.

Again, occasional bursts of gunfire burped from the rapidly approaching chopper. Quickly, I changed frequencies on the radio and tried one last time for a radio response. Not a thing, there would be no response.

Reaching for one of the smoke grenades on my equipment harness, I glanced back toward the area where the patrol was located.

One of the Americans from the patrol was coming out of the jungle and he appeared to be in a hurry. *What is he doing?* I wondered.

Even though I couldn't tell who he was yet, he was distinguishable as an American simply because his size was much larger than that of the average Vietnamese. As he came closer he became easily recognizable. It was the young medic from the orientation course who had been a few men behind me in the patrol column.

Whatever he wanted, the urgency of his message was evident on his face as he neared me, but just as he opened his mouth and before he could communicate anything, the chopper passed just to our north. It couldn't be seen, even from the clearing. But, it was very low, close, and loud as a seemingly indiscriminate spray of machine-gun rounds once again ripped into the trees around us. At that moment, I was hit and knocked completely off of my feet and to the ground. A bullet hadn't struck me. The medic who was afraid I might be hit by the incoming gunfire had tackled me.

As we rolled along the ground, I asked, "What are you doing out here?"

"I came for you, sir," he said.

"Why? Has someone been hit?"

"No, but we're afraid you'll get hit out here. You need to come back into the tree line."

Rolling over onto my stomach and propping myself up on my elbows, I said, "Listen. They've stopped shooting."

Jumping to my feet quickly, I got a momentary glimpse of the American UH-1 helicopter as it crossed and disappeared over the far end of the clearing. I pulled the pin on the red smoke grenade and prepared to throw it.

The sound of an occasional angry curse could be heard from the jungle where the patrol had taken cover not from enemy fire, but from friendly fire. While it would kill you just as quickly as enemy fire, the unlikely term "friendly fire" was applied to bullets or ordnance that emanated from American or allied sources.

"Come on, sir, throw it from the trees. You've got to get out of this clearing," the medic urged.

Just as I prepared to heave the small olive green can that would pop and belch a huge cloud of bright red smoke into the sky above us, something happened.

"Listen to that," I said. "They've moved away."

The chopper sounded as though it was now several kilometers beyond our strung-out patrol, and it was no longer firing.

"You know, I don't think they've actually seen us. They aren't attacking or they'd be all over us," I said.

◆ ◆ ◆

We were intentionally in a location where recent enemy activity had been reported through both Vietnamese and U.S. intelligence channels, so our frustrating situation was possibly due simply to poor timing and poor communication. It was unlikely, but one of the other headquarters in Nha Trang could have requested the chopper's mission, whatever that was, or it could simply be passing through on its way to another destination. Whatever the reason for its presence, unless the chopper pressed an attack that indicated we might have been mistaken for an enemy unit, it was best that the smoke grenade remain unused. If the enemy did see it, besides pinpointing our location, it might cause them to flee or, worse, prepare an ambush for us.

When the chopper's engines strained in another turn that sounded to be bringing it back toward us yet again, why and how it got there wasn't going to be as important as what I was about to witness. What would become remarkable were the continuing actions of the young medic over the next few minutes.

There wasn't anything really noticeable about what he was doing at first, but then it became very obvious. When we could tell the chopper was coming back, the medic began to move as he spoke, "LT, please . . . it's coming back. Let's get the hell back into the jungle."

The fact that he had moved to a position between the approaching chopper and me wasn't immediately perceptible.

"Come on, LT. That chopper could cut us down out here."

As the sound of the choppers' beating blades grew louder above and behind him and its pass became almost parallel, his movement was more deliberate.

The chopper's gunners weren't firing as the chopper passed, so I didn't throw the smoke grenade. But, as it passed, the young medic moved around me in such a way that he kept himself between me and the chopper. Based on the chopper's position in relation to ours, if we had received incoming fire, the medic would have been hit before and, probably, instead of me.

When I realized that he was making himself a human shield, I asked, "What are you doing?"

"I don't want you to get hit. You know the safest way back," he said. "If something happened to you, where would that leave us?"

I almost laughed but didn't, knowing the young medic hadn't been in Vietnam for much more than a week. It was easy to see that he was truly concerned. While admirable, his concern and daring deeds were for naught. Because he hadn't seen them, he had apparently forgotten that other A-502 advisors were with our patrol unit. Even if the other advisors hadn't been there, the Vietnamese would have easily led the unit back to camp, since they were acting as our guides. Additionally, as well trained as they were, any member of the orientation unit, including the medic, could have found his way back to camp with little difficulty. However, I'm sure that after being in-country for such a short time, walking through unfamiliar terrain wasn't something any of them really wanted to have to do.

Despite his needless concern, the medic's personal action and initiative on behalf of his unit spoke impressively about his character.

The chopper's next heard, but unseen, west-to-east pass was a little further north than it had been the last time. Also, its less frequent fire was no longer impacting near us.

166 | *Thomas A. Ross*

"I'm sure they don't know we're down here," I said, " and I'm fairly sure they must be running low on ammunition. Okay, you're right, let's get back to the trees and see what he does next."

When we rejoined the patrol in the jungle, one of the other lieutenants from the orientation group asked, "What do you think? Are they shooting at us?"

"No, I don't think so. And, as much as they've been firing, they're probably running low on ammo."

"Good!" he said. "I'm getting a little tired of this."

"Yeah, I know. Me too."

We all sat or crouched behind trees listening to the chopper and waiting for its next move. The experience was very much like sitting in a blacked room with an attacker you could hear, but couldn't see, and wondering whether or not he would find you.

Finally, though, concern of being discovered waned when the sound of the chopper dissolved into the southern sky, in the direction of Cam Ranh Bay.

After everyone stood up and we began reorganizing the patrol, I asked the medic again why he had come into the clearing. He explained that when he left the patrol, there was talk among the Americans about the uncertainty of the unit's exact location. Then, he said, "When I heard the chopper coming back, I was concerned about you getting hit and how we would get back."

"And, what about you?" I asked. "What if you'd been hit?"

"I don't know. I didn't really think about that."

✦ ✦ ✦

The medic's thinking might sound clouded or unusual now, but for Vietnam it was rational. Perhaps because many soldiers felt that there was diminishing support for those involved in the war, a unique bond of brotherhood seemed to develop. Whatever the motivation, the medic's reasons for acting were crystal clear to him, not at all unusual, and remarkably selfless. I ran into the clearing because I had to, not because I wanted to. It was my job; responsibility for the safety of the patrol was mine alone. The medic ran into the clearing because he wanted to, not just for himself, not just for me, but for others. His genuine concern for the safety of others is very likely among the many things that prompted him to become a medic.

Countless stories exist about men and women such as the medic, individuals whose thoughts and purpose were crystal clear in their own minds when they disregarded personal safety to act on behalf of another. In this story, the medic survived his actions.

Dale Reich, a member of a previous COC group, and others like him can't be asked the question, "Why did you do what you did?" The reason they can't be asked the question is because they didn't survive the situation in which they had willingly placed themselves. It is likely, however, that their thinking and purpose for what they had done were also clear. It is just as likely that they would have responded as the medic had: "I didn't think about what might happen to me."

Certainly, countless other stories of war, far more sensational or moving than this one, took place under decidedly more intense situations. If someone had been killed in the rain of seemingly less lethal, but equally deadly friendly fire, this would be a very different story. What is important to convey is the frequency with which Americans serving in Vietnam, often very young ones, displayed the qualities of courage and selflessness. Sometimes the results of their actions were tragic, while other times they were glorious. Today was simply a good day.

CHAPTER 12

Water, Water, Everywhere...

THE DONG BO MOUNTAINS stood tall and imposing against the magnificent star-studded southern sky, which was the only suitable backdrop for their enormous mass. Behind them, the night changed from deep purple in the east to a glowing bright blue along the horizon in the west. The air lacked its usual humidity and was occasionally stirred by a gentle breeze from the distant sea. It was the type of setting and evening meant to be shared by candlelight with someone special.

Unfortunately, while candlelight flickered nearby, anyone special to most of those Americans in Vietnam was more than ten thousand miles away. And, as beautiful and soft as the huge Dong Bo Mountains appeared from a distance, I knew how treacherous and deadly they had been to assaulting units in the past. Tomorrow, A-502 and its key CIDG companies would face the danger confronted by those who had gone before us.

My role as one of a handful of advisors for the Dong Bo operation would take me deep into the heart of the mountains that I had found so picturesque since my first day in Nha Trang. But, for the first time since arriving in-country, there were unusual feelings of apprehension about the coming mission. Every trip into the field could be danger-ous, but something was different about this one.

My feelings of foreboding were uncomfortable and little more than distracting, but not altogether unexpected. During the past several months we had gathered considerable intelligence about the vast mountain complex. Sergeant Koch had collected information from the camp's Vietnamese intelligence section and every other source in the Nha Trang intelligence network. Our operation would be mount-ed under less than favorable conditions, so we needed to know as much as possible about our objective.

For some time we had been trying to pinpoint the location of the VC base camp that we knew existed somewhere on the eastern-facing slopes of the Dong Bo Mountains. Finally, we had a break. One of our night ambushes had captured a prisoner who came from the moun-tain camp. During their interrogation of the man, the Vietnamese intelligence section convinced the prisoner to serve as a guide and lead us back to his base.

This opportunity was excellent, if true. My concern was that he might also be planning to lead us into a trap. After all, the moun-tains had belonged to the VC and NVA for years. It was difficult to believe that the captured soldier would lead us to the base camp, knowing his own people would probably kill him if he survived any ensuing battle.

Much of the information provided by the prisoner matched what we had already accumulated. His report of the VC strength in the mountains was about six to seven hundred men, approximately what we had estimated. Fortifications and supplies were also very good, as we expected them to be. Other than sharing the general location of the base camp, which he told the Vietnamese he couldn't find on a map, the prisoner hadn't told us much we didn't already know. His value was in his ability to lead us to the camp.

The fact that the enemy base was well manned and supplied had been demonstrated previously when they ran other allied units out of the mountains after inflicting significant casualties on them. We clearly understood the challenge we were facing.

◆ ◆ ◆

A month earlier, when the current assault into the Dong Bo's was being considered by Corp Command in Nha Trang, I had been asked to present a briefing on what we knew about the mountain complex. My presentation was given at First Field Force Headquarters to Lieutenant General William Peers and his staff officers. After discussing the suspected location of the base camp, its fortifications, estimated troop strength, supplies, and other details, the briefing was concluded with an outline of the South Vietnamese plan of attack. A-502 would be supplying the military advisors for the operation, which included me.

The plan, which sounded very weak to those of us who would serve as advisors, involved the use of most of Trung Dung's resources, three light Vietnamese CIDG companies, and some support platoons for odds and ends. In all, fewer than five hundred men would be used to attack what was believed to be a superior enemy force well entrenched in a position they had held and successfully defended for years. This option seemed almost foolhardy. There was, however, an alternate plan to attack the mountain complex, one that was tactically more sound. I asked General Peers if he cared to hear it.

"Absolutely, lieutenant," he said. "I want to hear everything you can tell me about that hell hole and how we can get rid of it."

With clearance to proceed, I wasted no time outlining a second option.

The Koreans, our allies on the north side of the Song Cai River, knew of the legendary enemy stronghold and they yearned for a major involvement. From our perspective, the most important part of their desire for a fight was their ability to commit almost three thousand men to such a mission. These would be exceptionally well trained and highly motivated soldiers. We had no such resources.

General Peers immediately recognized the tactical advantage of the Korean option, but pointed out that the Dong Bo Mountains were in the Vietnamese AO.

"I'm with you," the general said. "But the authority to give the mission to the Koreans rests with the Vietnamese High Command."

✦ ✦ ✦

The decision, tactically, should have been such a simple one to make, but politically, it was apparently impossible.

For the South Vietnamese High Command it may have been a matter of saving face. Whatever the reason, after taking several days to consider all the information and options, the final orders came down. CIDG companies 557, 558, and 559 and other Vietnamese support units from Trung Dung along with their U.S. advisors from A-502 would seek and attempt to destroy the enemy stronghold in the Dong Bo Mountains.

Aside from the war itself, this was the first time I can remember being personally affected by a political issue. The decision to send our units into the mountains had clearly been a political one, not a tactical one, and I was astonished by its absurdity. Word made its way to me from First Field Force that, because the Dong Bos were in the Vietnamese AO, they would appear weak in the eyes of allies if they didn't make at least one more attempt to find and destroy the base themselves.

With the Vietnamese going into the mountains, the American advisors from A-502 were committed to accompany them. The Americans would do what they had been ordered to do and exactly what they had been trained to do: provide the best support possible.

Because of my work on the operation plan and knowledge of the Dong Bo history, my presence on the mission was a given. So, looking out across the darkening mountains, I anticipated the next day with some trepidation.

Strange, but I had never given this much thought to my mortality prior to previous missions. Perhaps it is because of an innate will to survive, but military personnel often feel that if someone is going to die, it will be someone else. Whatever the cause of that phenomenon, I no longer felt exempt from serious harm, particularly because, with the VC prisoner as a guide, an encounter with a major enemy force seemed inevitable.

Watching as the mountains lost definition and became a silhouette against the starry Vietnamese sky, I organized my personal thoughts. As they fell into place, I began to feel an inner peace.

In anticipation of the coming operation, there had been both military planning and personal preparation. Earlier in the day, while in Nha Trang to coordinate artillery support, I made a visit to the Catholic chaplain who heard my confession. *If the worst happens*, I thought, *at least I am prepared to meet my maker.*

As I turned to leave the chaplain's office he offered his own mission support. "Lieutenant, I'm going to say a special prayer for your unit's safe return."

Everyone in Vietnam dealt with their fears and concerns in various ways. For me, it was a brief visit to a priest in uniform who simply listened as I cleansed my soul. Almost smiling when his promise of a "special prayer" was recalled, I realized, standing there alone in the dark, that my concerns about being killed had nearly vanished. While I still recognized the possibility intellectually, I was emotionally prepared for *whatever* was to come.

By the time the sun edged above the eastern horizon and illuminated our destination, we were already at our airstrip waiting for pickup. A short while later, we were being airlifted to a location about three quarters of the way up one of the western slopes of the Dong Bos. Our search-and-destroy mission was under way.

Since the VC prisoner was captured after we were given the mission orders, there had been a good deal of discussion about how we would proceed. We weren't sure what information disloyal Vietnamese in our own unit might have leaked. So, at the last minute, we decided to enter the mountains from above by helicopter, high on the west side of the mountain complex rather than from the low ground on the east side. That was where all the other previously defeated units had entered. If we had anything in our favor, hopefully, it would be some degree of surprise.

Clouds hung close to the mountain's summit as the old Vietnamese choppers began the many ferry trips it would take to get all of us to the drop-off point. In case the VC had lookouts on the mountain, which was generally southeast of our camp, we took off and headed directly west before circling around behind the suspected enemy location.

While it took a few hours to place everyone on the mountain, the process went smoothly. As soon as each chopper landed, its offloading unit organized and immediately started moving further up the mountain.

Thieu Ta (Major) Ngoc, Trung Dung's Vietnamese camp commander, would also serve as the Dong Bo mission commander. The senior American advisor was Major Richard Dubovick, who would soon replace Major Lee as A-502's commander. Having completed his tour of duty, Lee was scheduled to return to the States in only days. Major Dubovick was an even-tempered man who was less intense than Lee, but seemed equally experienced and militarily skilled. Because this mission was his first out of 502, my role was to provide him with whatever information he required. Along with Major Dubovick and myself, two Americans would advise each of the three CIDG companies.

We had been walking for about an hour and were on a very steep incline when I began to feel winded. The Vietnamese didn't appear to be affected by the climb at all, but the further up we went, the worse I felt.

How are they doing it? I asked myself.

After watching the two or three Vietnamese in front of me for a while, I noticed that for every one step I was taking, they were taking two or three. I changed my stride to a much shorter one. In only minutes, my respiration became less labored and more normal as we continued up toward the clouds.

As we neared the summit of the mountain on which we had landed, we actually walked into the clouds. It was like walking into a dense fog. The air was cooler and thick with humidity. Trees dripped with condensation—so much so that, at one point, it felt like rain as we were pelted by water droplets falling from the jungle canopy. If had known what was to come, we would have collected the precious liquid.

We followed our point unit quietly through the cloud layer and around the summit to a point on the southeast side of the mountain. We stopped there for a late lunch of cold C rations. While I sat on rock and picked at the contents of one of the tins, the aroma of cinnamon became very distinct.

"Do you smell the cinnamon?" I asked Light.

"Yes," he said. "It comes from the trees." He stood up and cut a small piece of bark from a nearby tree. Handing it to me he said, "Smell it, Trung Uy. It smells very good."

I suppose it was cinnamon, it smelled like cinnamon. Whatever it was, its aroma mixed with the fine mist of the low hanging clouds to give the air a pleasing scent. The surprise of a pleasant encounter was always welcomed in Vietnam. Since the war had been going on for so long, I expected to find the country torn up, with very little of anything pleasant or good. That wasn't the case. The country was beautiful, and pleasant experiences were frequent.

After a brief lunch, we moved behind the point unit down the mountain through jungle growth so thick that at times you couldn't see either the man in front of you or the one behind you. We were all hot and wringing wet with sweat when we finally broke into a clearing and onto a trail that ran along a narrow ridge toward another portion of the mountain.

Walking on trails in enemy territory was one of my least favorite things to do, even when it was quicker or there was no other option. The possibility of ambush always existed when walking on trails, because one of the easiest places to set up an ambush is along an exist-ing trail. In this case, though, traveling on the trail was a must situa-tion if we were going to reach the suspected base camp location quickly enough to take advantage of our element of surprise. We hoped to find the hidden camp and attack not later than the afternoon of the second day.

As we moved along the trail, everyone watched the jungle as it thinned on both sides of us. With the jungle opening, the pace quick-ened. No one wanted to get caught in an open killing zone. Ahead, on a short, straight part of the trail, I could see a dip and an open clearing in the growth on the right side. As each Vietnamese soldier reached the dip and the clearing, he bolted and ran across it. There was no sound of gunfire, but I wondered if a sniper was shooting at them.

When it was my turn to cross the open area, there was still no expla-nation for why everyone had run across it so quickly. One of the men about two persons ahead of me yelled something in Vietnamese, but I couldn't understand what he said.

They must know something I don't, I thought as I began my sprint. There was still no apparent reason for our hurry other than to sim-ply cross the clearing quickly. I couldn't understand why the soldier had cried out since we were trying to move as silently as possible. Then, about halfway across the opening, I discovered the reason for the hurry.

Whack! I was hit in the neck. The pain was excruciating, but I kept running, and was glad that I could.

At least I'm not dead, I thought. Quickly, I reached up on my neck to locate the wound and assess the degree of my injury. While I felt noth-ing unusual, I expected to see my hand covered with blood when it reached my line of sight. But when I looked at it, there was nothing—not a speck of blood on it. I couldn't understand what had happened.

After running back into the jungle on the far side of the clearing, the pain was still very intense. Again, my hand searched for a wound and source of the crippling pain, but nothing—no apparent injury.

Ahat, who was running behind me, had seen me grab my neck and knew I had been hit by something. When he came up beside me, I pointed to my neck. He pulled my collar down and looked for the wound.

"No shoot, Trung Uy," he said. Then he started making a buzzing sound.

I called Light back and asked him to check my neck and told him to ask Ahat what he was trying to tell me.

"Feel your neck now, Trung Uy," Light said.

Feeling my neck a second time, it was beginning to swell.

"You were stung by a hornet, he said."

As a young boy playing in the woods around my home I had been stung many times by both bees and wasps, but I had never experienced that kind of pain before. Even though the pain was intense, there was something for which to be thankful. I hadn't been shot.

A column doesn't stop for a hornet sting, so we continued moving along the ridgeline. It was almost dark anyway and nearly time to stop for the night.

When we finally stopped for the evening, each of the CIDG companies consolidated their positions and set up security. Major Dubovick and I picked a cavelike opening under a rocky overhang to spend the night. As we once again cut into cans for our evening meal, he asked, "How's your neck?"

"It doesn't hurt anymore. It's just a little numb feeling."

"Good, I guess that's better."

"Yes sir, it is . . . much better. I don't think I've ever felt a searing pain that intense before."

Then, pointing toward a small group set up not far away from the opening to our cave, the major said, "We have to make damn sure we keep an eye on that joker. He'd like to do more than sting us. He'll crawl in here tonight and crack our skulls with a rock."

He was talking about the VC prisoner who the Vietnamese had tied to a tree. It wasn't the VC that was going to injure the major that night, though. The rock that would get him would have another source.

We had finished eating and were both propped against the rocks to relax. It had been a long hike up the mountain to where we now rested. Eyeing our surroundings, the major noticed a small rock wedged between a couple of larger ones in the overhang above his feet. All three were wedged between two huge boulders. He pointed toward the smallest one in the center with the toe of his boot.

"I wonder if that rock's the keystone," he said, kicking at it. It didn't budge. Then, he kicked at it again. To our surprise, mostly his, the rocks suddenly broke loose and fell. One of them landed on his ankle. He grimaced, and I could tell he was hurt.

Slowly and gingerly, the major unlaced his boot and pulled it off. Again he grimaced as the boot slipped free of his foot. The boot had kept his foot from being cut, but it was swelling quickly and already showing signs of being badly bruised.

"Do you want me to get one of the medics?" I asked.

"No, it hurts, but I think it may be fine in the morning." The pain showed in the expression on his face as he rubbed the ankle, which was swelling even more.

"Are you sure you don't want me to get one of the medics up here to look at that? It really doesn't look very good."

"No, no. I can move it. I don't think anything is broken." Then, demonstrating his ability to move the blackening appendage, he wiggled it around a little. "I think it'll be fine by morning. Being able to stay off of it tonight will help."

Neither of us slept much that night, the major because of his ankle and me to check the perimeter and make sure the VC prisoner was still securely tied.

Nightfall in the jungle isn't just dark; it's very dark. Sometimes you could barely see your hand in front of your face. So, even though the prisoner was guarded, I never felt comfortable having him that close to us. Many times when I looked over at him, even though his form was barely discernible, I could see his eyes were wide open and moving around. Even when he appeared to be sleeping, I was sure he was just waiting for the guard to fall asleep. Because of our location and our mission, not many of the troops slept well that night. Everyone knew we were on unfriendly ground.

The next morning, light filtered through the jungle canopy to once again bring color and form to our campsite. The overnight rest did little to heal the major's injured foot. He couldn't do much more than hobble. When Thieu Ta Ngoc and I tried to convince him to let us medevac him out, he wouldn't hear of it.

"No," he said. "I'm staying till we find the base camp."

Since he wasn't going to leave, after a meeting with company commanders to review our attack plans, the unit began moving again. Dubovick limped along with it.

Based on information provided by the prisoner, we expected our recon patrols to find the enemy base camp by midmorning. When there was still no sign of it by noon, we began to believe we were being led on a wild goose chase.

By mid-afternoon, we still hadn't found anything of substance. A couple of our recon units had made contact with small enemy patrols and exchanged gunfire, but that was it. When we stopped for a break, it was easy to see that the Vietnamese had finally had enough of the rugged mountain terrain. Some of the officers felt certain the prisoner was intentionally misdirecting us and had no intention of taking us anywhere near his base camp. They questioned him and even threatened him with his life. He cried, apologized, and begged to live, claiming he had never come to the camp this way and was lost. None of us believed him, and some of the Vietnamese wanted to kill him anyway. Thieu Ta Ngoc intervened and didn't let that happen. He told his men that we would simply continue our search, and the prisoner would be handed over to the District Chief for punishment when we returned to Trung Dung.

Since our recon units had encountered and fired on the enemy patrols earlier, every VC and NVA soldier in the mountain complex would soon know we were there. Our element of surprise had been lost, and we had become vulnerable to attack ourselves.

Because our units might have to divide and move quickly, Thieu Ta Ngoc and I tried once more to convince the major to let us have him medevaced off the mountain. His ankle had become extremely discolored and so swollen that he could hardly walk. This time he agreed. He recognized that his condition was getting worse and that his presence could impede the unit if things suddenly got crazy.

We moved the major to a large boulder that hung out over the mountain. From there we had a commanding view of the Nha Trang Valley below. The boulder would serve as our LZ for the Dust Off helicopter.

The chopper took only about twenty minutes to reach us from the time our medic requested the pickup. Shortly after the call, we could see the helicopter clearly when it rounded the base of the mountains and started up to our location. We communicated frequently as the chopper made its way to the outcropping where the major was waiting.

Whenever warned of possible danger, the pilot displayed a calm, confident professionalism and simply replied, "Roger. Understand."

When he arrived and set up for his approach, we advised him one last time to use caution since we were uncertain about enemy presence. The pilot's only response this time was, "Roger. Get your man ready. We're coming in."

The speed and efficiency with which the medevac pilot and his crew functioned were smooth and practiced. The chopper swept in boldly and began to settle in on the outcropping. Because the rocks weren't level, the pilot only rested one skid and stayed at a hover. We loaded the major on board quickly and in only seconds he was on his way. He wished us well and showed us a thumbs-up as the chopper lifted off and began to rotate. Once clear of the rocks, the pilot dropped its nose and dove down between the mountain ridges toward the valley floor. Even though a great churning machine, it flew down between the ridges with the smoothness and authority of a soaring bird of prey.

While this one hadn't been a life-saving mission, there were countless others during the Vietnam War that were. As with the pilot and crew who had attempted to save the life of Lieutenant Dale Reich near My Loc a few months earlier, it took incredible courage and devotion to fly those slow-flying air ambulances. Lightly armed, they were easy targets for enemy gunners. Even though on mercy missions and clearly marked with large red crosses, many were blasted from the air. When that happened, another pilot and crew would confidently take their place.

With the major safely on board the chopper and on his way back to the field hospital in Nha Trang, the roll of Thieu Ta Ngoc's senior advisor fell to me. While I had come to know him very well, we hadn't worked this closely before. The roll of advisor to Thieu Ta had always belonged to A-502's camp commander. So, I had this opportunity to get to know him better.

When I asked how he wanted to proceed, Thieu Ta said he wanted to search for the base camp a while longer before requesting a planned resupply mission. Even though many of the men were already out of drinking water, he felt we needed to attempt to find the enemy base camp and attack before dark, which was only a few hours away.

"The VC know we are here now, Trung Uy," he said. "We must find them because, after dark, they will have a great advantage over us. These mountains are their home."

In agreement with his assessment of our situation, I shook my head and said, "Let's go find them."

We spent what remained of the afternoon without luck crawling over rocks, following trails, and chopping our way through jungle in search of the enemy hideaway. When it became early evening, I suggested to Thieu Ta that he call for the resupply.

Almost everyone was out of water, and in only a couple of hours it would be dark. If only we had taken advantage of the humidity and condensation of our moments in the clouds the previous day to collect water . . . but we couldn't have known at that point what we'd be facing.

When Thieu Ta agreed on the resupply, we sent a receiving unit to secure another large outcropping of rocks that projected out over a valley between two ridges. It was the only clear area available where we could receive supplies, other than the one higher on the mountain that we had used to medevac Major Dubovick. But it was now too far away, as was our preselected site. The original site had been chosen because it was close to the location where we expected to find the enemy base camp. We planned to use it to receive fresh supplies and reinforcements if and when required. We were now improvising.

Just before dark, big lumbering H-34 helicopters used by the Vietnamese began to appear in the air above the rocks, but their resupply mission soon turned into something more closely resembling a bombing mission.

Either because of updrafts from the valley beneath the rocks, lack of flying skill, fear of hitting the trees near the rocks, or a combination of all those factors, the chopper pilots couldn't get in close enough to deliver their loads. Time after time, each chopper tried to get in near enough to set down or hand the water containers and boxes of food out to the waiting troops, but none of them could make it. So, as a result, the chopper crewmen would simply try to drop the containers of water to the men on the ground. Unfortunately, when the troops attempted to catch the heavy containers being dropped from eight to ten feet above them they would pass through their arms and burst at their feet. There was water everywhere, but it quickly seeped into the dry hot rocks.

As the long day began fading to darkness, the crewmen became less cautious and simply shoved things out of the chopper door. Cases of sardines and rice fell into the jungle around us, and the ones that hit the rocks burst like bombs. When the resupply mission was over, cans of smashed sardines and broken bags of rice covered the rocks. As far as the much-needed water was concerned, we had only salvaged from the broken containers little more than a quarter cup for every man.

Thieu Ta was very angry about the results of the botched resupply attempt and called Trung Dung. He commanded an aid to arrange for another mission the next morning and threatened disciplinary action if it failed. That night was a long, dry, hungry, and sleepless one. The night also became a little crazy when an unexpected intruder attempted to kill a perimeter guard. We were expecting the NVA, but not this.

◆ ◆ ◆

At around two or three in the morning, the radio handset hooked to my hammock buzzed as I tried to nap. Occasionally, radio checks from Trung Dung's night ambushes caused it to crackle when the frequency was used. When the noise from the radio aroused my attention, I would also check to make sure the VC prisoner was still secured. That night, he was tied only about ten feet away. I had just checked him and put my head back down when the still of the night was broken by running footsteps and a frantic Vietnamese voice. In the dark, I didn't know if it was one of our troops or an incoming VC assault.

As the person ran in closer, he began to scream. His screams roused all of the Vietnamese around me, and many of them thought we were being attacked. They started yelling to alert everyone else. I still didn't have a clue about what was happening, but grabbed the M-16 lying across my hammock and rolled out onto the ground. Just as I hit the ground, the runner hit my hammock and fell right beside me. I grabbed him and Ahat jumped on him as he still chattered away.

"What is he saying, Light?" I yelled.

"He is one of our men, Trung Uy. He says a tiger tried to eat him."

"What?"

There was a frantic exchange of words between Light and the soldier, then a clearer explanation.

As it turned out, the man was one of our perimeter guards. He hadn't noticed it moving in or he may have fallen asleep. But, however it happened, a tiger had walked to within just a few feet of him before he saw it. When he finally did see it, he panicked, believing it was going to jump on him and kill him.

Things calmed down after the word of what had actually happened was circulated, but that took a while. I don't remember sleeping another wink that night. Occasionally, though, my eyelids closed just long enough to moisten my hot, dry eyes.

The next morning, when it appeared there was enough light to fly, Thieu Ta Ngoc summoned the second resupply. Unfortunately, because of an overcast sky that produced slightly higher winds than the day before, things didn't go much better than they had the previous evening. Water containers dropped from Vietnamese choppers that were once again hovering too high burst when they hit the ground.

As a crewman shoved one of the last water containers out of the chopper door, a thirsty and frustrated Vietnamese soldier raised his carbine as if to fire at the chopper, only to have it slapped down by one of his sergeants.

With a water resupply apparently impossible, we salvaged what we could of the food that was still scattered on the ground from the evening before and moved out. Hoping to find water in a mountain spring along our way, we headed for another location that intelligence had once targeted as a likely spot for the VC base camp. In reality, it had probably changed and been moved many times over the past several years.

Again, we spent the day walking and climbing up and down in the Dong Bo Mountains. We had nothing to show for our efforts, other than isolated contacts with very small enemy units, which had probably been dispatched simply to report on our movements. By the end of the day, we hadn't located either the enemy base camp or water. We were at the end of our third day in the mountains and were all very surprised that we had not encountered or been attacked by larger mountain-based enemy elements. It seemed the VC might intentionally be avoiding contact with us. But, we couldn't understand why that would be the case since we were on ground they knew extremely well. Previously, they had been very aggressive in their defense of the mountains.

That night, Thieu Ta Ngoc, fully frustrated, decided that we had no other good locations to check. He said we had been through or very near many of the areas Vietnamese intelligence suspected as likely locations to hide the elusive VC stronghold. He said we could spend weeks in the mountains at the rate we were moving and never be able to check all of them thoroughly, simply because of the dense vegetation and massiveness of the mountain complex.

Many of the Vietnamese were fatigued and some had become dehydrated and sick without water, so we obviously were not the fighting unit we needed to be. Thieu Ta decided we would try to make it out of the mountains by the next evening. Because our present location wouldn't permit a resupply, I suggested that we pick a slightly flatter place further down the mountain. The next morning we would take a different approach to ensure the success of a water resupply mission, which I suggested be brought by U.S. choppers. Thieu Ta quickly agreed.

While the night was uneventful, it was every bit as sleepless as the two previous nights had been. Near morning, though, I drifted off to sleep. When I awoke, the aroma of coffee was in the air.

Where did they get the water for coffee? I wondered, as I stretched and felt the cotton-dry sensation in my mouth. *Maybe someone found water,* I hoped. But I couldn't imagine why anyone would be cooking anything. Yes, I was sure the VC and NVA knew we were in the mountains, but telling them exactly where we were camped was insane.

As I got out of my hammock, I notice the coffee had a peculiar smell about it. Light was trying to open one of the smashed sardine tins he had put in his pack when I walked over to where he was sitting.

"Is that coffee I smell?"

"Yes, Trung Uy." Pointing to a small group of soldiers around a can of sterno, he added, "Some of those soldiers are making it."

"Where did they find the water?" I asked.

Making a grimace and shaking his head, he said, "They make it with pee pee,

Trung Uy."

"What?"

"Yes, I watched them do it," he said.

It was disgusting. They had made coffee out of urine. Yes, we had been out of water for a day and a half and my lips were dry and cracked, but I wasn't that thirsty yet. Nor was Thieu Ta, who ran up and kicked the sterno can. He yelled at the men who had been responsible for permitting the smell of coffee to drift over the mountainside, then turned to me and said, "We must move out of this area quickly."

A short while later, after hurriedly deciding on our path out of the mountains, the column began to move. We had only been in motion for minutes when one of the Vietnamese medics ran up to Thieu Ta to say that two of the men who had been drinking coffee were very sick. Thieu Ta showed little sympathy and told the medic to tell the men that if they didn't keep up they would be left behind. Then, barely fifteen minutes later, the medic returned to say that three other men were sick. They had become ill after sucking on trees trying to get moisture from the bark. Thieu Ta sent the same message to these men, and we continued moving toward the resupply site.

It took about two hours to reach the place we had chosen as our resupply site. While it was still jungle and wasn't level, it was reasonably flat. We would clear it with explosives, those we carried with us to blast the VC from their base camp. They would now be used to create an LZ in the middle of the jungle. While some of the Vietnamese soldiers chopped small trees, others placed the explosives near the base of larger ones.

I had taken the radio and climbed up on a large boulder near the edge of what would become our LZ to check in with 502. They were coordinating our resupply, and we needed to make sure they were ready. With their confirmation that everything was set, I clipped the radio handset on my web harness and turned to check on progress with the demolitions. Before I completed my turn, an abrupt change in my surroundings took place. I was little more that halfway into my turn when the world around me exploded.

Several of the soldiers walked past me on the boulder, so it was difficult to believe that no one realized that I was there. Maybe they thought I had moved or had been given the warning, I have no idea. But they set off the explosive charges attached to the trees—all at once. Chunks of trees, bark, branches, leaves, dirt, and small rocks filled the air. I crumpled and rolled off the large boulder down between two smaller ones, where I waited for the debris to quit falling.

Pulverized pieces of trees and earth fell for several seconds. A large branch that had been severed fell within inches of my head and because of its weight, was driven far into the ground. Finally, when it sounded as if everything had quit falling, I crawled out from under the trees and branches that had fallen over me. The boulders had kept me from being injured, but I was covered with small pieces of splintered wood and dirt, and my ears were ringing from the explosions.

After shaking my shirt out and letting my head clear, I examined the opening that had been created in the jungle. With all the stumps and fallen tree trunks, it was impossible to accurately pace the diameter of our new LZ. It looked a little tight, but appeared large enough for the choppers that would bring our water. We were all ready for a drink, so one of the other advisors made the call and got them started.

Once again, as so many times in the past, it was the 281st that would be responding to our call for support. When the choppers began to arrive over our hole in the jungle, the first pilot on site expressed some concern that the opening might be a little too tight. Normally, the touchdown area would be cleared to a diameter large enough to ensure several meters of clearance for the chopper blades. Additionally, stumps and remaining pieces of trees had to be short enough not to interfere with the landing skids. There was no problem with the height of stumps or trees, but once the first chopper was hovering above the opening it was obvious the fit would indeed be tight. Our estimate was that, at best, there would only be about a two- to three-meter clearance from the tip of the chopper blades to the edge of the jungle.

The pilot asked, "What are chances of making that hole a little larger?"

"I think we've used all our explosives to clear what you're looking at, but let me check," I said.

Thieu Ta Ngoc, confirmed that all our explosives had been used to make the LZ its present size. If we had to cut more trees it could take the rest of the day to clear some of the large ones that still surrounded the LZ.

"I'm afraid we've done the best that we can, but if you think it's too small, don't risk it," I told the pilot.

"It looks very close," he said. "Let's check your measurements. We'll try to get you guys a drink of water."

Evidently, the team member at 502 who had arranged our resupply had also shared the urgency of our situation.

The hovering chopper began descending through what now appeared to be a very, very small opening. As it dropped beneath tree-top level, its blades clipped leaves and pieces of small branches as it settled down through the cylindrical hole we had created in the jungle. Standing beneath the helicopter was much like being under a huge fan creating hurricane-force winds. My hair and clothing were being violently whipped in the turbulence. Looking up at the slowly descending chopper, I could see the copilot's head rotating quickly back and forth as he passed information to the pilot about their position inside the opening. Dust and dirt created a sandblaster effect on those of us around the chopper as it neared the ground. Huge trees littered the base of the LZ, and the pilot brought his chopper to rest across two of the fallen tree trunks that were laying parallel to each other. Once his chopper was stable, the pilot motioned through the window that it was safe to retrieve the water cans.

As quickly as we could, we off-loaded the heavy but welcomed water cans. As soon as all the cans were off, several sick and injured men were on-loaded to be ferried out. Then, directly in front of the chopper, just inside the tree line, I mouthed a thank-you to the pilot and copilot. Both shook their heads, and the copilot offered a familiar thumbs-up as they powered up.

Once again, we were buffeted by churning winds as the chopper ascended back into the sky. Then, one by one, the other 281st helicopters came down inside the small opening to drop off water. As each chopper descended toward the rubble at the base of the LZ, it was like sticking an eggbeater down inside an opening that was barely large enough to accommodate its spinning beaters. After each one touched down, sometimes maintaining a precarious balance across the trunk of the fallen trees, we unloaded the water as quickly and carefully as possible. Despite our dire need for the resupply, I was relieved when the last chopper cleared the top of the trees safely on its way out.

While we were distributing the much-needed water, it occurred to me that any one of the helicopters could have beaten its occupants to death if unbalanced by a branch falling through the rotor blades. The feat that each pilot and crew successfully completed was fraught with inherent dangers. I was amazed that they had actually attempted it when it would have been so easy and understandable for any one of them to say, "The opening is too small. We can't make it in safely."

Fortunately for us and for many, many others in Vietnam, helicopter pilots and crews had earned their "God's Own Lunatics" tag by doing more than they had to do and by going where they didn't have to go.

◆ ◆ ◆

As if another example were necessary, another chopper pilot I know was on a routine mission when he overheard a call for a medevac from one of our Special Forces LRP (long-range patrol) units. When he heard that no medevac choppers were available, he responded to the call and immediately diverted to the emergency. Even though he didn't have a medic on board, he knew the wounded men would have a better chance with him than if they had to lay on the ground and wait for a medevac that might be hours away from arriving.

The situation he encountered was very similar to ours. The unit had to create a landing zone in the jungle. After arriving and settling into the opening, the men were loaded onto his chopper. In attempting to clear the trees, he realized he had too much weight and couldn't rise above them. The obvious answer was to leave someone behind. But, for this pilot, that wasn't even a remote consideration. After trying once again to clear the trees, he was able to get within just feet of making it out. Dropping back into the jungle, he landed momentarily as he studied trees around the LZ.

"Don't be scared by what I'm about to do," he told his copilot. "I've done it before."

Powering up once again, he rose up into the opening. Then, as if using a lawn tool, he began trimming the tops out of the trees with the chopper's blades. When the opening appeared properly corrected, he settled back to the ground. Then, with his engine straining at full power, he ascended one more time and carefully guided his chopper through the stubble of the remaining treetops. Finally, they were clear.

This man did what he knew how to do and what he felt he needed to do, not for himself, but for the benefit of others. He could have easily landed and said, "Some of you have to get off. I can't get all of us out." The men who needed to get off would have done so for the safety of everyone else on board, but that isn't what this pilot did. He didn't take the easy way out; neither did the pilots and crews who brought us water and rescued our sick and injured men there on the mountain. The most important observation I can make about these men is that they were Americans simply being American.

✦ ✦ ✦

With bellies and canteens once again filled, we worked our way down the rugged northeast side of the mountains. Because of the weak condition of many of the Vietnamese soldiers, our movement out of the mountains was far slower than it had been when we entered. It was nearly dusk by the time we reached the river where boats were waiting to pick us up.

As we skimmed along the river's quiet, mirror-smooth surface, I looked at the reflection of the soldiers in the boat around me.

Noticing my own, it appeared slightly weary and a bit dirty. Then, as my gaze moved to the reflection of the mountains and onto the mountains themselves, it occurred to me that I had returned from the Dong Bos tired and dirty—but alive. *Surely, the chaplain's prayer must have been a very good one*, I thought, remembering the Nha Trang chaplain's promise to say a special prayer for our unit's safe return.

Interesting, but that was the first time since stepping foot on the mountain complex that I was reminded of my initial concern about surviving the mission. However, within days, it would be strangely surprising to discover just how close I had come to not surviving the experience. In little more than a month, everyone in the Nha Trang area would be reminded of just how deadly the mountains really were.

The reminder would occur when the Vietnamese High Command agreed to a joint allied operation to locate and attack the Dong Bo base camp. The operation would involve Vietnamese, American, and Korean units. The Vietnamese would provide a point unit to locate the legendary base camp. Americans would provide advisory and air support with the Koreans providing the main attack element.

The Vietnamese point unit would consist of troops from Trung Dung accompanied by members of A-502's Blue Bandit advisory team. The unit would be much smaller than ours had been in order to move considerably more rapidly.

Acting on newly acquired information, the point unit entered the mountain complex and quickly located the huge base camp, but with disastrous results. They sustained heavy casualties and my friend, Lieutenant Bill Phalen, was the unit's senior American advisor.

Even though he believed he and his unit were being sent on a suicide mission, Bill did what every other professional soldier in Vietnam did. He took his orders and carried out his mission. In Bill's case, with what was believed to be fresh and highly accurate intelligence, his unit was assigned the specific mission of locating the enemy base camp of the infamous North Vietnamese Army Regiment 18B.

It was common knowledge among Nha Trang military units that any foray into the Dong Bo Mountains was potentially dangerous and could cost one's life. While ours had been extremely lucky, Bill's wasn't nearly as fortunate. Upon locating the base camp a firefight erupted and lasted for torturous hours. During the battle, Bill was blown several meters down the side of the mountain by an exploding grenade. While stunned and wounded, he survived the blast that could have easily killed him. However, six of his Vietnamese soldiers were killed, and another seventeen were seriously wounded.

Having successfully located the enemy base camp, Bill and his CIDG Company 555 disengaged, carrying their dead and wounded with them down to the base of the mountains. There, they encountered the Korean 100th White Horse Division that was waiting to attack. The Koreans quickly moved into position and surrounded the mountain where Bill's unit had located the base camp. In a heavily supported massive assault, they cleared the mountain of its enemy inhabitants from bottom to top.

Intelligence gathered during the Korean operation revealed that the enemy base camp was far more than myth or legend. It was very real, and information supplied by the Koreans confirmed that the mountain complex had been occupied by the North Vietnamese Army's 18B Regiment. The regiment comprised the 7th, 8th, and 9th Battalions, the Dien Khanh VC District Force, and one sapper (demolition) company. The regiment even had a finance unit and a makeshift hospital in the multi-cave headquarters. Captured documents also indicated that, while assigned to the mountain unit, the 7th Battalion was actually in Cambodia on R&R (rest & recuperation) when the Koreans attacked.

Whatever the actual disposition of enemy units in the Dong Bo Mountains at the time of the attack, the 18B Regiment was functionally destroyed. While the Koreans suffered casualties of their own, they reported approximately seven hundred of NVA and VC killed, with none being reported as wounded.

The Korean mission, first suggested by A-502, was extremely successful. Besides destroying the enemy headquarters, it revealed the true size and makeup of the force that had been entrenched in the mountain stronghold since the days of the Viet Minh. It also explained why the Dong Bo Mountains had been such dangerous place to go.

Just as in any other war, American soldiers in Vietnam went where they were ordered to go regardless of any danger they might face, just as Bill Phalen and his unit had done. Then there were others, such as the pilots and crew members who brought us water and carried out our injured, who rather than orders seemed to rely on some higher and deeper calling.

CHAPTER 13

Life Spared

WHILE MANY YEARS HAVE come and gone since American soldiers served in Vietnam, nearly everyone who was there can cite several occurrences that still remain vivid in memory. The following is an account of such an event that causes me to simply shake my head when reminded of the episode.

✦ ✦ ✦

One morning not long after we returned from our patrol through the Dong Bo Mountains, I was on my way over to visit Thieu Ta Ngoc regarding an upcoming briefing we were scheduled to present to a group of visiting officials. About halfway up the steps to Thieu Ta's, I heard a commotion coming from near the Vietnamese radio room. Backing down the steps, I walked around the corner to see what was happening. Everything had grown quiet as I approached the doorway, but that changed shortly after I entered the room.

The Vietnamese were interrogating another VC suspect they had captured near the base of the Dong Bos the night before. They had begun to threaten him with the possibility of a death sentence if found guilty of supporting the Viet Cong, which is what caused all the commotion. The Vietnamese were yelling at the suspect and he was screaming, claiming that he had only helped the VC by carrying food and supplies to drop-off points in the mountains, but had never fought for them.

After being in the room long enough for him to get a good look at me, the VC suspect pointed at me and began chattering frantically in Vietnamese. He was almost yelling again. I couldn't understand what he was saying, but knew I was somehow involved in whatever it was. There was considerable back-and-forth conversation between the suspect and interrogator before the following story was related to me.

This man, along with two or three of his comrades and one or two armed VC guides, were on a routine delivery trip into the Dong Bos at exactly the same time we were there. While carrying supplies up the mountain, they detected our point unit. Fearing discovery themselves, the men quickly hid in the rocks and thick jungle growth. As we passed by, one of the VC soldiers noticed me in the slow-moving column. Recognizing me as an American, he leveled his AK-47 rifle on me and was preparing to open fire. Killing an American, any American, would have brought him special recognition at the base camp. In many cases a financial reward would also accompany that recognition. The suspect being interrogated quickly pointed out that he had saved my life by keeping the soldier from pulling the trigger. However, then as now, he was likely trying to save his own life as well. The interrogator said that the suspect claimed he argued with the soldier and told him that if he fired, they would probably all be killed. So, it was simply the fear of being killed by return fire from the men around me that kept him from shooting me.

After hearing the tale repeated by the interrogator, I was a little skeptical. I'm reasonably sure it showed in my expression, but the old Vietnamese sergeant who was conducting the questioning seemed convinced the man's story had merit. He had been on the mountain mission with us and expressed his belief in what the prisoner had just said.

"No, I think he is true, Trung Uy. He says to me the day and the place. The day is true, and I think also is true the place." While the interrogator's English wasn't clear, the implication of what he had conveyed was absolutely clear.

In the still of the darkened interrogation room, which had fallen quiet, I considered the old sergeant's assertion. *If the story is true*, I thought, *I wonder how much closer you can come to the event that actually takes your life.* Then I pondered the enigma of who lives and who dies in war, who comes home and who doesn't.

During the Vietnam War more than fifty-eight thousand Americans would meet a fate I had escaped. Each of those names appears on the Vietnam Veteran's Memorial Wall in Washington, D.C.

✦ ✦ ✦

Only days earlier, I had been amazed when two of our team members had survived a blazing close-quarter firefight. That incident began when Colonel Baer, Walt Three Zero, was flying an observation mission in support of one of our Vietnamese CIDG units. Sergeant Richard Bardsley and Sergeant John Key were the American advisors to the unit. They were returning from three-day patrol and were coming down mountain foothills into a flat area divided by a raised railroad berm. Colonel Baer, in his O-1 Bird-dog aircraft, was almost directly overhead when he radioed Sergeant Bardsley with a question.

"Blue Bandit Three Five, this is Walt Three Zero. Over."

"Roger, Walt Three Zero, this is Bandit Three Five. Go ahead."

"Roger, Three Five. Have you got troops on both sides of the railroad tracks? Over."

"Walt, Bandit Three Five. No, there shouldn't be anyone on the other side, but I'll check it out. Over."

With that, Sergeants Bardsley and Key headed for the railroad tracks. As the two started up their side of the berm, the men Baer had seen were coming up the other side. When Bardsley and Key reached the top of the berm, they were suddenly face-to-face with members of an NVA enemy unit. A fierce firefight immediately ensued at near-point-blank range. Each unit fired at the other, and both followed up by throwing grenades. During the exchange of munitions, the Americans either dove for cover or were knocked to the ground by one of the exploding grenades.

When the dust cloud created by the grenades had settled and calm was restored, the two Americans and their Montagnard radioman were the only ones standing. A heavy rapid-fire machine gun was lying on the ground next to one of the dead NVA soldiers. It had a bullet hole, put there by Sergeant Bardsley, directly through the center of its housing. The weapon was taken as a trophy from the battle and placed in our teamhouse where it also served as a constant reminder of our tenuous situation. It wasn't always the Americans who were left standing.

While he survived what amounted to nothing short of a Western-style shootout, Sergeant Bardsley didn't escape the encounter uninjured. During the firefight, his Montagnard radioman had taken cover next to him near the top of the railroad berm. In an attempt to return fire quickly, the radioman simply stuck his M2 carbine up over his head and started pulling the trigger, firing as fast as he could. Unfortunately, while pointed in the right direction, the muzzle of his carbine was only two or three inches from the steel railroad track. Every time he fired, his rounds hit the track and splintered into multiple pieces, which then ricocheted all around him and the two Americans. Sergeant Bardsley had to have several pieces of that ricocheting shrapnel removed from his back and shoulder. He was extremely fortunate that he hadn't been hit in the head or hit by a larger piece of the exploding projectiles, for how paradoxical if he were killed by one of his own men. Certainly, this would have been an unfortunate, but not uncommon folly of war—further complicating my consideration of the enigma of who lives, who dies, and why.

✦ ✦ ✦

When considering my personal experiences in Vietnam and, in particular, the incident in the interrogation room, I have sometimes imagined myself in the VC soldier's gun sight and felt his finger as he applied pressure to the trigger. For whatever reason, my life was spared, and I am very grateful that it was. That incident and other experiences in Vietnam gave me a tremendous respect and appreciation for life—all life.

CHAPTER 14

Take Them Alive

SEEING THEM IN ACTION would make their families and friends back home feel very proud, I thought, as I watched our medics examine a group of village children.

From time to time, as a part of A-502's MEDCAPS Program (Medical Civic Action Program), the medics would go out to the villages or they would invite the villagers to come to the dispensary at Trung Dung for examinations and treatment.

Jerry Arrants, A-502's senior medic, and his team of medics—Larry Freedman, Chuck McGill, and Juan Sotello—had all gone through an intensive forty-three-week medical training program back in the States. Besides the treatment of battle injuries, animal bites, diseases, and a host of other possible ailments, the training had given them the skills required to perform an array of surgical procedures under field conditions, if necessary.

These men, who wore the green beret and the uniform of a military advisor, not only performed their healing skills, but they taught them as well. Members of the camp's CIDG units were selected by our medic team based on interest, education, and aptitude for medical training. Those selected trained and worked in the camp's dispensary, which had been set up and run by our medics. Because of the unique requirements of soldier, teacher, and healer placed on the A-502 medics, it was not unusual to find them carrying all of the tools of their trades at once, a rifle, a pencil, and a stethoscope.

On this day, Sergeant Freedman and Sergeant McGill were working with the children of Trung Dung's Vietnamese soldiers and camp workers as well as those from surrounding villages. Their tone of voice and manner inspired trust and confidence as they tended to their tiny patients. Small children, who frequently arrived hurt and crying, often left with a smile and a good-bye wave for the *bac-si* (doctor) who had taken care of them.

The bedside manner of our medics was only surpassed by their skills and tenacity. On another day that I will never forget, I watched as Freedman and McGill worked under emergency conditions with the focus of skilled surgeons. Pop had been hit by a large military transport truck. He was on his motor scooter riding to Dien Khanh village for supplies when the huge vehicle struck him. Larry Freedman and Chuck McGill would combine their medical skills in an effort to save Pop, a man for whom every American in camp had great affection.

It all began when one of our CIDG soldiers came roaring into the camp on his motorcycle and skidded up to the team's dispensary door. He started yelling in broken English that there had been an accident out on the road. When Freedman ran out in response to the screaming, he was told that a large truck had hit Pop. He yelled for McGill, and the two took off in a military ambulance they acquired in some kind of trade with another unit, the details of which were never quite clear.

When the two men returned with siren yelping and blue light flashing, I became involved. When I ran over to see what had happened, Freedman yelled, "It's Pop! He's been hit! Help us get him inside!"

With that, he disappeared into the dispensary to prepare a treatment table. By the time I reached the back of the ambulance McGill already had Pop and the stretcher halfway out.

"Grab that end!" he yelled, nodding toward the unattended end of the stretcher.

After carrying Pop into what became an operating room, I watched the two Special Forces medics as they fought desperately not to take a life, but to save one. Pop's legs had been horribly crushed by the truck and looked like ground hamburger meat. They were recognizable as human appendages only because they were still attached to his torso. Pop had lost a tremendous amount of blood, which was still pouring from his catastrophic injuries. His soft brown Asian skin was now a washed-out, light ashen gray. Despite the feverish efforts of Freedman and McGill, I knew I was watching Pop die.

Working against the monumental odds facing them, Freedman and McGill moved around what was left of Pop's lower extremities, communicating in calm but loud voices as they worked. The two men attached transfusions, tied off profusely bleeding vessels, cut flesh and sawed bone. The dispensary began to look more like a butcher shop than an operating room as pieces of Pop's legs fell from the table.

As I looked at his face, which appeared as that of a corpse, in my imagination his skin color slowly returned, as did his warm familiar smile. I remember the day that he served lunch to one of the Red Cross girls that was visiting the team. Pop had put a flower on the rim of her plate and beamed as he placed it before her. Imagining the return of his smile would be easier than imagining life in the team-house without him.

As word of the accident spread around camp, team members quickly began gathering around the dispensary. After coming in and seeing Pop on the table and how severe his injuries were, Bill Lane became enraged and angrily declared, "Nothing good ever happens in this country."

I understood Bill's cynicism clearly. I was becoming cynical myself. If sent, I would have fought in the last battle for Vietnam, but this war seemed far from any resolution and I could see what it was doing to our country. I was looking at what it had done to Pop and didn't care to watch it anymore, so I went outside to wait with the rest of the team. Vietnamese medics were now assisting in the effort, and there was nothing I could do anyway.

It seemed like hours, but sometime later Freedman emerged from the dispensary. We all waited for the expected news of Pop's death. Freedman looked weary and was still wiping blood from his hands as he raised his head. "Pop will live," he said. Upon hearing those words, a roar spontaneously arose from the small gathering.

As I turned and walked away from the dispensary, I decided my teammate and friend Bill Lane was wrong. Good things did happen in Vietnam, and American medics were responsible for an important share of them. This day was a good day. While seriously injured, Pop had been saved. There were other days, too, when the medics provided medical treatment for the children and adults in the surrounding villages that would have otherwise been unavailable to them. More good days were still to come—days that would give meaning to my service in Vietnam.

✦ ✦ ✦

Many ailments that Vietnamese villagers suffered were a result of poor diets and lack of medical care. Because rice was their basic or, often their only, food, they also lacked many of the vitamins and nutrients contained in fish, meats and vegetables required for a healthy diet.

When the villagers did come by fresh meat, regardless of what kind it was, nothing was wasted. The Vietnamese villagers' lesson of "don't waste anything" had been taught to me one night in a small village a few weeks earlier.

Vietnamization, the act of turning all responsibilities for the war over to the Vietnamese, had just begun. The number of advisors at 502 was being reduced, and schedules often only allowed for one American advisor to go out on a night ambush with each of our Vietnamese units. Such was the case for me when my next ambush rotation came up. I was scheduled to serve as the only U.S. advisor to one of my favorite old Trung Sis (sergeants). Being the lone American with the unit didn't bother me at all. By this time, I had been in-country for many months and felt comfortable with the assignment. Besides, I knew that if anything happened, there was plenty of support on the other end of my radio.

It was between dusk and full dark as we walked across rice paddy dikes toward our ambush site. The night air was still hot and laden with humidity. My skin was moist with beads of perspiration as I slapped at mosquitoes buzzing around my face and neck. Flickering candlelight could be seen in the small village ahead, the village where Trung Si lived and where we would be setting up our ambush for the night. Our men would be set out along the south side parallel to an approach used by looters believed to be VC.

When we reached the village, the old Vietnamese sergeant told me our position would be in the center of the ambush, which wasn't far from his house. He then told me that he had asked his wife to prepare a special meal for us, knowing I would be with him that night. As usual before a night ambush, I had already eaten at camp. But, because it would have been impolite and a dishonor to the Trung Si not to accept the extremely rare invitation to a Vietnamese soldier's home, I would eat again.

After establishing the ambush and reporting our exact location to 502, we went to Trung Si's home for dinner. His wife greeted me warmly at the door to their tiny dwelling and gestured for me to enter. The table, as the rest of the house, was lit only by candlelight. There was no electricity. The small dinner table was set with a humble flower centerpiece, painted rice bowls, Oriental soup spoons, and chopsticks.

When Trung Si's wife served dinner, it consisted of a heaping bowl of rice, chicken soup, and warm Ba Mui Ba (Vietnamese beer) for Trung Si and me. Sipping a spoonful of hot broth, it didn't taste or smell quite like anything Mom used to make. Even so, I complimented Trung Si's wife on her wonderful soup. In spite of the fact that she spoke no English, she smiled broadly and thanked me in Vietnamese. Then, spooning deeper into my bowl, I felt a large piece of chicken and began lifting it to the surface of the soup. As it emerged, I discovered that special surprises had been placed in my bowl. Pausing to let my spoon rest on the edge of the bowl, I reached for my beer glass and pondered what to do with the surprises.

After taking a drink of my beer, I looked back down at the chicken head lying in my soup spoon. Its glazed blue eye appeared to stare straight up at me. The head didn't look appetizing, nor did the chicken foot that was hooked to the spoon by its claw. My method of dealing with the situation was to simply let both slide off my spoon and back to the bottom of my bowl. Not wanting to hurt the feelings of Trung Si's wife and knowing I was probably the only American ever invited to his home, I hoped to leave a good impression of my visit. So, eventually, I ate everything . . . except the foot and the head. Later, Trung Si told me they had been used to give more flavor to the soup. One thing was certain, none of that chicken had been wasted. Every piece of it had been used, from head to toe.

✦ ✦ ✦

Continuing to watch our medics treat the village children, I noticed something interesting. The medics themselves appeared to be gaining something from the healing process in which they were involved, a great sense of satisfaction. How do I know? The look on their faces just after putting a treated child back in its mother's arms told everything.

The medics were a special blend of sensitivity and courage. Sergeant Freedman, for example, besides being a skilled medic, was also a seasoned military advisor. When he wasn't conducting one of his many monthly MEDCAP visits, he served as a primary advisor to Vietnamese Combat Reconnaissance Platoon 58 and saw action with that and other units on a number of night ambushes and patrols. He was a man the Vietnamese liked, trusted, and respected. Freedman, Sergeant Arrants, and his entire team of medics were a unique breed of men.

My observation of the MEDCAPS program was interrupted by our radioman.

"Lieutenant Ross, Walt Three Zero is on the horn for you."

"Okay. Tell him I'm on the way."

When I arrived at the radio room and called Walt Three Zero, he sounded fairly excited. "Zero Two, I've got two VC suspects in the open. Can you get out here?"

"Where are you?"

When he gave me coordinates for his location, I realized it was going to take a chopper to get to the area he was circling. Because of the demand for them, it could be difficult to obtain a chopper unless it had been previously scheduled. However, the 281st AHC always seemed to come through for us. They had a chopper available and dispatched it immediately.

The men of the 281st, whose company designation was "Intruders" and whose motto was "Hell from Above," were divided into three platoons. "Rat Pack" and "Bandits" were lift platoons, which means they were used primarily to deliver troops to a battlefield. "Wolf Pack" was a gunship platoon, which means they were primarily used to cover the lift platoons during troop insertions and extractions. They were also called upon to provide cover and/or support for ground units. They were like having a big brother, and I was always more comfortable when they were nearby.

The pilots and crews of these UH-1 helicopters sat exposed to any and every danger on the battlefield as they entered and exited. The pilot and copilot sat in a cockpit surrounded by little more than Plexiglas, clearly visible to any enemy gunner who might be on or near their LZ. While they had small armored shields on both sides and under their seats, it was always my opinion that they provided little more than psychological protection. On the lift platoon choppers, the two crew members, who also served as door gunners, sat on each side of the helicopter manning .60-caliber machine guns, fully exposed with no protection beyond the flak vests they wore.

The pilots and crew of these extremely vulnerable aircraft were supremely courageous men who never failed to respond to A-502's calls for support or help. Their bold and frequent intrusions into dangerous situations confirmed the appropriateness of their "Intruders" designation. But their response to our most recent call for assistance would demonstrate that they weren't just bold, they were skilled, intelligent, and compassionate.

✦ ✦ ✦

With the 281st inbound, eight Vietnamese Special Forces members of The Eagle Team, our quick response unit, were alerted and told to meet at the chopper pad. The radio operator called Walt Three Zero, and told him to try to keep his targets in sight until we arrived.

The chopper pilots who served in Vietnam had long since won my admiration, but the performance and discipline of the pilot and crew of the 281st chopper flying this mission were truly admirable. It only took them about fifteen minutes to reach us and about the same to get to the place where Colonel Baer was circling.

On the way out, I told the pilot we needed to capture the VC alive, if possible. It had been a while since we had received any fresh intelligence information, and this offered us a great opportunity to learn what was going on in Charlie's head out west.

"Just show us where they are," the pilot said.

"They ought to be somewhere under that 01," I told him, then checked in with Colonel Baer.

"Walt Three Zero, this is Zero Two. We're coming in on you from the east. Can you see us? Over."

"Roger, I've got you."

"Do you still have your targets?" I asked.

"Roger, I just chased them into that abandoned village directly beneath me. They ran into one of those houses down there."

"Okay," said the chopper pilot. "Let's go find 'em."

Then, he swooped down toward the village like an eagle after a fish near the surface of the water. My insides felt as though they had stayed somewhere a few hundred feet above us as we continued our dive toward the village.

"Let me know when you see our targets," the pilot told his crew as he finally leveled off.

After making about three passes over the village at around fifty feet, one of the door gunners spotted the two men.

"I've got 'em at five o'clock running between two small houses," he said.

The gunner had barely gotten "five o'clock" out of his mouth before the pilot pushed the chopper up around to the right and back down. It felt as though we had gone from one direction to the exact opposite instantaneously, and I wasn't sure exactly where my insides were that time. We all just hung on as the pilot maneuvered to locate and lock in on our prey.

We were still coming out of our "U" turn when the copilot said, "Yeah, I've got 'em. They just ran behind that house with the blown-out roof."

"Be alert," the pilot said to his door gunners. "We're going to rock around behind that house."

That's exactly what we did. The nose of the chopper continued to point directly at the house as its tail started to swing around. In just a few seconds we were looking at the backside of the house and the two VC suspects. When they turned to run, we could see they were in civilian clothes, but it was similar to clothing we had seen on VC before. Because they were turning, our view was obscured. We couldn't tell what kind of weapons the men were carrying.

Obviously, they were trying to elude us and bolted for the corner of the house. Darting around the corner and along the side of the dwelling, they crossed an open area and ran toward yet another vacant house. But this time they were in full view as they made their crossing. The door gunner swung his M-60 machine gun around and had the two in the center of his sites the entire way. I watched the face of the young door gunner, whose focus on the men was intense. He had his M-60 pulled in tightly against his shoulder. His right hand gripped the weapon firmly, and his index finger covered the trigger. I wanted the men alive and was concerned he was going to fire. One or two bursts from his weapon, and the chase would have been over. The two men weren't very fast on their feet and would have been very easy targets for the door gunner if his intent had been to kill. Despite the intensity of the situation, the gunner never opened fire and simply kept his weapon trained on them as they ran into a house.

"Were those carbines they were carrying?" the pilot asked.

"Yeah, I think so," the copilot responded. "I could have nailed them," he added.

The pilot circled the house to make sure his quarry hadn't run out the back door. When he saw there was no back door, he said, "We've got 'em." Then, he moved back around to the front side of the house and hovered in a position that, once again, gave the left door gunner an ideal firing position. Immediately, three Eagle Team members moved with their M-16s to the chopper door to provide backup for the door gunner.

The pilot was hovering at little more than twenty-five feet off the ground. Dust was blowing everywhere, and the door gunner had his M-60 machine gun trained on the front of the house to cover the door and two opened windows.

In our low hovering position, though, our chopper was an easy target for the two men inside the house if they chose to duel. We waited to see either the men or their weapons. Then, finally, we saw their faces looking up at us.

When I waved and yelled for them to come out, they backed out of sight. When they appeared at one of the windows again, I waved and yelled once more for them to come out. But, as they had done before, they simply backed out of sight. That went on one or two more times. Then, the pilot very calmly said, "We'll run 'em out."

The pilot's next action was unorthodox and, frankly, amusing. He moved the chopper to a position directly over the house and set it down on the roof. Then he bounced on it a couple of times. When he roosted on the roof the next time, it started to collapse under the weight of the chopper, and the two men burst out of the house unarmed with their hands in the air. The pilot then quickly moved off the house and set the chopper down in front of it.

As soon as the chopper's skids hit the ground, three members of the Eagle Team and I jumped out to retrieve the two men. Since we were without a gunship for covering protection, we didn't hang around. As quickly as everyone was back on board, the pilot lifted off with the quarry bagged and uninjured.

✦ ✦ ✦

The two men that the pilot and his crew had skillfully captured could have been killed by either of the two door gunners on multiple occasions. But, given the challenging mission of capturing the two alive, that's exactly what they had done.

Even Colonel Baer who had stayed close at hand and had seen the capture called with compliments for the chopper's pilot and crew.

"Zero Two, Walt Three Zero. Over."

"Roger, go ahead Walt Three Zero."

"Tell your pilot that was some mighty fancy flying. I especially enjoyed the rooftop landing. Ask him if he learned that at flight school. Over."

The pilot, who was monitoring the frequency, grinned as he listened to Baer's remarks.

"Tell him that one came out of our hat."

"Walt Three Zero, this is Zero Two. I'm told that one wasn't in the book."

After thanking Colonel Baer for his tip on the two VC suspects, who were now prisoners, our communications were ended. But, with shared feelings of satisfaction, the Air Force 0-1 Bird Dog and Army UH-1 Huey flew together back toward Trung Dung.

It had been a good day that started with healing and ended with mercy, an unusual day in Vietnam.

PART II

The Rescue

CHAPTER 15

A Promise Made

IT WAS HAIRCUT TIME. My hair had grown almost three inches long on top, and I was sure Major Lee would say something if it grew any longer. Lee was a disciplined man who believed an officer's hair should always be neat and closely trimmed, even in a combat zone. Mine was neat, but long enough to comb. A trip to the barber was in order.

It was about 1000 (10 a.m.) when I left the small two-chair barbershop operated by a couple of the camp's Vietnamese soldiers. I was still brushing hair off my neck when Sergeant Koch came walking up at a quick pace. He was in a hurry.

"Sir," he said, as he waved a salute.

"Good morning, Sarge. How does my haircut look?"

"Fine, LT. It looks real good."

So much for our exchange on my haircut. He obviously had something more important to talk about.

"LT, we just got a call from My Loc. They say some VC have surrendered to them. They want you out there ASAP," Koch said.

"Fine, grab a jeep and let's go."

Koch went after a jeep. I went for my gear, and in a few minutes we were headed west to My Loc. On the way to the somewhat remote outpost, I asked Sergeant Koch what he thought about the call he had received. We never had anyone offer to turn themselves in as VC before.

"So, what do you think, Sarge? Seems a little strange, doesn't it?"

"It sure does. Nothing like this has happened as long as I've been here," he said.

"Well, I guess we'll find out what's what soon enough."

Upon arriving at My Loc, we were taken to a spot near the main bunker where the three men who had turned themselves in were sitting. Immediately upon seeing the trio and after talking with them via an interpreter for just a few minutes, we had a much clearer understanding of what was happening.

The men weren't VC at all. They were Montagnard tribesmen. They claimed they had been used as slaves by the VC for years and had escaped almost two days earlier. The three hadn't made their way through the jungle to turn themselves in as VC. The desperate journey was attempted for a much more important reason.

Two of the men found Chieu Hoi (pronounced "chu hoy") passes in fields near their village that had been dropped from allied aircraft in hopes that VC or North Vietnamese soldiers would find them. The small leaflets were part of a joint military Psy Ops (psychological operations) program. They promised a warm reception and good treatment to enemy soldiers who would quit fighting and turn themselves in to allied forces.

The Montagnards found the passes and thought that, if they could make their way to the allies and turn themselves in, they might be able to obtain help for their village.

Now that we knew who they really were and why they were there, we asked the villagers to tell their story through our interpreter. What followed was a tale of servitude and abuse. According to what we were told the VC and North Vietnamese had made slaves of not just these three men, but the entire village as well. For the past eight years, the villagers had been forced to carry ammunition and supplies as well as grow food to be used by various enemy units passing through the area.

Their story of captivity included tales of brutal beatings and other more violent atrocities perpetrated on village inhabitants.

Mang Quang, the primary spokesman and apparent leader for the three, was a village elder who claimed to have been kept restrained in the village. He explained through the interpreter that after years of abusive captivity, he had grown weary of the VC treatment and began to defy their orders. Rather than killing him when he became defiant, they told him that he would serve their needs better as a living example for the rest of the village. They responded by beating him and keeping him tied to a post at night for the better part of two years. He had rope burns and the other two men as witnesses to support his story.

Mang Quang said he recently convinced the VC of his contrition and asked to be released from his in-camp duties and released to work in the fields. He said he decided to make the plea after his two friends told him about the information contained in the Chieu Hoi passes they found.

Early in the morning after the VC released him and allowed him to return to the fields, he and his two friends quietly disappeared into the dense jungle. They hoped to find the allies and the things promised on the pieces of paper they carried with them.

In spite of the fact that the three had been successful in their attempt to reach our outpost, Mang Quang was noticeably upset as his story continued to unfold. The reason for his distress was quick to follow and easily understood. He explained that, when they released him to work the fields, his captors gave him an extremely stern warning about checking in on a routine basis. They told him that if they hadn't seen him in three days, they would kill his family.

Mang Quang said the VC would think he slept in the fields one or two nights since that was a common practice and because he had just been released. But, if he didn't return by the third night, he felt sure they would know he had run away and would very likely carry out their threat to kill his family. One of the other Montagnards quickly added that the VC routinely threatened all of the villagers. He said that was the reason they came to us. They wanted to "turn themselves in" because they needed help for their village.

The Montagnard interpreter, translating the villagers' emotional plea, turned to me and repeated it in English, "He says they are not able to defend themselves or their families from the VC Trung Uy. They need help because they don't want their wives or children to be hurt anymore." His lips were quivering as he spoke the last words of the villager's plea for help. I believe it was mostly anger, but he appeared visibly shaken by the story he had just translated. He wasn't the only one. Sergeant Koch and I were both moved as well. There was little doubt that we would have to respond in some way.

Having grown up in a very close and loving family, I was more moved by Mang Quang's emotional expression of fear about his family's safety than I showed. I wasn't sure exactly what we were going to do yet, but with defenseless families involved, some action seemed required.

After Sergeant Koch and I discussed the magnitude of the commitment we were about to make, I told the interpreter to tell Mang Quang and his friends not to worry.

"Then, tell them," I said, "we will go get their families."

After the translation was complete, Mang smiled widely and nodded his head. Then, he took one of my hands with both of his and squeezed it tightly and spoke directly to me in his native language. As he spoke, a feeling of tremendous responsibility swept over me. Without understanding his words, I knew exactly what he was trying to communicate to me. The interpreter confirmed that when he translated Mang's words.

"He is giving you very great thanks, Trung Uy, for helping him and his people."

Nodding, I returned his smile.

"Tell him I understood what he said. Then tell him we are very glad to help. That's why we are here."

It may seem naive, but as a young American army officer, I was very proud to speak those words, because that was exactly why I was there.

Looking at the three villagers huddled together and giving thought to the situation, I began to realize the scope of the challenge we had just accepted. Then something else came to mind. *These three half-naked, half-starved mountain villagers have just given us an incredible opportunity,* I thought. This wasn't going to be an attack to kill or a search-and-destroy mission. It was going to be a rescue, a mission with an objective to save lives.

Any military man or woman will tell you that they would rather save a life than take one. This was exactly the opportunity I had hoped for, but hadn't really expected. It was a chance to do something truly meaningful with my military training, and three small, beaten men had dropped it in our laps. While they had been beaten physically, though, they had not been beaten mentally. They were husbands and fathers whose courage was as great as their love and concern for their families. These qualities and emotions could easily be read in the things they said, as well as in their faces.

With our promise made, the reality of timing suddenly struck us. "If it took them two days to find us, you know what that makes today, LT," Sergeant Koch said.

"Yes, I do," I said with concern. "It's the third day."

If we were going to do something for the villagers and, in particular, Mang Quang's family, we were going to have to do it very quickly.

Since we had to go to work immediately, I explained our need for help from Mang Quang and the other two men. Speaking to the interpreter but looking at Mang Quang, I said, "Tell him before we can help his people, we need help from him. We need to know how many villagers there are and exactly where the village is located."

Trying to determine the location of the village turned out to be more difficult than one might imagine. Mang Quang's first response to my question about the village wasn't much more than a wave of his arm, gesturing generally to the west, and a grunt.

"He says, it's out there." The interpreter said.

"Well, that's a start," I replied.

Clearly this wasn't going to be easy. It would, however, turn out to be a textbook scenario, just like the ones taught at the Intelligence School back at Fort Holibird, Maryland. At Holibird, they used actors who were dressed and trained to behave as Vietnamese, even VC and North Vietnamese, in various scripted scenarios. Students were asked to assume that information in the script was real and to conduct themselves as though the actors were actually Vietnamese with valuable intelligence information. The student's task was to gather as much information as possible from them using various interrogation methods taught at the school. Some of the actors posing as VC and NVA were often so convincing and provocative that student interrogators became enraged and were ready to fight then and there. The class was extremely interesting, and the value of its practical application was about to be proven.

The questions posed to the Montagnards as related here are meant to serve as an approximation of the actual exchange in composite form, simply to demonstrate the tedium of the process.

✦ ✦ ✦

I asked Sergeant Koch to get our map from the jeep, which turned out to be of little help. After showing it to Mang Quang and trying to explain what it was and how it worked, he looked at me and shook his head. He had no idea how to read a map. Again, he gestured toward the west and repeated his "out there" grunt, which was met with a chuckle from an amused Sergeant Koch.

Anticipating the answer to my next question, I asked it anyway.

"If we flew in a plane 'out there' and we flew over the village, could we see it from above?"

I knew my guess was correct when Mang Quang responded by shaking his head negatively back and forth.

"He says, 'No. The jungle is very big and very thick. The village is very well hidden under the trees,'" the interpreter said.

Obviously we needed to begin with basics.

"Okay, good. Now, ask him to describe the land around the village. Is it flat? Are there hills?" Before I could say more, the interpreter understood what I was asking and began the questioning.

"He says their village is in the hills near the base of some mountains, Trung Uy."

"Good. Now, ask him where the morning sun was when they left the hills. Was it beside him, in front of him, where? Ask him to show us with his arm. Ask him to point to where the morning sun was in the sky."

As the interpreter translated, I could tell Mang understood the question and why it was being asked. He immediately began shaking his head up and down and gesturing with both arms, indicating both the direction they walked and the sun's relative position.

"He says they walked that way and the sun was over there."

"Good!" I said smiling.

The smile was to let him know the information he was giving us was helpful. It was obviously going to take a while to sort things out, and if he didn't think we were accomplishing something, I was concerned that he might become frustrated.

With Mang Quang's motions indicating that the trio had started out walking northeast, the next question was asked, "Where was the sun on the second morning?"

"He says it was straight in front of them. They walked toward the rising sun," the interpreter said.

With our first few questions we were able to determine that the village was roughly two days' walk away in mountains somewhere in the southeast, not near enough information to plan a mission. The long series of questions continued with Sergeant Koch taking notes and asking his own questions as we proceeded.

"Did they sleep at night? If so, how long?" I queried.

"They slept, but not very long, maybe only a couple of hours. They wanted to keep moving in case the VC were following them," the interpreter said.

"Did they walk to the outpost on trails or did they have to make his way through the jungle?" I asked.

"They came through the jungle, but sometimes they found trails," came the response.

"Were they able to walk in a straight line or did they have to go around hills or mountains?"

"They went around some hills and walked over some small ones. But, he says they mostly walked straight."

"Good, Mang Quang. Very good!" I encouraged him.

Sergeant Koch added his encouragement by patting him on the back. Mang smiled broadly, obviously pleased that he was helping.

Mang Quang was indeed providing helpful information, but it still only narrowed the location of the village to a vast area far to the southwest of Trung Dung. The exact distance he covered would depend on how many hills he walked over, how many and how far he had to walk around, how long he stopped to rest, along with a host of other key factors.

Pausing momentarily to consider my next question, I was half staring at the map. Then, my eyes focused above the edge of the map toward the direction of the Song Cai River, which ran through the valley. That gave me an idea. The village, in order to survive, would need a water source.

Maybe it's near the river, I thought.

Realizing the river might be seen from the hill where we were, I stood up from the customary squatting position we had assumed to talk. Turning to face the river more directly, I motioned to Mang Quang and the interpreter to come beside me. Then, putting my hand on Mang's shoulder, I pointed toward the river and traced its flow through the valley until it disappeared in the west.

"Is there a river near your village?" I asked through the interpreter.

He smiled again and said, "Yes."

I picked up a stick and drew a long slowly curving line in the dirt. "This is the river," I said.

Then, scratching an "X" on both sides of the river, I asked my next question.

"On which side of the river is your village?" pointing first at the one X and then the other.

"That side or . . . this side?"

Mang didn't hesitate. He quickly pointed to the X on the south side of the river. Then, he spoke as he continued to point.

"He says the village is on the hills in the jungle above the river, Trung Uy."

When asked if there was anything else around the village besides the river that would help us locate it, we were given an important graphic response.

Mang Quang took the stick from my hand and scratched some marks of his own in the dirt. He drew some small inverted "V's" on the south side of the village. As he drew, he spoke to the interpreter and continued to draw some larger "V's" on the south side of the smaller ones.

"These are the small hills where the village is located," the interpreter said, pointing to the small Vs. Then, he pointed to the large Vs.

"He says these are the higher mountains beyond the village in this direction."

Then he gave us the information we needed to pinpoint the village from the air.

Still scratching with the stick, he drew several squares.

"What are those?" I asked.

"Cornfields, Trung Uy. He says there are many cornfields around their village," was the response through the interpreter as Mang handed the stick back to me.

Of course, I thought, *those must be the fields where they found the Chieu Hoi passes.* I thought for a moment or two studying Mang Quang's drawing before asking my next question.

"Are there any cornfields near the village other than these?"

"No," Mang indicated, shaking his head back and forth very definitely.

Even though he was primitive with no formal education, it was obvious that he was very bright. Mang Quang seemed to realize that he had given us enough information to find his village and his family.

✦ ✦ ✦

Sergeant Koch and I finally agreed that that we had what we needed to complete the puzzle and find the village. As important as knowing its location, though, was the need to find a place to land close enough to the village to reach it quickly.

Sergeant Koch and I had both become concerned when Mang first described the village as being in the hills under the jungle canopy. We were afraid we would have to land some distance away and move through the jungle. That could take a great deal of time. If we were unable to reach the village quickly, the VC would have more than enough time to kill or move the villagers before we reached them. They would also have time to set up an ambush for us or, at least, prepare for our assault.

Now, however, there was no need for concern about where we would land. The cornfields, which Mang Quang told us were located in close proximity to the village, were an unexpected bonus and more than we could have hoped for. They would serve as ready-made LZs. We would land in one of them and from there we would move immediately to the village and, hopefully, effect the rescue.

With a reasonably clear idea of how we would locate the Montagnard village and how we would get to it, we considered another important issue. Once more I turned to the interpreter. "Ask Mang Quang about the enemy soldiers. How many are there and where are they?"

Mang's responses were long and fairly detailed. Among other things, he indicated that a large unit had left the camp only a few days prior to his escape. He also told us that the absence of troops and some of the guards had made it easier for the trio to slip away undetected. Mang then said that, normally, the soldiers were posted on trails as well as in various places in the jungle all around the village. But, now, he believed there could be no more than thirty to forty men guarding the entire area. If that were true, it would be another unexpected break.

Sergeant Koch and I both asked several more questions regarding the disposition of the soldiers around the village. We also asked Mang and the other two men for their best description of the weapons used by the enemy soldiers.

All Mang and his friends described were light weapons. Apparently, the larger unit had taken all the bigger pieces with them when they left the village. That was extremely welcome information.

Now, we only had to hope the main body didn't return before we arrived the next day. However, even with the bulk of the enemy unit apparently at another location, the remaining unit of "thirty to forty" soldiers could prove very resistant. A well-commanded unit of that size, defending on its own jungle terrain, could inflict significant casualties on our force.

If a large portion of the enemy unit was concentrated in identifiable areas, an air strike might help to eliminate the threat. But, according to Mang Quang, they weren't. And because of the dispersal of villagers throughout the area, the possibility of utilizing an air strike was virtually eliminated.

During the questioning it had become clear that in order to be successful and hold casualties to a minimum, we would have to move swiftly and strike with surprise. We needed to do whatever we were going to do early the next morning.

Now agreed that we had all the information we needed to plan the operation, Sergeant Koch and I also agreed that in order to be "out there" the next morning, where Mang had first indicated his village was located, we needed to get to work on a plan quickly.

"Okay, Sarge. Let's head back to camp and get started. We've got a lot to do and not a whole lot a time to get it done."

We loaded Mang Quang and the other two men into the jeep and started back to camp. We drove down off My Loc hill with considerable anticipation of what we were about to attempt.

✦ ✦ ✦

On the day of my encounter with Mang Quang, I had been in Vietnam for more than seven months. While having been involved in an array of missions, there were no particular feelings of meaningful accomplishment. With fewer than five months of my tour remaining, I had begun to believe that it might expire before anything of substance would be achieved. While never being quite sure what form it would take, it was always my belief that the opportunity to do something of merit would be easily recognizable when it arose. And it was. This was it.

✦ ✦ ✦

As Americans, we are a helping people. This statement is easily proven true by simply observing our actions whenever there is a disaster somewhere in our country or in some other part of the world. We are quick to respond and among the first to send help. Very simply, our nature is to respond when others are in distress, and this is one of the qualities that defines us as Americans. It's in our blood.

✦ ✦ ✦

If Mang Quang's family was to be saved, there were only hours in which to act. In order to be successful, this operation would require an extremely quick response.

CHAPTER 16

Gathering the Team

IT WAS NOW ABOUT 1400 (2 p.m.), and with so much to do, the speed at which Sergeant Koch was driving us back to Trung Dung suddenly seemed awfully slow.

"Is this as fast as we can go, Sarge? We really need to get back to camp."

"Are you saying you want me to go a little faster, LT?"

"Yeah, if you think this thing will go any faster."

"You've got it. Hang onto your beret."

✦ ✦ ✦

Because the road was still wet from a morning rain, the wheels spun when Sergeant Koch changed gears and mashed the accelerator pedal. The Montagnards grabbed the backs of our seats to hang on as our speed increased and thrust us all backwards.

"Sarge, you know this is a unique opportunity."

"Yes, sir. You're right. But how are we gonna pull this off? It's too far to walk and make it in time. So, we're gonna have to use choppers. If the VC or NVA are there, even thirty or forty, as these guys say, we're gonna have to prep the LZ. Hell, LT, their people will scatter into the jungle along with the VC. They'll think we're shooting at them, too."

"Yeah, you're right. There's a lot we're going to have to think about. That's why we need to get back to camp as quickly as possible."

Koch nodded, and we continued bouncing and sliding our way toward Trung Dung.

As we made our way back to camp we had many things to consider. While enthusiastic about the possibility of a rescue mission, I couldn't help shake the possibility that what we had been told might simply be part of an elaborate trap.

✦ ✦ ✦

When we reached Trung Dung, I went straight to the radio room in the teamhouse. During the ride in, I'd thought about the problem of alerting the people in the village to our rescue attempt. Sergeant Koch had recognized a problem we would have to resolve.

I called the Eighth Psy Ops headquarters in Nha Trang and asked if they had an aircraft capable of broadcasting a recorded message via loudspeakers. They told me the Air Force had one they used from time to time.

"Is it available for a mission tomorrow morning, and can you help record the message?" I asked.

The response was yes to both questions.

✦ ✦ ✦

One of our radiomen was checking on the availability of air support while I went looking for a ride from the 281st Attack Helicopter Company. We would need them to transport our rescue unit to the village. Their participation was essential if the mission was, literally, to get off the ground. However, the serious possibility existed that, for more than one reason, they would be prevented from being involved.

On the way back from My Loc I was looking over my map and realized that, based on the information gathered from Mang Quang, it was likely that the village would be found far beyond the western border of the map. Since that would be well outside our AO, the 281st would not be required to fly so far out. Additionally, because the Montagnards were civilians, the 281st would not be flying in support of an American military mission. That could be a problem if a military mission developed somewhere else and required the unit's choppers. Added to these issues were the facts that we weren't sure exactly where we were going, and we were uncertain about precisely what we would find when we arrived. So, a "We can't help you" response was a distinct possibility.

When the radioman answered at the 281st, I asked him if they were available to fly a mission early the next morning. He said there was nothing on the schedule, but asked me to "wait one" while he put his duty officer on the radio. The ops officer asked for the details regarding our mission request.

I told him everything. I told him what we knew as well as what we didn't know. I also told him there would be no artillery support and no air support. Artillery wouldn't reach that far, and I had just been advised that air support was unavailable.

There was a long pause on the radio as the ops officer at the 281st was obviously considering his response. Then, "You know you're giving us pretty short notice for something this big, right?"

"I do. But this just fell into our laps, and we feel that if we are to have any advantage we have to be there at first light."

There was no hesitation in his next response.

"I agree. I think we have to be there early."

Obviously accepting the mission, he went on to assure me that everything would be arranged for wherever the mission took us.

"Everything you need will be there tomorrow morning and it will be there on time. I'll be flying one of the choppers myself," he said. "I want to be a part of this one." This was a typical response that A-502 came to expect from the Intruders.

❖ ❖ ❖

With the transportation arranged, the next requirement was the troops who would utilize the transportation. That meant a visit to

Thieu Ta, whose authorization was needed for the Vietnamese units to be committed to the operation.

While his authorization would be required, Thieu Ta's approval wasn't really a concern. We had developed a very warm relationship during my time as an advisor at A-502 and particularly during our time together on the Dong Bo Mountain mission.

✦ ✦ ✦

At the end of my tour in December 1968, I went to say good-bye to Thieu Ta Ngoc. I gave him my address and told him to call if he ever got to the United States. After sharing a few memories of our experiences together, we shook hands and I left to catch my ride to Cam Ranh Bay and the flight home. When the government of South Vietnam collapsed in 1975, Ngoc, his wife, and their four children fled the country with thousands of other refugees. They escaped with what they were wearing, almost no money, and not much more than a few phone numbers. One of them was mine.

After moving through various refugee camps, they were relocated to one in Huntsville, Alabama. Ngoc and his family reached Huntsville late in the evening, but he found a phone and called me to let me know they were in the United States. His call was a surprise. Although I had wondered about them many times while watching the news of his country's fall, it had been nearly six years since we last spoke.

Ngoc wasted no time telling me that the only way they could leave the camp was if a sponsor could be found for his family. When he asked if I had any ideas, I told him not to worry. "You just found your sponsor," I said. Since Huntsville was about a six-hour drive from my home in Pensacola, I told him to expect me to arrive at about lunchtime the next day.

For a few weeks, Nguyen Quang Ngoc and his family stayed in my home. During that time we found him a job and a place for his family to live. Ngoc, as he wanted to be called, was able to make contact with some of his family living in France, and they sent him money to help him with his new start.

While they were living with me, Ngoc and his wife, Kim, who resembled a delicate china doll, woke up early every morning. They would clean the house and work in the yard. I often found them on their hands and knees picking weeds out of the yard and flower beds, which was their way to return a perceived favor. Even though I made them quit cleaning or picking weeds every time I found them doing it, the very next morning they would be at it again.

When Ngoc left Vietnam, he was a colonel and held a very important position. He and Kim owned two homes and lived a respected upscale lifestyle, yet while they were in my home, they never hesitated to take the most menial tasks upon themselves.

While we lived in Pensacola, our families became very close. Since then, Ngoc and Kim's children have had children, and we've both moved a number of times. The last time I heard from Ngoc, he was—ironically—trying to return to Vietnam. If the tables were turned, I suppose I would be trying to make it back to the United States.

◆ ◆ ◆

After completing arrangements with the 281st, I left the radio room and walked across the camp to Thieu Ta's command center, where he also maintained a residence. Even though he was eating a late lunch when I found him, he motioned me in when he saw me.

"*Ciao,* Trung Uy. How are you today?"

"I am fine, Thieu Ta. How are you?"

"Good, good. I am good. You want to have lunch with me, Trung Uy?"

"No, Thieu Ta. Thank you. But there is something I do need. I need some help."

"Tell me what you need, Trung Uy."

"I need about two companies of your best soldiers, Thieu Ta," I said.

Then I told him the villager's story and explained why the troops were needed. I ended my explanation by telling him that this mission was very important to me personally, but also to the other Americans.

"Why is this mission so important to you, Trung Uy?" he asked.

My answer was brief. I told him that this mission, for once, would give our troops the chance to use their weapons for good—to save lives, not take them. Also, helping the Montagnards would give our A-502 team the opportunity to do something that would make us very glad we came to Vietnam.

At the end of a brief silence, Thieu Ta placed his chopsticks across his plate, wiped his mouth with a cloth, and dropped it beside his rice bowl. Then he turned to face me.

"Trung Uy," he said, "you can have whatever you need."

"Thank you, Thieu Ta. Thank you very much."

"Will you direct this mission, Trung Uy?" he asked.

"Yes, I will."

"Good. Then, I will command the Vietnamese forces. We will go on the mission together since it is so important to you."

"Very good, Thieu Ta. I am glad you will be with us."

After, thanking him again, I turned to leave.

"I am going to Nha Trang now to make a recording with the Psy Ops people, but I will see you this evening to make final plans."

"Okay, good. Then, I will see you tonight, Trung Uy."

I saluted and moved on to the next piece of the puzzle.

Putting A-502's various operations together was often like assembling a puzzle. Each one was a little different than the last or the next, but the process was always the same. You put the easiest parts together first. Then, the trick was trying to make all the remaining pieces fit. The next piece of this puzzle was one that would be key.

I hadn't worked with the Psy Ops people before, but I knew exactly how their plane would fit into the mission. It would be very important to the success of our operation.

Sergeant Koch had identified a significant problem regarding the operation on the way back from My Loc. His concern was valid about how we would alert the villagers to the rescue attempt. Because we would be firing on or around the landing zones to suppress any enemy activity, our action would likely cause significant alarm among the villagers.

In spite of our worthy intentions, the villagers would probably flee deep into the jungle when they saw or heard us approaching, unless they were somehow advised of our intentions. Alerting the Montagnards to exactly what was happening would be the responsibility and the mission of the Psy Ops pilot.

Our plan was to tape record a message to the villagers that would let them know that the soldiers had come to rescue them, not to kill or hurt them. At first, we considered having our Montagnard interpreter tape the message. Then we were struck by the logic of having Mang Quang do it. He could identify himself to the villagers and, hopefully, that would give credibility to the message as well as helping to calm the villagers as the sky overhead filled with helicopters. Mang Quang could also give specific and familiar directions to the pickup point. This particular part of the puzzle would fit well.

After leaving Thieu Ta's, I collected Sergeant Koch and Mang Quang, and we left for Nha Trang. The drive was going to take a while, so I began to work on a script for his message and the timing of its use.

By the time we reached the Eighth Psy Ops headquarters, they were ready for us and we were ready for them. The message was prepared along with a plan for its broadcast during the mission. I had also finished a basic outline for the overall mission; prior to making the tape, we would need to have a sequence of events in order for Mang Quang to tell his people what was happening.

We reviewed our plan with the Psy Ops team, which was also carefully explained to Mang Quang so that he would understand why and what he was to do.

Our attempt to rescue Mang Quang's family and the other villagers would begin when we lifted off from Trung Dung's small airstrip at 0600 the next morning. We knew generally where the village was located, so we planned to fly west through the valley after liftoff.

We estimated the village to be twenty to thirty kilometers west of My Loc on the south side of one of the Song Cai River's forks. Since he had not crossed a wide river on his way in, we would simply stay south of any wide ones. Mang Quang's job would then be to pinpoint the location of the village once we found the cornfields, which would be our most important landmarks. Mang Quang was very confident that if we could get him to the cornfields, he could show us the location of the village.

During our earlier conversations, Mang had described one particular cornfield that was on a hill above the village and higher in the hills than any of the others. We picked that hill to serve as our landing zone. It might also give us the advantage of holding the high ground if we encountered trouble. The hill would also be an easily recognizable gathering point for those people who may not be in the village when our troops landed.

As we continued to review the plan, I explained that after we found the cornfield, we would mark it with smoke for the gunships. They would then make a couple of passes firing their guns and rockets to discourage the VC from interfering with our landing. If the gunships received no significant return fire, Mang's message would begin to be broadcast, and the slicks, lightly armed helicopters, would move in immediately to begin offloading troops.

As troops continued to be offloaded, Mang's message would tell the villagers why we were there and urge them to come to the cornfield as quickly as possible. Once we had gathered all the villagers, we would fly them to Trung Dung and safety.

✦ ✦ ✦

With the Psy Ops team ready to tape, I asked Mang Quang if he understood what we were going to do. He shook his head and indicated to the interpreter that he did. With everyone prepared, we began to record the message we would use the next morning.

Before handing the script for the message to the interpreter, I told him to once again ask Mang if understood what we needed him to do. When he indicated that he did, I handed the script to the interpreter. And as I did, I asked him to help Mang put the message in his own words to make sure the villagers would understand it. Mang and the interpreter rehearsed the message a number of times. It was brief:

> *This is Mang Quang. This is Mang Quang. I have returned with help. The guns shoot at the VC . . . not at you. Move quickly to the high cornfield where the soldiers are landing. They will protect you. Move quickly.*

The message was necessarily brief since the plane with the speakers was a propeller type and would be flying fairly fast as it pasted low over the thick jungle. The plane would have to fly low to ensure that the message could be heard clearly through the dense jungle canopy.

Additionally, even though the message was short, it wouldn't be possible for the entire message to be heard on one pass. The pilot would have to fly over the same area a number of times for it to be heard in its entirety. If the terrain were as rugged as we expected, this mission would be very challenging and dangerous for the pilot.

After about the fourth or fifth rehearsal, Mang nodded his head and told the interpreter he was ready.

The technician who was making the tape for us turned the recorder on and motioned to Mang to begin speaking. Without any other prompts, Mang Quang repeated the message into the microphone exactly as he had rehearsed it.

When Mang Quang finished speaking, the interpreter appeared pleased.

"Perfect. He did it perfect the first time, Trung Uy." Even the interpreter was proud of Mang's effort.

"Good job," I said, patting him on the back and showing him a wide smile, the international symbol of approval.

He seemed pleased with himself, but I believe he was also amused by what we had asked him to do because he began to laugh.

He had seen and heard the VC radios before, but as it turned out he had never seen a tape recorder before. He knew he was to speak into the small box we provided the words he had practiced. But, he hadn't fully understood why until we played the tape back for him a little later.

When he heard his own voice coming from the recorder his eyes opened wide. He pointed at the recorder and, as if questioning, he repeated "Mang Quang? Mang Quang?"

He laughed a little, then put his hand on the recorder and began shaking his head and repeating his own name softly.

When the tape finished playing, I had the interpreter explain that we would play his message loud enough for the villagers to hear when we went for them the next morning.

Mang Quang began shaking his head up and down.

"He says, this is good, Trung Uy," the interpreter said, "He says it is good his people will hear him."

"Good. Tell him he did a very good job and that we will now return to Trung Dung."

◆ ◆ ◆

It was getting very late in the afternoon and we needed to get back to camp before dark. I still needed to coordinate and finalize plans with Thieu Ta Ngoc.

I thanked the Psy Ops technician who had made the tape for us. He said he was glad to help and that he would rerecord the message several times so that it would play continuously while the pilot was flying over the village. Thanking him again, I handed him the information the pilot would need to link up with us the next morning. At the same time, he gave me the pilot's call sign.

"He's a good man. You'll be glad he's with you."

"I look forward to meeting him."

After exchanging salutes, Sergeant Koch, Mang Quang, and myself got back in the jeep for the return trip to Trung Dung.

Occasionally, on the way back to camp, Mang would repeat his name and shake his head. Apparently, he was still trying to determine how his voice had been trapped in the small box.

When we reached Trung Dung, I asked Sergeant Koch to reunite Mang Quang with his friends and arrange for them to have something to eat and a place to sleep. Then, I walked over to Thieu Ta's where we spent most of the evening finalizing our plans.

After being confident we had resolved multiple aspects of the operation, including contingencies for the unexpected, I left Thieu Ta and walked back across the compound to our teamhouse to review the operation with the other U.S. team members who would be involved.

While it was in no way unexpected, the enthusiasm of our team members for what we would be attempting was remarkable; everyone was willing to go. However, the only ones going were the regular advisors to the units Thieu Ta had selected for the mission, which meant only about eight Americans including myself. Everyone else would remain at Trung Dung on standby in case of an emergency requiring reinforcements.

By the time the briefing was finished, there was little left of the night. It had been a very long day. With map and notes in hand, I walked down the hall to my room to get some sleep, but at the end of the hall, rather than taking the familiar left turn into my room, I went out the side door of the teamhouse. My walk was short and only took me out far enough to see down toward the airstrip where it was all going to start the next morning.

The air was still as I stood, a single figure in the darkness starring into the vastness of the night. There were no sounds except for the occasional bark of a dog in one of the nearby villages. Looking up toward the stars, the only companions to the night's black sky, a few quiet moments were spent reflecting on the occurrences of day and wondering what the next one would bring.

CHAPTER 17

Going "Out There"

SLEEP CAME QUICKLY AFTER falling into bed, but it didn't last long. The morning virtually to burst into being. The stars were replaced by loud, churning helicopters. The 281st was arriving. Outfitted for the mission and standing about where I had been the night before, I watched the choppers as they passed over my head one by one. Bright camp lights illuminated their olive-green underbellies and the spinning blades that held them in the early dawn sky.

It was a beautiful morning, with the sun creating a shimmering yellow-orange glow across the eastern horizon. The sky was clear except for a few small white clouds off in the distance. Our mission would have a good start. The weather was perfect. Now it was time to go.

Pre-mission checks had been completed, and the troops were at the airstrip. I motioned to Mang Quang and his two fellow villagers that it was time to go. They jumped down off the front of the jeep where they were perched like a flock of small birds, and we started walking toward the airstrip together. We hadn't walked far when Thieu Ta and his driver came around the corner of one of the buildings in his jeep.

"Oh, Trung Uy. Good morning."

"Good morning, Thieu Ta."

"You want a ride to the airstrip?"

"Sure. Thank you."

I motioned Mang and the other two to get into the back of the jeep and jumped in beside them.

When we reached the edge of the airstrip, we stopped on a small rise that provided a slightly elevated view of the runway. That's where we got out of the jeep.

In front of us and slightly below us, ten troop-carrying helicopters were lined up with their blades spinning. Three gunship helicopters, which would fly protection, circled overhead. More than two hundred troops with full combat gear and an assortment of weapons were assembled all along the runway.

The collection of men and equipment at the airstrip created an image of power and strength. My senses became keen as I watched troops making adjustments to their equipment and thought about the purpose for which they would be used. Significant amounts of adrenaline began pumping into my bloodstream.

Scanning the runway, there was astonishing detail to everything that I saw and heard. A myriad of things were almost simultaneously perceptible. Our U.S. advisors could be seen working with their Vietnamese counterparts to prepare the troops. Rifle bolts slapped shut and radio checks were audible as final equipment checks took place. Mixed with things that could been seen and heard were the alternating smells of helicopter exhaust and fresh air. The exhaust fumes would intrude on the fresh morning air blown in from the South China Sea. Then it would fade, only to return with the next wind shift. Much was happening, but nothing seemed confused. It was an amazing experience.

My memories of this unique moment and the experience remain clear and vivid. I had felt the grip of fear and knew what it was like to believe my death could be imminent, but this experience was very different. While standing there on the small rise surveying the assembled force, I momentarily experienced a strange feeling I had only heard others describe.

Soldiers, both young and old, have described and expressed a multitude of unique feelings just prior to going into battle. These feelings have ranged from near numbness to shear terror, and each is easily understandable. The cause for the feeling I had heard described and the one I experienced is more difficult to articulate or rationalize. That day, for a fleeting moment, I experienced the feeling of invincibility. Despite all of the trappings of war before me, I was absolutely certain neither harm nor death could chink the armor of whatever force had enveloped my body. The feeling was exhilarating for the few seconds it lasted, and I marveled at its almost intoxicating effect.

Was the feeling of invincibility caused simply by an excess of adrenaline or just the general feeling of invulnerability experienced by nearly all youth, particularly when they are behind the wheel of a speeding car? I would rather believe that it was based on a belief that our cause was just and noble. After all, who could be hurt or killed on such a worthy mission?

Whatever the cause of the amazing feeling, I had the good sense to recognize my mortality. Still, for the very short time it took the reality of my true vulnerability to replace the brief illusion of invincibility, I savored the feeling that would never again be experienced.

Regaining my grip on reality, I echoed Mang Quang's first directions to where we would find the village and the families.

"Let's go, Thieu Ta. They're out there."

We walked the rest of the way down to the runway where Thieu Ta went to check on his men while I went to the waiting helicopters to meet the pilots.

✦ ✦ ✦

"Good morning! How is everyone?" I asked upon approaching the gathered aviators.

"Good" and "Fine" came the quick and crisp responses.

"Great! I'm Lieutenant Ross, and I'm glad you all could be a part of this operation. Thanks for coming on such short notice."

"That's what we're here for," one of the group said as he stepped forward to introduce himself.

"Hi, I'm Bandit Leader. I'll be your flight leader, Lieutenant, and I'll also coordinate the Wolf Pack gunships for you."

The man, whose name I recall as Wehr (I'm not even sure he ever told me his name), seemed confident. Whatever his name, it later became obvious why he was the leader.

"Excellent. It's good to meet you. Your assist on this is going to make the entire mission possible."

"Well, Lieutenant, there's something I'd like you to know. When our pilots and their crews heard this was a rescue mission, everyone wanted to be a part of it. I hope nothing happens anywhere else today. There won't be many people left back at our base to respond. So, just tell us what you want us to do."

"We're glad you're all in on this. Here's what we think is going to happen," I said.

Then, spreading my map out on the hood of a nearby jeep, I began to brief the pilots.

The briefing started with an outline and explanation that once we located and marked an LZ, the Vietnamese major and I would initially coordinate everything from directly overhead in the leader's chopper.

✦ ✦ ✦

While I knew Mang Quang wanted to be on the ground looking for his family and I wanted to be there with him, it was essential that we establish and maintain as much control as possible. My opinion was that, of the three Montagnards, Mang Quang knew the most about the area where were going, so he needed to be with Thieu Ta and me. One of the other two Montagnards would go in with the point unit while the third would remain at Trung Dung and serve as a backup guide for the reinforcements. He would also be available to the meet incoming villagers we expected to be sending back to Trung Dung.

✦ ✦ ✦

Everyone was told that it was important to be flexible and that we stay mobile in the command chopper in case something unexpected occurred and plans needed to be changed quickly. Because we wanted to have maximum flexibility in command and control, Thieu Ta and I decided we would begin directing the operation from the air. We would simultaneously survey the other cornfields as alternate LZs for incoming troops or for reinforcements. If reinforcements were required, we would land and lead them in to wherever they were needed.

Point by point, we went through each step of the operation as it was expected to unfold, down to our return to camp. In finishing the briefing, I mentioned the most important part of getting the mission started.

"The key to getting on the ground and finding the village," I said, "will be locating the cornfields. So, as we head west, whoever sights them first, please alert the command chopper so our villager can point out the one we need to prep for insertion."

I paused, then asked, "Are there any questions?"

When no one responded, the flight leader repeated, "Any questions, guys?"

Everyone shook their heads, indicating there were none.

"I guess not," he said. "We're ready to go."

"Good, so are we. We just need to wait for—"

My remark was interrupted by the high-pitched sound of the engines announcing the arrival of the Psy Ops speaker plane as its pilot made a low pass over the field.

I finished what I had started to say, "—that guy."

As he pulled up over the end of the runway, he checked in on the radio.

"Bunkhouse Zero Two, Zero Two. This is Tracer, this is Tracer. Over."

"Roger, Tracer. This is Zero Two. Are you ready? Over."

"Roger. I'm loaded and ready to talk. Over."

"Good. Are you clear on the mission, Tracer? Over."

"Roger. Understand I'm to stay with you to the target and follow your direction for delivery of my payload. Over."

"Roger. Tracer, that's it. Stand by. We're coming up to meet you."

Turning back to the pilots, "That's everyone. We're set. Let's go find 'em and bring 'em back!"

The briefing broke up, and the pilots started back to their choppers just as Thieu Ta walked up.

"Are we ready, Trung Uy?" he asked.

"We are, if you and your men are."

"We're ready."

I folded my map, which I expected to be useless, and stuck it in my web gear.

"Okay, then. Thieu Ta, you can load your troops."

While Thieu Ta passed the order down the line for his men to get on the choppers, I had Mang Quang and the interpreter get aboard ours. Ngoc and I stood on the runway beside the helicopter waiting for the troops who were going with us to finish loading.

We weren't taking everyone. A backup force would remain behind and ready on the runway in case we had been lured into a VC trap or received unexpected resistance. They would serve as reinforcements who could be moved in quickly. That had been one of our contingencies for the unexpected, but hopefully one we would not be required to use.

Once the choppers were loaded, we climbed aboard and I plugged the cable on my flight helmet into the communications outlet on the chopper. This, as usual, would permit me to communicate with the pilot and other U.S. units involved in the operation. Thieu Ta had his radio, which would give him access to the Vietnamese units. A quick radio check with everyone was accomplished while the choppers powered up. Then, it was time.

"Zero Two, this is Leader. We're ready."

"Roger, Leader. Let's go."

With its blades cutting through the hot, humid Vietnamese air to create lift, our helicopter began to rise off the ground. It moved forward down the runway picking up speed. Then, dropping its nose slightly, it rose effortlessly up over the camp wall and the trees beyond.

We flew over the village outside the camp, made a slow turn to the west, and headed out through the valley.

I motioned for Mang Quang to move over by the door with me so he could see out and help direct our flight. With the wind whipping his jet-black hair and clothing, he didn't appear to be comfortable that close to the door. But, with a death grip on a piece of the chopper's framing, he nodded affirmatively when asked if he was all right.

On our way west, we would fly directly over My Loc. It would serve as our first point of reference for Mang Quang on the reverse trip to his village. Then, with him acting as guide and using the information he had given us the day before, we would attempt to retrace the route he had taken to reach us.

We passed to the south of the Korean base on the way to My Loc. It was on the top of a hill that had been bulldozed so that there was little or no vegetation on the hilltop, which was smooth and rounded. Five or six rows of barbed wire ringed the base to provide some protection against a ground attack. Their artillery was inside the wire and pointed skyward in various positions around the hill.

Colonel Chang's Korean guns would do us no good this day, though. The artillery we had so often been able to count on in our normal area of operation wouldn't be able to reach us this time. We were going so far west that we would be far beyond the effective range of any artillery.

In fact, the only immediate fire support we would have was the three gunships that flew above us at a slightly higher altitude. Other air support, Spooky, had been prearranged on a standby basis in case we encountered serious trouble, another contingency. The only problem was that air support of any kind was on a first-come, first-served basis. Even though Spooky had been alerted and was prepared for our operation, if someone else got into trouble, he would properly be dispatched to assist that unit.

That situation only made the operation that much more challenging. It also made an important statement about the American advisors who had volunteered for this mission, knowing that it might have to be completed with the individual skill and equipment they each carried. The amazing thing was that every advisor at Trung Dung wanted to come. Even my battle-worn buddy Phalen wanted to stick his neck out yet again and asked, "Why can't I go, too?"

"You've been into enough stuff." I said, "Just stay here and clean my room."

Before we flew over My Loc, I asked the interpreter to remind Mang Quang about his role. We would show him the outpost where he had first found our soldiers. Then his job would be to try to show us the way back to his village.

After the interpreter finished speaking, Mang responded by eagerly shaking his head that he understood.

As we neared My Loc, I looked down on the rice paddies surrounding the small outpost and thought about Dale Reich, the lieutenant who had been killed during a night ambush. The site where his unit had been set up was along one of the paddies below. It came to mind that the enemy unit responsible for his death might be the same one responsible for holding the Montagnards. That unit had approached our ambush from the west, the same direction from which Mang Quang had traveled in his search for help. If it was the same enemy unit, they had been armed the night of the ambush. During our questioning of Mang Quang, he indicted that they were away from the village on some unknown mission, which hopefully was still true.

We passed almost directly over, but a little north of, My Loc so Mang would have a wider view of the valley. After pointing down to the outpost, it was a little surprising to see him lean out the door to look ahead. He pulled his head in and looked back at My Loc, which was behind us by then. Again, he leaned out the door to look forward. Then, slowly looking back toward My Loc once more, he moved his arm back and forth along our direction of flight, indicating that we were going the right way.

I looked out both sides of the helicopter for the other choppers. There were five slicks flying in echelon formation trailing back to the right and four back to the left. We were at the point of the "V" formation. There were two gun-ships a little farther out on the left and one the same distance out on the right. Tracer's speaker plane was above everyone and a little behind us. Our mini air armada was an impressive sight.

As we flew west out through the valley, Mang continued to lean out the door. Occasionally, he smiled as he pointed toward things on the ground and told the interpreter he knew where we were. I was glad, because there were a lot of people, his and ours, depending on his ability to find the way.

More than once, I hoped that Mang's recognition of terrain features was accurate and that he was guiding us correctly. Since he had never flown before, things must have looked very different to him from the air, but he seemed quite confident as he guided us over the jungle below. Occasionally, he would look ahead, down, back, and then gesture with his arm for slight changes in our direction of flight.

Further ahead in the valley, hills began to rise from what, behind us, had been flat valley floor. The large valley we had followed began to split and forked into a number of smaller ones. I moved up to the opening between the pilot and copilot seats.

"See anything yet?"

"No," the pilot said, "but we're about to come up on twenty klicks past My Loc. Isn't that where you thought our search pattern should begin?"

"Right," I responded.

"Okay. I'm gonna pass the word to the rest of the flight."

"Roger, go ahead."

He pressed his radio switch and alerted the other pilots.

"This is Bandit Leader to Bandit Flight. We are entering our target area. Let me know if you see anything that resembles a cornfield."

There was a tug on my shirtsleeve. When I turned around, Mang Quang was pulling me back to the door. He began pointing toward a valley that doglegged off to the left of our direction of flight. He seemed excited. When I saw a river in the valley he was pointing toward, I got excited too.

"Leader, our guide wants to go up this valley that doglegs off to the southwest."

"Roger, we'll bring it around."

We had barely entered the smaller valley when Tracer called. Because his plane was faster, he was now ahead of us and considerably higher than we were. He could see further out in front of us.

"Zero Two, this is Tracer. Over."

"Roger, Tracer. Go."

"I think I've got your cornfields. There are several patches on the low hills out at about eleven o'clock. Over."

"Roger, Tracer . . . we're looking."

I moved back up between the pilots.

"Did you hear that?" I asked.

"Roger."

The pilot/flight leader, who was seated in the left front seat, saw them first.

"Ah . . . yeah, I've got 'em."

He put two fingers up and pointed out through the plastic nose bubble. Then I could see them.

"Yes, I see them, too."

Then I pointed them out to Mang Quang, who very enthusiastically indicated that we were indeed on target.

"Leader, this Zero Two. Our guide says that's the place."

"Okay. We'll move in a little closer and then I'll orbit the slicks until we mark the one you want to use as our LZ. Is that okay?"

"Roger, that's fine," I said.

As we flew into the valley and toward the cornfields, I let Tracer know that he'd found our target.

"Good work, Tracer. That appears to be the place."

While the flight leader gave instructions to the other chopper pilots, I told Thieu Ta we had found the cornfields and that he could alert his units. Then, while he called his men, I alerted the other four U.S. advisors who were each on four of the other nine choppers.

✦ ✦ ✦

When we were in close proximity to our target, the flight leader gave his instructions for the slicks to break off, circle, and hold their positions.

"This is Bandit Leader. Everyone on my left, break and orbit left. Everyone to my right, break and orbit right. Guns, stay with me."

After the choppers broke away and formed two spinning circles behind us, the gunships moved in closer to provide protection as we began to descend toward the widely spread-out cornfields.

I called Tracer to keep him with us.

"Tracer, Zero Two. Stay with us, but maintain your altitude above us. Take this opportunity to look the ground over."

"Tracer rogers."

I moved back over near Mang Quang, whose map in the sand had been as good as any printed on paper. Looking out the door toward the cornfields, it was obvious immediately which one was the high one. Mang and I pointed to it at the same time. We looked at each other and I gave him a thumbs up.

I don't think he understood the gesture because he smiled, grabbed my thumb, and began shaking it.

"Okay, Leader, we've got the LZ. It's the highest one on that ridge at about ten o'clock."

"Roger, I see it," he said.

"Let's check it out."

"Okay, we'll take you in low. If it looks good to you, throw your smoke."

"Roger. I'll be ready."

✦ ✦ ✦

Out the side doors, the gunships could easily be seen. They were staying right with us. It was like having a couple of big brothers with you to deal with any bully problems.

"Wolf Pack Leader, this is Zero Two. We're going to mark the LZ. If we don't take ground fire, we'd like you to put a few rockets and some gunfire on it to discourage Charlie. If we take fire, we'll identify your new target from the center of the LZ. Over."

"Roger, understand. The Wolf Pack is standing by."

As we drew nearer to the cornfield, the pilot prepared for our approach.

"Wolf Pack Leader, this is Bandit Leader. We'll make this a wide turn. You can line up behind me and we'll make the approach single file. When we pull out, the target is yours. Over."

"Roger, Bandit Leader. Understand. We're lining up on your tail now."

We completed the turn and started down with the three gunships in a staggered line behind us. Our two door gunners moved their .30-caliber machine guns back and forth over the jungle that was rapidly rising up beneath us. They searched for any threatening targets as we closed the distance to the cornfield. We were quickly getting low enough to the ground to see leaves on the jungle trees, which had been individually undefined from a higher altitude. At the same time, we were well within the range of enemy light arms fire.

Removing one of the smoke grenades from my web gear, I positioned myself back at the door behind the pilot. Looking ahead, the cornfield could be seen clearly. It was steeper than we had hoped, but it would serve our purposes. When we were almost over it, I pulled the pin on the grenade, took a tighter grip on the top of the door, and leaned out far enough to ensure it wouldn't hit anything on the chopper when it was thrown.

We had kept our promise to the small Asian man at my side, and now we were Out There. The pilot pushed his chopper into a steep approach, diving directly toward the cornfield. It was early in the morning and as a light white mist was still rising from the steaming jungle beneath us, we struck. As we swooped over the center of the field, I threw the grenade.

"It's gone," I told the pilot. Immediately, he pulled up sharply.

We quickly gained altitude as we circled back to the north. Looking out the door across from me, red smoke could be seen billowing up from the cornfield. The Wolf Pack gunships were given the all-clear to attack. By pouring fire onto what would soon become our LZ, we hoped to intimidate any nearby VC or NVA into clearing out of the immediate area, making safer for our troop-carrying choppers to land.

"Wolf Pack Leader, this is Zero Two. Your target is marked. Over."

"Roger, we're going hot now."

One by one, the Wolf Pack gunships attacked the cornfield, firing into the smoke. Each rocket marked its path by leaving a trail of white smoke until it disappeared into the cloud of swirling red smoke where it exploded upon impact with the cornfield.

As we circled around behind the gunships, Wolf Pack Leader was pulling up and out after his attack. I let him know we had not taken any ground fire and wanted to clear the area quickly.

"Wolf Pack Leader, Zero Two. We took no ground fire. If you guys don't take any, one pass each will be enough. Over."

"Roger, understand. We didn't take any either. If the next two aren't hit, we'll move out of the way."

Now it was now almost time for Tracer.

"Tracer, Zero Two. Can you see what's happening down here? Over."

"Roger, my seat is front row."

"Good, when that last gun pulls out we're going to make a pass so that our guide can point out the village location. When we have that location fixed, we will direct you to it, over."

"Roger. Tracer is standing by."

When the last gunship emerged from the cloud of smoke that hung over the cornfield, we headed back down so that Mang Quang could point out the village position under the thick jungle trees.

As we again dove toward the cornfield and jungle surrounding it,

Mang Quang, who had become comfortable with flying, was now leaning out the door with his face in the wind like a dog out a car window. He was smiling broadly and looked triumphant as he pointed an outstretched arm down into the jungle. He now appeared bold as he led us to his village.

After completing our flyover of the jungle, we regained altitude, but there was a problem. We would have to make two more passes before we were sure the problem was resolved because, on the first one, Mang pointed toward three different places. At first, I thought he was disoriented or confused, but when he pointed to exactly the same three places on each pass, I began to suspect that our mission had just been made more complicated.

Even though the answer was anticipated, the interpreter was told to ask Mang why he was pointing to different places.

As it turned out, he wasn't confused at all. What Mang referred to as his village was actually divided into three separated living areas on two different terrain features. They were in the same general location, but one portion of the village was on the ridge below the cornfield and two were on the ridge just a few hundred meters to the west of the cornfield. Mang had identified all three for us.

While we gained altitude after our last pass, Thieu Ta Ngoc and I quickly adapted our plan to the new circumstances. Since we weren't sure what was waiting for us, we decided not to divide our troops and try to send them in three different directions at once. Until we did know what resistance we would encounter, we didn't want to commit the reinforcements waiting at Trung Dung.

We decided to have our men go to the portion of the village located below the cornfield first and then, depending on what happened there, we would either send them to the other two or call in the reinforcements.

Regardless of what happened next, we had found our way Out There. Everyone was ready to get on the ground.

CHAPTER 18

Go Find Them

WITH OUR ORIGINAL PLAN slightly adjusted, it was time to bring Tracer down.

"Tracer, Zero Two. Over."

"Roger, this is Tracer. Go ahead."

"Tracer, it seems the village is spread out. One part is about two hundred meters below the cornfield and the other two are on the ridge west of the field. One of those is at almost the same level as the cornfield, and the other is roughly two to three hundred meters further down the ridge. Over."

There was a pause as Tracer checked the ground.

"Ahh . . . Roger, I have the area marked."

"Good. When you get down there, make several passes over the village locations. Then work a little further out until the troops are on the ground. Over."

"Roger, I'll make room."

"Okay, Tracer, the stage is yours. We're calling the slicks in now. Over."

"Roger, Tracer is coming down. My speakers are live . . . now."

Then, like a hawk after a mouse, Tracer swooped down from his perch high above us. Mang Quang's voice could be heard booming from Tracer's speakers as he dove past us on his way down.

◆ ◆ ◆

Hearing my conversation with Tracer, the 281st flight leader radioed the slicks and pulled them out of their circling formations. He gave them directions that would put them on a course to the LZ. The cornfield was now officially our LZ.

Moving back to a seat in the center of the chopper next to Thieu Ta, I told him the slicks were on the way.

"Good," he said, "my men are ready."

Looking out the door, we could see Tracer beginning his run. He passed very low across the ridges just below the field. Then he rolled and made a looping turn and passed over them again. When he made his next run, I couldn't believe it when he disappeared down over the hill on which the cornfield was located. He flew out of sight down between the ridges. When he emerged on the other side of the ridge, it appeared as though he was coming almost straight up from the river bottom.

Tracer continued to make pass after pass over and between ridges, down small valleys, and through the river bottom. I was sure he was going to rip the wings off his plane on one of his passes through the jungle. He wasn't flying over it as he flew through the river bottom. He was down in it, below treetop level.

Later, when I asked him why he flew so low, he said he wanted to make sure the villagers could hear the tape.

Tracer's demonstration of flying acuity was no less impressive than that of the marines who attacked the Dong Bo hilltop. He wasn't up in the wild blue yonder where the air force anthem suggested he should be. Instead, he was as close to the villagers as he could be without putting his wheels down and landing.

With Tracer's passes carrying him further away from the field as the slicks approached, I asked the flight leader to take us up to a higher altitude. From further up, we would be out of the way and would have a better vantage point from which we could see everything as it happened.

As they neared touchdown on the LZ, I became concerned for the first few slicks. If we had been lured into an ambush or if the VC were simply holding their fire until troops began to offload, the ones going in first would be the most vulnerable.

First Lieutenant Mike Sullivan, who had been responsible for different areas at A-502, was on the first slick into the LZ and would be the first U.S. advisor out on the ground. He was the perfect man to have down there. He was a serious, experienced soldier, having been in-country for almost a year. He would provide stability for a tenuous situation and was responsible for organizing security around the LZ as troops on other incoming choppers continued to be off-loaded.

Sullivan was from Columbus, Ohio, and was a stocky, barrel-chested young guy who was an intense and very focused person. Even while he was in Vietnam, he lifted weights to stay in shape. He seemed to enjoy being a part of the Special Forces, but he sometimes took issue with the less formal or unconventional methods of SF operations.

Mike started his military career with a regular infantry unit, then requested a transfer to Special Forces. After receiving SF training at Fort Bragg, he was assigned to the Fifth Group and A-502. Prior to coming to the main camp, he served as the senior advisor of our Binh Tan outpost on the river near Nha Trang. He was a good man, and I was glad he had accepted the challenge of advising the point unit, which would likely be the first to encounter any enemy resistance. I was certain that Sullivan would prove to be a fierce opponent for anyone unfortunate enough to challenge his unit.

✦ ✦ ✦

From a vantage point several hundred feet above the humming actively below, we could see the slicks making their final approach to the LZ. They had white stripes painted on top of their blades that made them stand out against the steaming, dark-green jungle. They looked like spinning tops as they moved over the jungle canopy.

A fine morning mist was still rising from the jungle when our troops began hitting the ground. Immediately after the first 281st slick landed, we could see Sullivan and his unit fanning out across the cornfield, now our LZ. I scanned the edges of the open area for flashes, which would indicate enemy gunfire. But, there were none—at least, no automatic fire. A couple of the slicks reported hearing semiautomatic gunfire, but they were unable to determine its location.

The lack of enemy fire was welcomed, but not surprising. If, indeed, there was only a small enemy unit down there, disclosing their position could have meant immediate death. The three Wolf Pack gunships alternately swooped in, proving cover for each landing slick. Rockets or heavy gunfire would have rained in on any VC or NVA troop bold enough to make his location known.

While the gunships provided protection for the off-loading slicks, Tracer, who was unarmed, continued his daredevil passes over the treetops and through the valleys further away from the LZ.

"Tracer, this is Zero Two. You're doing a great job. Don't hit a tree!"

"No problem, I'm trying to figure out how to make money doing this."

When I told him to "Join the circus," we could hear him laugh as he once again disappeared behind a ridgeline.

Focusing my attention back on the LZ, I could see the last slick coming up out of the cornfield. It rejoined the others and they all turned toward Trung Dung, where they would land and stand by with the reinforcements in case help was needed.

"Bunkhouse Zero Two, this is Zero Eight." It was Sullivan. "We've got the LZ secured and all units are on the ground. We're beginning to move now. Over."

"Roger, understand. Good luck and keep us posted."

"Roger. Zero Eight, out."

This was a critical time. Would the villagers come to the cornfield or flee in fear?

Temporarily, at least, theirs would be a position of terrible conflict. They were already on the ground with people who had abused them and who they knew to be their enemy. Now they were being confronted by an unknown group of soldiers who were descending upon them from the air. Our hope was that they could hear and understand Mang Quang's familiar voice being broadcast from Tracer's speakers and would try to reach the cornfield as his message directed.

Sullivan, with his Vietnamese counterpart at his side and one of the three villagers acting as guide, directed the rescue units to begin moving down the ridge toward the village. Once the units moved off the cornfield and disappeared into the dense jungle, they were very much on their own. The slicks had gone to refuel, so an extraction or reinforcement, if necessary, would take some time. There was no artillery support, and the thick jungle into which the units had vanished now obstructed the vision of the pilots in the Wolf Pack gunships. If an enemy unit was encountered, the fight would likely be intense and at very close quarters.

We could do little for the men on the ground after they moved into the jungle, except pray for their safety.

✦ ✦ ✦

Thieu Ta and I circled above the gunships that were moving their very low passes further down the ridge. They worked like a team of hungry wolves searching for prey as they attempted to intimidate any VC or NVA who might be in front of our advancing units.

Tracer's passes were on the ridges above, below, and on each side of Wolf Pack's swirling movement. While they had never worked together before, the movement between Tracer and the Wolf Pack appeared choreographed.

The ground units hadn't been out of sight long when Thieu Ta's radio came alive with chatter. I heard it, but was still looking down on the jungle when he tapped me on the shoulder to get my attention. He held up a finger for me to wait. I was sure he must have been receiving information from his men on the ground.

"Trung Uy, they have some people," he said. Then, pointing to Mang Quang, he repeated, "My troops have found some of his people."

At about the same time, Sullivan called with a similar report. "Zero Two, this is Zero Eight. They're coming to us."

Amazingly, within approximately twenty minutes of the first troops landing on the LZ, the villagers were hurrying to meet them. Mang Quang's message had obviously been heard. Tracer had delivered it through the dense canopy to the jungle floor.

✦ ✦ ✦

Later, after the operation had been completed, one of the American advisors told me that when one small group of villagers approached his unit, a couple of them were pointing into the air and saying, "Mang Quang, Mang Quang." It was clear that they had heard the tape being broadcast clearly enough to recognize Mang's voice.

✦ ✦ ✦

The news of Mang Quang's people meeting our search teams was great news, and I wanted to share it with him. When I called his name, he turned from the door where he had been anxiously watching the activity beneath us. I asked the interpreter to tell him that his people were coming to the field. Mang questioned the interpreter, then he looked at me and smiled and shook his head to confirm that he understood. After hearing the news, he quickly turned back to the door. His gaze appeared locked on the cornfield.

While Mang looked for villagers who had not yet emerged from the jungle, the interpreter told me that he had asked if his family had been found.

If the villagers were indeed coming to us, Thieu Ta and I decided it would be better to move our units back to the LZ. In case the villagers were coming from all three locations as well as other work sites in the area, it made more sense to consolidate on the LZ and provide a secure base where they could be protected. Since the action had begun far better than expected, creating a strong collecting point would be preferred to walking around in the jungle looking for the villagers. If they didn't come or weren't able to reach us, we would then move the units back out in whichever direction seemed appropriate and resume our search. Additionally, with the LZ strongly secured and covered by Wolf Pack, if our rescue unit were attacked, the entire team would be available to defend or counterattack.

❖ ❖ ❖

"Zero Eight, Zero Two, over."

"Roger, this is Eight. Go."

"Eight, your counterpart is getting orders now to move back up the hill. Make your base on the LZ. We're going to have you wait there since the villagers seem willing to come to you. Over."

"Roger, understand. We're turning around now. Out."

❖ ❖ ❖

Sullivan and the rescue units moved back to the LZ to wait for new arrivals. And, sure enough, in they came. In twos, threes, and small groups of fours, fives, and sixes, the villagers made their way up the hill to the LZ.

We absolutely couldn't believe what was happening. Despite the tactically poor layout of the village, the mission was running very smoothly. When we saw the villagers beginning to gather on the LZ, the gunships were backed out a short distance so we could go down for a closer look. We flew down and circled the field at treetop level and, as we did, Mang Quang became very excited and waved to the villagers below. To let them know where he was he began yelling his name and continued to wave. I'm not sure they could hear him, but some apparently recognized him. They began pointing and waving back toward our chopper.

The sight of villagers waving at Mang Quang was remarkable. I felt very glad we had been given this unusual opportunity.

With Mang still waving, we regained altitude so the Wolf Pack gunships could return to their close cover of the LZ. They were still behaving very much like big brothers and immediately swooped in as we cleared the area.

◆ ◆ ◆

After we had been over the village for some time, our flight leader began to be concerned about the gunship's fuel supply since they had done "a lot of fuel-burning flying." After checking with Wolf Pack Leader to confirm their fuel status, he suggested that they return to be refueled one at a time, which would leave two of them with us all the time. With no one voicing an objection, the guns were sent back one by one to have their tanks refilled.

We stayed on site, watching as villagers continued to emerge from the jungle and gather in the cornfield. While we circled overhead, we sent small patrols out to sweep the area around the cornfield. We wanted them to make sure the VC weren't moving in and told them to look for villagers while they were out. We remained overhead until all of the gunships had returned fully fueled. Then, we made the trip to have our own tanks refilled.

◆ ◆ ◆

Upon our arrival back over the cornfield, Sullivan advised me that the flow of villagers had stopped. He also said the patrols we had sent out were no longer encountering any of them. When I asked him to take a count of the villagers, he reported back shortly that eight-two were with him on the LZ.

After Mike's count, the interpreter was asked to advise Mang Quang of the number and ask him if that was everyone.

Mang said yes, he thought so, but he wasn't sure. He explained through the interpreter that the villagers had been kept separated for a long time. Some had escaped, and others had been killed or taken away. Since he had been closely guarded and his access to the other villagers had been restricted, he wasn't really sure how many were still in the area.

The assembled crowd on the ground appeared to be large enough to fill a small village. So, with no other information on which to estimate the total number of villagers in the area, and since no other villagers were arriving or being sighted, I asked the flight leader to alert his Bandit slicks that we were ready to begin the pickup.

When the slicks began to arrive we watched as the lead chopper made its approach to pick up the first group of villagers. As it neared the LZ, I called Tracer to release him for return to base and thank him for a truly incredible job, but he didn't want to leave.

"I'd like to stick around until they're out, Zero Two."

"Roger, stay as long as you like. We're very glad to have you here."

Then, when the first slick began to touch down, the flight leader urged a quick pickup.

"Bandit Two, this is Leader. Get in there, get 'em, and get out. We don't want to lose them now. Over."

"Roger, Leader. They won't spend another night out here. Over."

"Roger, they're under your wing now."

As each of the remaining slicks began to touch down, the guns swooped in and out to provide the same very close cover they had given when the troops were offloaded. This time the slicks were carrying out a precious cargo of men, women, and children, but they were more than that. They were families who now had a chance of life in freedom without fear for their safety or their lives. Among them, we hoped, was Mang Quang's family, and it was clear by watching what was happening on the LZ that the men of the 281st weren't going to let anything happen to any of them.

We were all pleased with the results of the day, but Mang Quang appeared the happiest of all. His face almost glowed with the knowledge that his family was safe.

The flight leader became a little concerned that the gunships were staying too close together and too close to the ground.

"Bandit Leader to Wolf Pack Leader. You guys are pretty tight down there, aren't you?"

"Roger, Bandit. We are. Just covering our families in case Charlie decides he wants them back. Over."

The flight leader laughed and responded, "Roger, Bandit understands. Take care of your families."

Listening to the exchange between the pilots, I realized how personal this mission had become for all of the Americans involved. Tracer didn't want to leave until the villagers were extracted, and the guns were literally going to hover over them until the last one was out.

During the course of my tour of duty, I experienced a number of unique feelings. Some, I hope, I will never experience again. While certain emotions are more difficult to describe than others, the feelings I experienced while listening to the exchanges between these very seasoned combat pilots is fairly easy to describe: an incredible pride just to be in the presence of men like these.

Every man involved in the operation knew what his individual mission required. From the time the mission began it was clear that a serious battle would be required to keep them from accomplishing their assigned tasks. They had come to find families and take them to safety—precisely what they had done.

CHAPTER 19

No Joy

AFTER ALL THE VILLAGERS had been taken back to Trung Dung and the last troop was picked up from the LZ, our small air armada turned east and headed home. Everyone was feeling very good about what had happened. We were able to find the cornfield with relative ease, the troops had been inserted quickly and without incident, the villagers responded to the broadcast far better than we had hoped, and everyone had been extracted without a single casualty. Villagers would tell us later that enemy soldiers had hidden in the jungle, fearing they would be killed. The rescue had been an extraordinary success.

Considering the events of the day as we churned our way back to camp, I was amazed and thankful that our rescue effort had gone so smoothly. When the choppers dropped us off at Trung Dung, however, we discovered that the results weren't as good as we first thought.

As soon as we cleared the spinning helicopter blades, Mang Quang, with me close behind him, went directly to the area being set up for the villagers. He couldn't wait to see his family. I followed him through the crowd as he searched for their faces. He was so excited, he looked as though he might burst with joy before he found them. But, while others celebrated their newfound freedom, this expectant husband and father would have no joy.

After making several passes around and through the crowd of villagers, Mang wasn't able to find his family. They weren't there. For whatever the reason, they hadn't reached the cornfield and were still out there.

I asked one of the U.S. advisors keeping the head count if all eighty-two were in the assembly area. He said he had just counted and that they were all there. He was sure because our medics were bringing gear down to do a medical check on everyone, and they had asked him to confirm the number.

Mang Quang wilted like a dying leaf before my eyes when he confronted the agonizing reality that his family was still missing. He fell to his knees, grabbed his head with his hands, and started saying something I couldn't understand. Then, he began to cry.

His heartache was compelling. I quickly turned to the interpreter.

"We're going back! We're going back! Tell him quickly that we will go back for his family. We will return with the morning."

When Mang's crying changed to sobbing, it became difficult for the interpreter to understand and translate what he was saying.

"Trung Uy, he says his family will die before morning. The VC will know he brought the soldiers, and they will kill his family. He says you could give him ten million piasters [Vietnamese currency], but he would give it back. Without his family, it would mean nothing to him."

At that point, I felt as if my own heart had been ripped out. The exhilaration of the day had instantly turned to frustration and deep disappointment. While eighty-two freed Montagnards stood all around us, we had clearly failed this man who prompted our actions.

Watching and listening to Mang Quang there on the ground in front of me, it was obvious that he believed his family would not live through the night. He wanted no wealth or much else without his family; even life might not be important to him at that moment.

◆ ◆ ◆

While the urge to return to the village right then was strong for all of us, it simply didn't make sense. It was already too late in the day. By the time we readied everyone to go again and relaunched the mission, it would be dark when we reached the cornfield, assuming we could find it in the dark. Even if we could find it, we didn't need to be searching through the unfamiliar jungle at night. Furthermore, we didn't know the terrain as the enemy did, so even a small VC unit could inflict heavy casualties on us.

Kneeling beside Mang Quang, I put my hand on his shoulder.

"Mang . . . Mang Quang."

Slowly, as he swiped at his face with his hands, he turned to look at me. His face was covered with tears and dirt rubbed off from his hands.

I spoke to him softly, but confidently.

"Your family will be fine." The interpreter began translating immediately without being asked. I spoke slowly so that the interpreter could translate simultaneously as I attempted to console the small, crumpled man.

"They are probably hiding in the jungle. I am very sure our planes and soldiers scared the VC. They had to protect themselves. That would have given your family time to run away and hide in the jungle." Then, pausing for a moment, I continued.

"Mang, we will not leave them out there. The VC will not expect us to come again so quickly. When the sun returns to your village, we will return with it. And we will find your family."

He seemed to calm, so I kept talking.

"Mang, do you see these men behind me?" I asked, gesturing toward several of our team members who had gathered around us.

"They say with me that the VC will not keep your family. Tomorrow night, your family will be here and they will be with you, and they will be safe."

When the interpreter finished translating my last remark, Mang looked at me and, as if testing the degree of my conviction, "Yeah, Trung Uy?"

Those were the first words he had spoken to me directly that I understood.

"Yeah, Mang Quang," I said with feeling and a much stronger voice. There was no need for the interpreter to translate.

✦ ✦ ✦

In my attempt to make Mang believe, I had convinced myself that we would find his family. But a few moments later, after considering things said in my zeal to console him, I became very concerned. I wasn't sure what would be said to him the next day if his family couldn't be found, had been hurt, or—the worst—killed. What words could possibly be offered to explain why I had been wrong about their safety? All I was certain of now was the need to keep him busy until the next morning.

✦ ✦ ✦

Once again addressing him, I said, "Mang, in the morning we will help you find your family. But, now, we need you to help us. We need to take care of the villagers who are here. Will you help us do that?"

He nodded, took another swipe at his face with each of his forearms, and, together, we stood up. I explained to Mang Quang, who was regaining his composure, that I needed to go make plans for the next day, but would return a little later.

One of our medics had been on standby for casualties and/or a checkup of the villagers when they arrived. He was standing nearby and immediately stepped up and said he would take care of Mang and would keep him occupied. The medic handed him some medical supplies and asked him if he would help with the care of the other villagers. Again, he nodded.

Knowing he was in very good hands, I patted him on the back and started for the radio room.

As I walked away from Mang Quang, I realized something very important I had just learned from him. A man's capacity to love and care about his family has very little, if anything, to do with how primitive he may act or appear. If anything, the importance of family to someone without all the trappings and distractions of modern society may be even greater.

Republic of South Vietnam —1968

ADVANCES IN COMMUNICATIONS technology brought television pictures of the Vietnam War into America's living rooms. Advances in photographic technology miniaturized cameras to pocket size. As a result of this technology, I began carrying a small camera with me on parachute training jumps at Fort Bragg.

My first attempt at airborne photography was an effort to capture the opening of my own parachute. Unfortunately, I made this attempt during a training jump from a Lockheed C-141 Starlifter, a huge air force jet powered by four Pratt & Whitney TF33-P-7 turbofan engines. Because of the aircraft's necessarily faster than usual air speed, the sudden jerk caused by the rapid opening of the parachute ripped the camera from my hands. I am confident that a hunter or naturalist will one day find that camera in the North Carolina forest where it fell.

In Vietnam, as a function of my role as S2 and S3, I often carried a camera in my pocket to document various missions and key terrain in A-502's area of operation. After Sergeant Gordon Gilmore, a team member, built a darkroom in one corner of the team's motorpool, he taught me to develop my film and print pictures. Some of those photographs appear on the following pages. The picture of the 281st resupply and those of the Montagnards were taken and contributed by then First Lieutenant Bill Phalen, who took thousands of pictures while he was in Vietnam.

SFOB (SPECIAL FORCES OPERATIONAL BASE)
5th Special Forces Group Headquarters — Nha Trang, South Vietnam

THE CITADEL
Home of Special Forces Detachment A-502's main camp —
Khanh Hoa Province, South Vietnam

BUDDHA HILL
Buddha sitting atop a small hill in Nha Trang keeping watch over the city

BUDDHIST TEMPLE
Brightly painted temple near 5th Group Headquarters

ON PATROL
"Light" Interpreter/Radioman (last in line) — In a stand of elephant grass

IN SEARCH OF ENEMY BASECAMP
Dense Jungle — Dong Bo Mountains

RE-SUPPLY
281st Attack Helicopter Company delivering supplies to A-502's outpost in the Dong Bo Mountains

NHA TRANG VALLEY
Photographed from a rock outcropping high in the Dong Bo Mountains while awaiting a medevac

FRIENDS
First Lieutenant Tom Ross and Ahat, Montagnard radioman/bodyguard

THE BEAST
Armored fighting vehicle created by two A-502 team members

MILITARY COUNTERPARTS
ROK Captain Lee and First Lieutenant Bill Phalen, A-502 "Blue Bandit" Team Leader

GATHERING THE TEAM
Some of the A-502 and 281st team that would attempt the rescue

NEW HOPE
Some of the first Montagnard families to reach safety

THEY MADE IT HAPPEN
281st pilots and crew with Montagnard families rescued in the Valley of the Tigers

CHAPTER 20

We're Going Back

WITH YET ANOTHER PROMISE made to return to the mountain village to find Mang Quang's family, much work was to be completed. My first stop would, once again, be our radio room.

On my way to our small communications center, several team members who had heard we were back in camp stopped me along the way. They all wanted to know where the Montagnards were and what they could do to help. They were all told to see the docs (our medics), who would need a great deal of help.

Finally reaching the radio room, my first call went to the 281st. The Bandit flight had only been back on the ground in Nha Trang a short while at the time of my call. I asked for the flight leader and quickly told him the situation. After hearing my explanation, there was no need to ask for anything. He gave a direct and simple response.

"Tell me where you want us to be . . . and when."

"Same place, same time . . . tomorrow morning," I said.

"We'll be there."

It was that easy.

✦ ✦ ✦

With the 281st signed on to another mission, Tracer was the next person who needed to be found. After tracking him down, his response was very similar to the one given by the 281st.

"I know where," he said. "Just tell me when."

◆ ◆ ◆

Two major parts of our return to the Montagnard village had been quickly resolved. The only thing remaining was the manpower and Thieu Ta's approval to use his troops again. So, once more, I went visiting.

While he couldn't go on the mission himself because of a meeting in the city, Thieu Ta said to take whatever was needed in the way of troops. He said he would send his next senior officer as my counterpart.

After leaving Thieu Ta's, I started back to find Mang Quang and check on the Montagnards. I had just gone past the teamhouse when Specialist Miller, the radioman, called out to me.

"Lieutenant Ross."

"Yes. What's up? If your radio is broken, I don't work on radios."

Miller chuckled a little and said, "There's a Lieutenant Orians on the radio who says he needs to talk to you."

"Okay, let's go see what he needs."

Frank Orians was the PIO (public information officer) for the Fifth Group in Vietnam. He was a nice guy who I liked and had worked with from time to time. Whenever he had a VIP visitor at Fifth Group Headquarters who wanted to see a Special Forces camp, he would often call me to arrange a visit and briefing.

"Roger, this is Bunkhouse. How can we be of service? Over."

"So, what have you guys got going out there? Nha Trang's buzzing about some kind of rescue 502's got under way. Is that true? Over."

My conversations with Frank were always a little less military in nature.

"Roger, it is. We brought out eight-two Montagnards today. They tell us they've been used as slaves by the VC for several years."

"Damn, I wish we had known this sooner. We need press coverage on this," Frank said.

"Well, you've still got time. We're going back tomorrow. We've just discovered that there are still other families out there. If you have media available, they're welcome to ride along," I answered.

"I don't know who's around, but I'll find out and call you back."

"Frank, I have to tell you, in view of what's being reported back in the States lately about search-and-destroy missions, this is the kind of story the American public needs to be told. Everyone involved in this operation is putting his life on line for these people. It's happening out in the middle of nowhere, in unfriendly country with little or no support."

"Okay, okay, it's late in the day. Let me get on it and see who's available. When are you leaving tomorrow to go back?"

"Zero six hundred. That's six in the morning for you."

"Yeah, yeah. Okay, I'm going to work on it right now. I'll get back to you before morning."

"Roger. If you find someone, you can send them out with the 281st. They're providing our ride."

"Good, good. I'll get back to you as soon as I can."

"Roger, I'll be right here. Zero Two, out."

✦ ✦ ✦

This development was unexpected and fortuitous. Recently, there had been a great deal of international coverage about search-and-destroy missions carried out by U.S. troops in Vietnamese villages. One such mission in a village named My Lai would become infamous and synonymous with all of the worst occurrences in Vietnam. American soldiers mercilessly killed all or most of the inhabitants of My Lai.

Search-and-destroy missions required U.S. troops to go into areas suspected of being controlled by the VC or NVA to search for the villages from which they might be receiving support. If and when such villages were located, they were destroyed, usually burned to the ground. Unfortunately, to save the lives of loyal South Vietnamese as well as those of American soldiers, the seemingly obdurate action was necessary. However, the indiscriminate killing of unarmed civilians was not policy and was absolutely unnecessary.

Because there were few good stories to tell, everyone at A-502 knew that media coverage with its often graphic pictures of search-and-destroy missions couldn't be doing much for morale back at home. Even we knew that negativism regarding the Vietnam War was mounting. News and mail from home made it obvious that since the Tet offensive of January, support for us and for our efforts had begun to deteriorate more rapidly. We felt our story was a good one, and we hoped Frank Orians could find someone with the press who would tell it.

✦ ✦ ✦

As the screen door to the teamhouse slapped shut behind me on my way back to the Montagnards, the last thing on my mind was press coverage. If we got it, we could share a good story with family, friends, and our country. If not, nothing was lost since the deed was infinitely more important than the story anyway.

When I reached the Montagnards' new temporary home, they were being fed dinner. I had the interpreter ask them if everything was good. When he did, many smiled and almost all shook their heads up and down while adding various guttural sounds of approval. This was probably one of the best meals they had enjoyed in years.

I asked our senior medic, Sergeant Jerry Arrants, if his team had checked everyone. He said that they had seen almost everyone and would check the few remaining before they left. I thanked him for his effort and walked over to where the Montagnards were being served. Taking a bowl of rice, I went with Mang Quang and sat cross-legged on the floor with several of the villagers. Mang appeared much more relaxed than when I left him. However, his thoughts were obviously on those far to our west, and he would not be at peace until his family had been found.

I stayed with the Montagnards until sometime after dark. Several times during the evening Mang Quang would go to the far end of the long shelter and look out into the darkness to the west. He was silhouetted against the darkness by the light of a nearby campfire as sparks from the fire flickered and crackled into the black night sky. It was fairly easy to guess what he was thinking about as he stared off into the distance. But, it wouldn't be until years later, when I had a family of my own, that I could even begin to imagine how he felt.

It was time to go back to the teamhouse when the Montagnard mothers began putting their small ones down for the night. Preparations still needed to be made before the next morning when, we would once again try to find Mang's wife and children and other families that we now knew remained.

✦ ✦ ✦

At the teamhouse, I found my way to the refrigerator and helped myself to a cold Coca-Cola. Then, sitting at a table near the radio room, I began writing the operations outline for the next day's mission.

A good portion of the outline was finished along with most of my Coke when I heard Frank Orians's call come in over the radio.

"I'll get it," I said to Miller, pushing my chair back.

He gave me the handset as I walked through the radio room door.

"This is Bunkhouse. What's up in the city tonight? Over."

"Ha! Not much. That's for sure, and I know. I've been all over trying to find a news team. There's no one in town."

"Well, don't worry about it. You did what you could. We're going back with or without a news team and whether or not it ever receives coverage."

"No, I know it," he said, "but I hate it. You were right, even Zero Six [06 was the call sign for Colonel Arron, the CO of Fifth Group] feels this is an important story that we want to tell. And we are covering it. We began working on a release this afternoon. So, I'll try to catch up with you late tomorrow to see what happened."

"Roger. I hope we have more good news for you. The family of the man who was our guide today is still out there, and we all really want to find them. That situation is truly a very sad one. Over."

"Well, I wish you luck and hope you find them. Good luck, Zero Two. You and your team take care."

"Roger, no problem. I'll talk to you tomorrow. Zero Two, out."

✦ ✦ ✦

Unfortunately it appeared there would be no media coverage. *This would a great opportunity to share a little positive news with our country and our families*, I thought.

Coverage of the Montagnard mission wouldn't be a report describing killing or destruction. It would be a good story, an uncommon tale and the kind that rarely reached the States, but since their presence had never been anticipated anyway, the absence of press would make little difference to anyone involved in the mission. A commitment had been made to a small, dark-skinned Asian man by a small group of Americans who were going to see that it was met. We were going back, whether or not anyone else ever became aware that we made the trip.

CHAPTER 21

On the Rocks

THE FIRST LIGHT OF morning had just begun to brighten the eastern horizon. I was sitting on the hood of a jeep at the airstrip looking over my notes when elements of the 281st's Bandit lift platoons dropped in over the fort's north wall. Dirt, grass, and dust blew everywhere as they settled down on the runway in single file. Then, as they had the day before, Wolf Pack gunships cut circles in the humid morning air as they circled Trung Dung. Jumping down off the jeep, I went to meet the flight leader so we could go over changes in what we had done the day before.

The blades were still spinning when I reached the lead chopper. I was surprised to see a different face.

"Good, morning. It's good to see you. Where's the other guy?" I asked.

"There was a last-minute change, and we'll be taking you out today. We're the Rat Pack!" the new flight leader said proudly of his unit. "Our guys wanted in on this thing yesterday, so we're all glad to be able to get in on the action today."

"That's great."

As the rest of pilots walked up, I again welcomed the new team.

"Good morning. Welcome to A-502. We're glad more of you are going to get in on this."

There were several "Us, too!"–type responses, and then we quickly started the briefing.

My first comments were directed to the flight leader.

"Let me go over some things that will happen today."

"Okay," he said.

"See that guy over there?"

"The major?"

"Yes. His name is Lee, and he's my boss. He'll ride out with you. Sullivan, the lieutenant who—"

Just then, Mike Sullivan walked up.

"Oh, here he is right here. Good timing, Mike. I was just about to tell them you would lead the flight out."

"That's right," Mike replied.

Then, again speaking to the flight leader, "You can hang back or take a forward position, just as long as the boss gets a good look at what's going on."

"Okay, fine. We'll make sure he sees it all."

"Good. Then, as soon as you get Lieutenant Sullivan and his troops in, send the slicks back for me and my guys."

"Okay."

"We will go in on another cornfield I noticed yesterday. It's near a place where our Montagnard thinks his family might have gone to hide. From there, we will sweep east through the portion of the village on the western ridge and link up with Lieutenant Sullivan on the original LZ."

Confirming his understanding of what was to occur, the flight leader recapped.

"Okay. So we're taking them out and inserting them wherever you were yesterday. Then we're to come back for you, and you'll show us where you want to go in. Correct?"

"Exactly, and there are some other things you and the other pilots need to know."

Since this was a new group, we discussed many things, and the pilots were given the opportunity to ask questions. Just about the time we finished the briefing, Tracer roared overhead.

The radio on the radioman's back came to life with Tracer's check-in.

"Bunkhouse Zero Two, Zero Two, this is *T-r-a-c-e-r*, over." He drew his call sign out with a little more flair than he had the day before. He seemed to be feeling the fresh exhilaration we were all experiencing with the prospect of finding Mang Quang's missing family.

"Roger, Tracer. This is Zero Two. You sound ready to go again this morning. Over."

"Roger, get those things crankin' and let's go get the rest of 'em!"

Looking at the group assembled around me, I mimicked Tracer.

"Let's go get the rest of 'em."

Then, I turned to Sullivan.

"Go ahead, Mike. They're all yours. Take 'em out."

"Okay, we'll see you out there."

Everyone climbed onto the choppers. Major Lee got on the flight leader's, and Mike Sullivan was on the second one back. Sullivan, with the Montagnard who had been with him the day before, would take the lead once airborne to direct the flight west to the cornfield. With the standard serious look on his face, he gave me a thumbs-up sign as they lifted off and started down the runway.

Feeling left behind, I watched as, one by one, the choppers cleared the south wall and turned west. When the choppers were no longer visible in the distance, I went to Mang Quang, who was sitting on the edge of the runway. His legs were folded up against his chest with his arms wrapped around his knees. He was motionless and very quiet as I walked up to him.

"Mang Quang!"

I smiled and tried to appear positive and enthusiastic as he struggled to force a smile in return. There was little question that we were both concerned about what we would find upon reaching the village.

The night before, when visiting with some of the other Montagnards, they told appalling stories of things the VC and NVA had done to them over the years. So, as positive as I attempted to be, I truly feared for the safety of Mang Quang's family, and he appeared to fear the worst. Waiting gave both of us too much time to ponder his family's fate. We were more than prepared for the choppers to return so we could get on with our part of the mission.

Patting Mang on the back, I left him and started walking up and down and back and forth on the runway. Every now and then, I would look toward the western horizon and glance at my watch. One time, only two minutes had past. It seemed like fifteen.

Finally, the flight of helicopters could be heard approaching from the west. We immediately got our troops ready to go. As quickly as the choppers settled in on the runway, troops began loading. In less than five minutes we were on our way back to the village.

✦ ✦ ✦

Upon reaching the mountainside, I could see Lee's chopper circling where Thieu Ta and I had been the day before. When we came in, we passed a little north and slightly downhill of the original LZ. Sullivan called as we passed by and said they had encountered no problems and had secured the LZ. "A few villagers have already walked in," he said.

The news was welcomed and immediately given to Mang Quang. With word of villagers arriving at the cornfield, life appeared to come back to his face. We both knew it meant the VC hadn't killed everyone after we left the day before.

When we neared the cornfield, which was overgrown with tall elephant grass, I pointed it out to the pilot. "Put us in there," I said.

As we turned on approach to what was to become our LZ, the pilot asked, "Zero Two, do you want to light it up?" He was asking if his door gunners should fire into the field, if for nothing more than intimidation.

"It couldn't hurt," I said.

"Go ahead."

With that, the command to fire was given and the door gunners opened up, pouring M-60 machine-gun rounds across the thick stand of elephant grass.

Because there were stumps scattered throughout the tall grass, the choppers couldn't land. So, when we were as low as we could get, I jumped and Mang Quang came out right behind me. The draft created by the beating chopper blades whipped the grass and dried corn stalks in every direction. I squinted my eyes and moved out about ten meters in order to direct the off-loading troops toward my Vietnamese counterpart, who began placing them in perimeter positions on our new LZ.

The door gunners continued to provide covering fire as the chopper lifted out of its hover and circled away from us. I moved a little further into the field to act as a marker for approaching choppers while my Vietnamese counterpart continued to direct his men around the perimeter.

Almost every copilot on the incoming choppers gave some kind of positive gesture before departing. The copilot on the last one formed words with his mouth that would never be heard through his windshield or over the roar of his chopper. But, even with the grass and dirt blowing everywhere, I could see well enough to note clearly what he was saying. His simple but appreciated words were "Good luck." Acknowledging my understanding, I showed him a thumbs-up and nodded. His gesture of encouragement was the last I saw of him as his chopper moved away and passed directly over me.

Once everyone was on the ground, we pulled our perimeter in and moved directly into the jungle and toward the village. Sergeant Giao Phan, one of Thieu Ta Ngoc's most experienced platoon leaders, would lead the point unit. Mang Quang and I, along with my Vietnamese counterpart, were near the front of the column. The other American advisor and his radioman were toward the rear of the column.

According to Mang, in order to reach the village, we would only have to cross one small valley and a stream, and to go up the ridge. I asked him to take us into the village by a route the VC would least expect us to be using. He said he knew a way, but it would be difficult.

He wasn't wrong. The jungle growth was so thick at one point that we had to get down on our hands and knees and crawl through it for some distance. Finally, we could see the sky again when we reached a small stream at the bottom of a ravine.

The water in the steam was chest deep. It had been stirred and muddied by the eight to ten members of the point unit ahead of us. When I reached the far side, I realized that more than mud had been stirred up by our crossing. There were nearly a dozen leeches on my forearms. They were disgusting to look at, but no reason to slow down. Pulling myself up into the jungle, I flicked them off and kept moving.

I had only taken a few steps into the thick growth on the other side of the stream when the hair on the back of my neck began to stand straight up. We were walking on a trail that had been very well traveled. It appeared to be the jungle equivalent of an interstate highway. I signaled up the line to stop the point unit. When I turned back to see where Mang Quang was, he was just coming up out of the stream with Ahat the radioman and Light the interpreter close behind him.

When they reached me, I put my hand on Light's shoulder and spoke quietly.

"Ask Mang if we are close to the village."

Mang spoke in a whisper and gestured ahead up the trail on which we were standing. A translation didn't seem necessary, and there was no surprise when it came in a whisper as well.

"Trung Uy, he says we are very close. The village is at the top of the hill. He says this trail will take us straight up to the village."

I asked Light to pass Mang Quang's information up to the point unit and tell them to be alert. The same word was then passed to those behind us.

After enough time had passed for the message to reach the point unit, the signal was given for them to begin moving again.

As we moved up the trail, the jungle opened a little and wasn't quite so thick. I hated being on the trail. Since first entering the service, I'd been taught to say off trails whenever possible. They're great places for booby-traps and ambushes. But, searching both sides of the trail for signs of either, I noticed a number of large flowers standing out against the vivid green of the jungle.

The setting appeared to contradict any concern about booby traps or ambushes.

No wonder the Montagnards picked this place to build their village, I thought. *It is beautiful; this could be paradise.* The thought had barely dissolved and I had only taken about ten steps when paradise exploded and gunfire ripped through the jungle.

Instinctively, I dropped to the ground and waited to see if the jungle around me was going to erupt with the gunfire of an ambush. When it didn't, I got to my knees and tried to look up the trail, but because of a bend, I could only see as far as two men—about ten meters.

It's the point unit. They've made contact, I thought.

In addition to the sound of the point unit's M-16s, the distinctive blooping sound of their M-79 grenade launchers could be heard. That was followed by the sound of impact further up the trail. I hadn't been this close to so much noise since the days I had visited the artillery battery.

The explosions and gunfire up ahead were loud, and they were close.

✦ ✦ ✦

Later, thinking about the first few seconds of the incident on the trail, I considered what happens to the human body and mind in that type of situation.

Science has shown that the instinctive will to survive causes various body organs to rise to full function. Lungs work like billows as respiration increases, and the heart pounds in the chest as it pumps blood to other body parts demanding more oxygen.

While it flows undetected, the effects of adrenaline released into the bloodstream are unmistakable. Just prior to the contact, I remembered feeling a little tired because of our rapid and rigorous trek through the jungle, not to mention a lack of sleep during the last couple of nights.

But once the gunfire erupted and I crouched on the trail trying to determine the seriousness of our situation, a tremendous feeling of energy surged. I suspect that it was simply the result of a human brain preparing my body for a fight-or-flight response in order to survive.

◆ ◆ ◆

In spite of all the things happening inside and around me, spontaneously my thoughts merged and focused. I considered what actions to take.

Gunfire was still coming from up ahead. I had no way to help or give intelligent direction without knowing what was happening, and the only way to know what was happening was to go up the hill and find out. I jumped to my feet and started up the trail.

Moving around the two or three Vietnamese soldiers who were directly in front of me, I began making my way toward the front of the column. Maneuvering up the trail, my eyes focused ahead and snapped alternately back and forth. With my thumb, I flipped the safety on my M-16 to the firing position and watched the jungle for enemy soldiers.

At the same time, in anticipation of having one of the enemy appear, I kept thinking, *Don't shoot a villager by mistake.*

After reaching the turn in the trail, I looked back. Mang Quang and Light were right behind me. Then, turning back to go around the curve, I slammed into one of our Vietnamese soldiers who was running back down the trail. For a split second, I thought he was a VC and almost shot him just before slipping to the ground.

We were at a steep incline, and the trail was wet and slippery because water from a stream further up was running across it. Grabbing at plants, small trees, branches, and anything else I could get my hands on, I struggled to pull myself up the incline. But, as I tried to move up, I ran into more of the Vietnamese soldiers from the point unit who were coming back down the trail. When they reached the wet area, they used it like a slide and came down on their backs and behinds.

Two or three times, I was knocked off my feet and was covered with mud by the time I moved past the wet area.

Finally reaching dry ground, I continued moving carefully up the steep trail. None of our men were anywhere to be seen, but I could still hear occasional gunfire. Not all of our point unit had come back down the trail, which meant Giao and some of them were still somewhere up ahead.

I kept moving and hoped that when I did find them they weren't jumpy and wouldn't shoot me by mistake when they saw me come up behind them.

As we worked our way up the trail, the radio Ahat was carrying became active.

"Zero Two, this is Zero Eight. What's your status? Over."

Sullivan had heard the gunfire and was trying to reach us to find out what was happening. Still huffing and puffing and trying to determine what was happening myself, there wasn't a time to stop to talk. But as we kept going, I turned around and pulled the handset off of Ahat's web gear.

"Eight, this is Two. We're going uphill and I don't know what's happened yet. Over."

Because we were under dense jungle and on the opposite side of the ridge from him, Mike couldn't hear my transmission clearly.

He asked me to repeat, "Zero Two, can you say again? Over."

"Roger, Eight. There's something going on, but I'm not sure what. Over."

He still couldn't understand. "Two, speak slowly. I can't read you."

I knew he was trying to determine whether or not we needed help, but there was no time to attempt further communication with him. Speaking slowly enough for him to understand, I said, "Stand by, Eight. Zero Two, out." Then I passed the handset to Light.

Just about that time, a couple of explosions occurred that sounded like regular grenades or enemy rockets, and they were within meters. There was no way to determine who was shooting at whom or what, and I still couldn't see anything. Glancing back down the trail, only Mang Quang, Ahat, and Light were with me.

Further down, it appeared that the Vietnamese had regrouped and were trying to follow us back up. Hopefully, that was the case.

Just as we reached a sharp turn in the trail, Mang Quang reached up and grabbed me and we stopped. There was no gunfire, not a sound. The haze of smoke and smell of gunpowder filled the air, so I knew we must be right on top of whatever had happened.

Mang whispered so low to Light that I couldn't hear what he said. Light leaned over to me, and while gesturing around the turn, he whispered.

"Mang Quang says that if you look around this turn you will see his village."

I looked at Mang and shook my head up and down. Then I moved in close against a tree and leaned around the turn in the trail. There they were.

Sergeant Giao and about five or six of his more experienced men were just ahead.

They were squatting on the trail just inside the tree line.

One of the soldiers protecting their rear saw me and, to my relief, he recognized me. He tapped Giao on the shoulder and pointed toward me. When Giao saw me, he motioned for me to come up with him. My trio of shadows, Mang, Ahat, and Light, followed me around the turn and up the trail to the place where Giao and his men had stopped.

When we reached Giao, I whispered a greeting to him in Vietnamese. "*Ciao,* Trung Si."

"*Ciao,* Trung Uy."

Giao could not speak English well, so, in Vietnamese, he asked Light where the rest of his men were. Light told him that we had passed some going down, but that he thought they were coming back up.

Giao was obviously angered that some of his men had run back and the others had not yet arrived. He turned to the soldier who had seen me approaching and told him to go back and bring the rest up quickly. He told Light to tell me that when they arrived we would secure the village.

Watching Giao's man go down the trail, I noticed the others come around the turn. I tapped him on the shoulder and pointed toward them. Then, I pointed at the two of us and into the village. He nodded his head up and down.

Simultaneously we stood up and began moving from the tree line into the village. As we moved in, I ran my thumb along the safety on my M-16 to make sure it was still in the off position and ready to fire.

The village was compact. There were six open huts built very close together under the dense growth of jungle. As we moved through the huts searching for someone who looked like they belonged to Mang Quang, I turned quickly this way and that. My index finger rested securely against the round, smooth curvature of the trigger.

I kept expecting either a VC or Montagnard villager to jump out in front of me and hoped there would be time to determine quickly enough which was which. I didn't want to kill a villager and didn't want a VC or NVA soldier to kill me.

The corner of one of the huts housed something that looked like a storage area. I thought I heard movement coming from inside and began moving toward it.

Giao's men were now pouring into the village, and there was a fair amount of chatter as the Vietnamese coordinated their movement into and through the village. I wasn't sure if I had really heard something or if my imagination was being creative. It could easily have been the sound of my own heartbeat pounding in my ears.

Very carefully, I reached for the cover to the storage area. Just as I snatched it open, there was a tremendous explosion right behind me. Dust and an assortment of debris blew everywhere.

Many times I wished my ability to speak and understand Vietnamese was fluent. I understood enough to know that amidst the occasional gunfire and yelling, there was concern about a hole in the ground that someone else had discovered.

Light had taken cover under a table not far away, so I yelled to him. "Light, what in hell is going on?"

"Some soldier is saying he saw a VC go in a hole. He threw a grenade in the hole."

"What hole?"

"A hole in the ground . . . over there," he said, pointing as he spoke.

I rolled around to see where he was pointing, but could only see some large rocks.

Getting up on my knees to take a better look, I could see holes around the base of a huge rock outcropping.

With my rifle pointed toward the holes, I stood up and moved over to see if there was anything in them. As I moved around looking in each one, there was nothing and no one to be seen, but they appeared to go very deep. I told Light to ask Giao to have a couple of his men stay behind to keep an eye on the holes while we finished searching the village.

As it turned out, there was nothing in the storage area I had been about to check when someone tried to crack the earth in half. But worse, there was no sign of Mang's family or any of the other families. The only people anyone had seen were a small group of VC who were surprised by Giao and his men when they came up the trail toward the village.

After a brief exchange of gunfire and grenades, the VC had quickly disappeared down one of the many trails that ran off in various directions away from the village. As I checked one of the trails near where I was standing, I noticed movement in the jungle. From my vantage point, I had a relatively unobstructed view for some distance up the trail. The movement was perpendicular to and toward the trail. If the movement was a VC trying to exit the area, I was about to have a very clear shot. Raising my M-16 shoulder high, I leveled it up the center of the trail, again made sure the safety was off with my thumb, put my finger on the trigger, and waited for whatever was about to cross the trail.

✦ ✦ ✦

Years before, while on one of our rabbit hunting trips, my grandfather had offered advice on what to do in exactly this situation.

"If you see a rabbit running toward the trail, wait till he gets there. Then, as he crosses it, take your shot and make a clean kill. Not even a rabbit needs to suffer," my grandfather said.

♦ ♦ ♦

Standing positioned in the jungle foliage along the edge of the trail in order not to be seen, I waited for my shot as my quick-moving target approached. A small beam of filtered sunlight had made its way through the thick jungle canopy and was shining in one of my eyes, so I moved slightly. The nearer the movement got to the trail, the more the pressure on my trigger finger increased. The jungle was hot and steamy, and insects buzzed around my face. Perspiration was dripping down my forehead. *I hope it doesn't get in my eyes*, I thought. *As quickly as he's moving, I'm only going to have one shot.* Then, at that instant, my target burst from the jungle, thrusting back leaves and vines. *Fire, fire, fire!!!* was the screaming instinct to protect myself, but my eyes drew wide open. In a space of time too infinitesimal to measure, my finger straightened and came clear of the trigger. Standing dead center in my sites was a small Montagnard boy who quickly dashed off the trail and back into the jungle on the other side. In a long slow sigh, I released the deep breath I had been holding in anticipation of my shot and thanked God that I hadn't killed the child.

Later, we learned that the boy had become separated from his parents who were on their way to the cornfield, and he was simply trying to catch up with his family when he crossed the trail.

♦ ♦ ♦

Back in the small village I rejoined Mang Quang, who was upset that we had not found his family in or around this part of the village. He expected them to be hiding around here if they were still alive. Through Light, I told him we would continue our search and reminded him that several villagers had already reached the other cornfield and were safe. Maybe his family was there, too.

It was a little gruesome, but I also asked Light to tell him to look around. There were no bodies and no blood. "No one has been killed here," I said.

Mang looked around, then shook his head and agreed that was a good sign.

I had just finished encouraging Mang when the rear part of our column arrived at the village. The American advisor who had been with the rear element of our column walked over and wanted to know what he had missed.

I was giving him a quick rundown on what had happened when Lee called from his chopper. They were passing almost directly overhead. The jungle was so thick that we could hear them but couldn't see them. He was checking to see if we needed anything after Sullivan had called him to report the gunfire and explosions he had heard.

"Bunkhouse Zero Two, this is Bunkhouse Zero Six. Over."

"Roger, this is Two. Go ahead, Six."

"Is everything okay down there? Eight said he thought you were in contact. Over."

"Yes, we were briefly, but everything is fine now. We're getting ready to move on toward Eight's location. Over."

"Okay, these guys need to refuel. I'm going to have them drop me off on the way in. Good luck. Bunkhouse Zero Six, out."

"Roger. Thank you. Two, out."

When they passed low over the trees on the way back in, the leader let me know he would be back.

"Zero Two, this is Rat Pack Leader. Stay safe. We won't be gone long."

✦ ✦ ✦

We rested for a few minutes while I finished telling my team member what he had missed and what we were going to do next. Then I found

Sergeant Giao to tell him we needed to move on up the ridge to the other field.

Giao shouted a few orders, and in a couple of minutes we were on our way again.

✦ ✦ ✦

Since we knew a number of VC with weapons were still around, we left the village on one of the trails, but quickly moved back into the jungle to avoid providing them with an ambush opportunity.

As our column chugged through the undergrowth like a slow-moving centipede, the sound of Tracer's engines roared and the speakers blared down into the jungle each time he passed over us just above the treetops. It was surprising to hear how well the tape could be heard through the jungle canopy. It made me feel better about the prospects of Mang's family hearing it and knowing they must reach the cornfield. Hopefully, we would find them before we got there.

I was just getting ready to push a thick growth of leaves aside when a hand suddenly appeared in front of my face, the hand of the soldier in front of me. Our movement had halted.

Motioning for Mang, Ahat, and Light to follow, I made my way up the column to find out why we had stopped. When we reached the front of the point unit, Giao was standing next to a Montagnard family. Turning quickly to Mang Quang, I waited for a reaction, but it wasn't his family. It was, however, a family to which Mang was close because he was obviously very glad to see them.

The small family had heavy-looking baskets that were filled with their personal belongings. They were trying to carry them up to the cornfield as Tracer's tape directed.

The baskets were far too heavy for the children, though, and they were having a difficult time trying to move them. They had stopped to rest when Giao and our unit happened onto them.

When Mang Quang asked if they had seen any of his family, they told him, "No." They said they hadn't seen any of his family since the afternoon before. They also said that when Mang's voice told them to go to the cornfield, everyone ran to gather what they could and then started toward the field, but for many with children and old people, it was a long way and everyone couldn't make the trip. Those who hadn't reached the field in time had gone into the jungle to hide from the VC.

The place where the family stopped to rest wasn't far from the cornfield where Sullivan was waiting. It was a good time to let him know we were nearby and would be coming out of the jungle soon. We didn't want any of his team to mistake us for a VC unit and start shooting.

While alerting Sullivan to our pending arrival, I asked if any more villagers had arrived. "Yes, about twenty more," he said. Because we hadn't found them, I could only hope that Mang Quang's family was among them. Before continuing, we distributed the family's baskets among our soldiers and, once more, started up the ridge. It only took about fifteen minutes before we popped out of the jungle and onto the base of the cornfield.

As we neared the top of the cornfield where it was a little more level, the Montagnards could be seen gathered together near the center of the field. I scanned the gathering, looking for a family that appeared to be missing a father. There didn't appear to be anyone in the group of villagers that matched the description Mang had given of his family. I was terribly afraid we were about to experience the same heart-sickening disappointment of the day before.

Then, deep into the crowd I spotted a woman and two children sitting on a pair of rocks. Turning to Mang Quang, who was also looking for the faces of his family, I put my hand on his shoulder and pulled him toward me. Then, pointing into the moving group toward the woman and children, I asked, "Mang Quang's?"

He looked and tried to see where I was pointing. For just a moment the crowd in front of the woman and children separated enough for him to catch sight of the three. When he turned back, there was no need for him to answer. His eyes started to well with tears and his face appeared to glow. He smiled with a tremendous expression of relief.

"Yeah, Trung Uy . . . Mang's." I patted him on his back and said, "Go!"

Mang had covered about half the distance to where his family was sitting on the rocks when they saw him coming. One of the children yelled something that must surely have been the equivalent of "Dad" or "Daddy" in English. Then, they all jumped off the rocks and ran to meet him.

I don't believe I've ever seen a happier person in my life than when Mang Quang was reunited with his family. The reunion was warm and emotional, and it was a special privilege just to witness. Mang had expected the worst possible outcome for his family, but was experiencing the very best.

We were all relieved that the man who was responsible for our rescue attempt had been rewarded for his leadership and bravery with the greatest prize he could have been given, the safe return of his family.

Walking past them over to a flat place on the cornfield, I dropped my equipment and sat down on the ground. It was nice not to be walking uphill anymore. I looked out over the valley and could see Tracer still out there broadcasting. The two gunships on station were making wide passes around the area still looking for potential targets. Shading my eyes from the sun with one hand, I looked off in the distance. Two other choppers were coming in our direction.

"That's Rat Pack Leader and the other gun coming back from refueling. They just radioed in." Sullivan had come up behind me.

"That's what I thought," I said.

Gesturing toward Mang, he asked, "Is that his family?"

"Yes. They look glad to see each other, don't they?"

"Yes, they do," he said.

"How long has it been since the last villager walked in?"

"About forty-five minutes."

"Okay, let's have someone ask the villagers if they know of anyone else who is missing. Depending on the response we get, we'll decide how much longer to stay. We'll be sitting ducks here if we hang around long enough for the bad guys to move in on us. And, if that NVA unit comes back while we're here, we'll really have a problem."

"Okay, we'll check now," Sullivan said.

I took a drink from my canteen and got up to walk around and take a count of the Montagnards.

Most of the villagers were sitting as I wandered through the group counting and smiling. Many seemed pleased to be where they were. Others appeared frightened and uncertain about their future. A few acted suspicious, as if they thought that maybe they had simply traded one set of captors for another.

Light walked up with a bullhorn and asked the Montagnards if anyone knew other people who were missing. A few names were called out, but Mang Quang said he had seen them at Trung Dung. They had been picked up the day before.

Eventually, after several other names were discussed, we realized no one really knew exactly how many villagers there were. We had been told that the villagers had been separated and denied any frequent contact for purposes of control. So, it seemed the VC's strategy of separating the Montagnards into the smaller groups had been effective.

Over the years, since they had been kept from communicating freely, the villagers had become uncertain of their own numbers. For that reason, it would have been difficult if not impossible for the unarmed Montagnards to organize any successful attack against their captors. Also, Mang had told us that he knew some of the Montagnards had run away and fled deeper into the jungle to escape VC control. It became clear that until we got the villagers in one place to make some kind of list, we weren't going to know whether or not we had everyone.

If we called for a pickup at that moment, it would still take almost two hours to get everyone out. That would allow additional time for any straggling Montagnards to reach us. It was late in the afternoon and rain was moving in from the coast. Time to go had clearly arrived. We would do our accounting of the villagers at Trung Dung.

Walking over to Ahat, I took the radio handset and called our flight leader, who since returning, had been circling above the Wolf Pack gunships overhead.

"Rat Pack Leader, this is Zero Two. Over."

"Roger, this is Rat Pack. What can I do for you? Over."

"Take us home. Over."

"Roger, I'll call for your taxis now."

"Thank you, we'll be standing by. Out."

A couple minutes later, the flight leader called back. "Zero Two, Rat Pack Leader, over."

"Roger. Go ahead, Leader."

"Your ride is on the way. ETA approximately two-five minutes. Over."

"Roger, we'll be ready."

"Zero Two, Leader. I've got some guys who want to know if our man (Mang Quang) found his family."

"Roger, Leader . . . he did. They're standing right here with him now. Over."

"Great! I'll pass the word."

On his next pass overhead, the crew of the lead chopper could be seen looking down toward us, so I pointed to Mang and his family. The pilot responded without using any call signs.

"Makes you feel real good, doesn't it?"

"It sure does," I said.

✦ ✦ ✦

No other Montagnards appeared before the last chopper left the cornfield. Until that chopper cleared the LZ, the ever-watchful Wolf Pack gunship pilots and their crews circled overhead providing protection. In all, another 41 villagers had made their way to the cornfield and, now, the last of them were headed for safety.

✦ ✦ ✦

For a second time spirits were high as we flew back to Trung Dung, but they became even higher when we reached camp and the two groups of Montagnards were reunited. Joy created by the long-overdue reunion of the village caused a spontaneous celebration.

While it seemed of little importance to the Montagnards who reveled in their new taste of freedom, everyone who took part in the mission knew we had been far more fortunate than we had any reason to expect. We had taken no casualties in only minor skirmishes in a place far outside of our normal area of operations. Now, despite any risks that may have been faced, the men of A-502 offered the Montagnards more than their exceptional military skills.

As the villagers continued to greet each other as if long-separated relatives, I watched our team members distribute food, drink, and bedding and marveled at the respect and kindness with which these seasoned military men treated the primitive families. With warm smiles and unexpected gentleness, some even helped make beds for smaller children who had obviously been made weary by their experience. These scenes were never captured on film or reported back home, which may have made their occurrence so much more sincere and genuine.

By going where they had gone, the men from A-502, the Bandits, the Rat Pack and Wolf Pack from the 281st, and Tracer from the 8th Psy Ops had all risked a great deal—the ultimate. Watching as some of them shared in the joy of the moment, I wondered, *How could anyone ask more of those men?* But, before the week was over, that's exactly what I would be doing. This time, would-be rescuers would find themselves in need of rescue.

CHAPTER 22

Ice Cream and Little People

AFTER WATCHING THE MONTAGNARD reunion for a while from a distance, I went to the teamhouse and asked one of the Vietnamese cooks to ice tubs of soft drinks. When they were ready, he helped me load them into the back of one of the jeeps. We then drove the cold refreshments down to the tent, where the Montagnards were introduced to Coca-Cola.

While the villagers began to relax in their new surroundings, Sergeant Arrants and his team of medics moved through the new group doing checkups. They took their time, applying Band-Aids and kindness as necessary.

Other team members arrived and passed out clothing they had gathered from here and there while still others helped prepare food that had been distributed.

Sergeant Koch went to one corner of the tent and began the task of creating a list of everyone who had been rescued. When it was finished we would visit with each of the adult Montagnards to determine how many, if any, were still missing.

While almost everyone else on our team was busy healing, clothing, and feeding, I took one of the cold Cokes, walked about twenty meters away, and crawled up on a stack of sandbags. Leaning back into the bags, I looked over toward the tent where 123 Montagnard villagers were being cared for by a group of Americans who acted more like hosts at a party than soldiers.

✦ ✦ ✦

I found great satisfaction in what had occurred during the last two days and, in particular, about what was continuing to happen at Trung Dung. With the ongoing scene of warm human interaction before me, I wondered who was benefiting most from the experience(the Montagnards or our team members. For a few moments my mind yielded to things philosophical, not necessarily a unique occurrence during a time of war when there was more than enough time to contemplate one's situation.

The events of the last two days were a side of war one rarely, if ever, has the opportunity to see. *I am fortunate to witness this,* I thought.

The crying, pain, wounds, fear of death, and death itself that the Montagnards said they had experienced in the past were, for the moment, replaced with laughter, healing, caring, good food, and the anticipation of a new life.

From my vantage point on the sandbags, I watched Lee, Lane, Vasquez, Phalen, Arrants, Freedman, Sotello, Trujillo, Stewart, Koch, King, Bardsley, Key, Miller, and all the others as they came and went in their individual attempts to make the Montagnards feel safe and welcomed. Watching them, I mused at how different the Americans were. They were black, white, and brown. They were Jewish, Christian, and who knows what else. Despite their differences in race or religion, though, they functioned as the team they were and with a single purpose as they cared for the Montagnards.

What an interesting phenomenon it is, I thought, *how human beings bond together during war or other times of trouble or disaster.* Differences seem to become less important during difficult and challenging times as focus shifts to similarities.

When we had free time, team members would sit around and talk about home. We talked about things we liked and things we didn't like. During one of those times I realized how distinctly different the men who made up the A-502 really were. Yet, they worked incredibly well together and acted as though they cared very much about each other's welfare. Our team represented a microcosm of the country from which we had all come.

Watching as another team member arrived with more blankets to be used for bedding, it occurred to me what an extraordinary amalgam of humankind Americans truly are. We are woven together into a wonderfully vibrant fabric from the threads of countless different ethnic origins. Even though we are a blend of differences, we share something that gives the fabric its amazing strength. Americans, like no others, share an unyielding determination to live in freedom.

Still watching while the Montagnards enjoyed their first day of freedom in many years, I witnessed firsthand the joy of living free. Before now, freedom was a word to me . . . a concept . . . a dream that brought the Pilgrims and other settlers to America hundreds of years ago and continues to bring them today. But now, it was more than a word, a concept, or even a dream. Freedom was real. I could see it.

My belief had always been that our efforts to perpetuate and ensure the dream of freedom was what made the United States great and gained it recognition around the world as the champion of human rights. But as a nation we are not perfect, and we do occasionally made mistakes. After many months in Vietnam, I was growing in maturity regarding political issues and was facing the possibility that this war might be one of those mistakes. It would have been easy for me to challenge Lord Tennyson's postulation that it is "Ours not to reason why. . . . Ours but to do and die." However, as I watched my fellow team members tend to the Montagnards, I felt reasonably sure of one thing. Whenever the United States offered to share our dream of freedom with others, men such as these would surely do the very best they could, as they had this day, to ensure that the dream became reality.

✦ ✦ ✦

My momentary drift was jolted to a halt when Miller skidded up in a jeep.

"Hey, LT."

We were often less than military formal at 502, so I returned Miller's spunky greeting.

"Hey, Miller. What's up!"

Looking toward the tent housing the Montagnards, he continued. "Looks like everybody did a great job today."

"Without question, they did an incredible job. I was just thinking about what everyone has been doing. The folks at home would be pretty proud of them. Don't you think?"

"Yes, sir, I do. And, you know I wanted to go, too."

"Yeah . . . I know," I said, laughing as I spoke, "Everyone wanted to go."

Then, wondering what he had come for, I asked, "So, Miller . . . did you need something or was this just a driving demonstration?"

"Oh, yeah . . . No. Lieutenant Orians has been calling all afternoon to find out what happened. He's on the radio now. If you can come back with me . . . he'd like to talk to you."

"Sure. Let's go."

We drove the short distance to the teamhouse, and I went to the radio room to give Frank a report on the day.

He was pleased that the villagers had been brought in, but was disappointed that immediate media coverage hadn't been available. He said he was going to alert the various in-country media bureaus for follow-up coverage and told me to expect visitors.

I told him we'd be ready and thanked him for checking on us.

After cleaning up a little, I went back down to spend the evening with the Montagnards and then, later, to get a good night's sleep.

✦ ✦ ✦

The next day, as we began questioning the Montagnards regarding the list Sergeant Koch had compiled the night before, it became apparent almost immediately to both of us that other families were still missing. Several of the villagers we visited with told us that people they had seen recently were not among the group relocated to Trung Dung.

After spending most of the day with villagers and interpreters, the count would be forty, forty-one, forty-two, or forty-three people still unaccounted for, depending on who you talked to. We thought one or two people might have been referred to by different names, but that made little difference. We were reasonably sure that between forty and forty-five people were still out there. That was a significant number and, like it or not, we knew we had to consider going back . . . one more time.

However, a serious problem now existed. Based on information obtained during questioning of the Montagnards, we began to believe that the enemy unit that had been using the village area as a base camp was part of the 18B Regiment. It was a well-armed and disciplined North Vietnamese Army unit. One of our units had faced elements of their 8th and 9th Battalions in the Dong Bo Mountains, and possibly these were outpost members or part of the 7th Battalion, which was away when the other two were annihilated.

Regardless of who was using the village, we couldn't make repeated trips so far outside of our AO into the same area without running the risk of being ambushed or encountering a larger unit.

After considering our dilemma, we decided to let the VC and/or 18B NVA think we were finished and wouldn't be coming back. We decided we would let a few days pass before attempting to rescue the remaining families, but we immediately began making arrangements for our final trip to the village.

When speaking to the 281st, Tracer, Thieu Ta, and the other advisors, there was no attempt to minimize the seriousness of the situation. Our predicament and the danger of returning a third time were made very clear, but no one flinched. Everyone agreed we couldn't just forget that the remaining families were out there. We would have to go after them.

✦ ✦ ✦

The days before our final trip were spent questioning the villagers about the various enemy units they had encountered during the past several years. They reported a number of units passing through the village en route to both northern and southern destinations.

During the questioning, we discovered the unit responsible for killing Dale Reich had very probably come from the village. While discussing some of their captors' most recent activities, two of the villagers mentioned that a few months before, the 18B unit had returned to the village after being gone only four or five days. The villagers overheard them discussing an ambush their unit had walked into while they were away. We felt reasonably sure the unit they had encountered was ours. The villagers said the unit had an unknown number of men killed and many wounded in that battle. They said two or three others died after returning to camp. The Montagnards were sure of this because they were made to dig the graves for those who died.

Team members quickly developed a desire for revenge when they learned that the enemy unit holding the Montagnards might also have been responsible for Dale Reich's death. While I understood and shared the feeling, I wondered if what we were doing might be the greatest moral revenge we could take on Reich's behalf. The enemy unit had taken one life from us. We had already taken 123 from them and planned on taking another forty or more. There was a difference, though. The ones we had taken would continue to live.

✦ ✦ ✦

After draining the Montagnards of intelligence information, we turned to lighter things. I took Mang Quang's children and several of the others up to the teamhouse where we dared to serve them chocolate ice cream. They had never tasted it before, and watching their reactions was great fun. Almost all of the children examined the brown concoction carefully and smelled it before they attempted to eat it. A couple of the team members encouraged them by helping themselves to a bowl and demonstrating that it was for eating. Their demonstration included a variety of sounds and facial expressions meant to show how good it was.

When the children finally began to eat it, there were those who loved it immediately and couldn't get it into their small mouths quickly enough. Then, there were others who tapped on it with their spoons or used their fingers to determine its exact nature before it reached their mouths.

By the time the ice cream was gone, the hands and faces of all the children were covered with chocolate. While our ice cream party required one heck of a mopping-up operation, the best was yet to come.

Coming from an industrialized country, we take so much for granted. Things that are commonplace to us may be inconceivable or appear fantastic to someone as primitive as the Montagnard children were. They had all been born and had grown to their young ages in the jungle. While I thought they might enjoy it or be amused by it, I was not prepared for their reaction when I turned on the television.

We seated some of the children on the sofa in our sitting area and the others on the floor in front of them. One of our team members had taken one of Pop's dishtowels and was teasing them by holding it in front of the television while we waited for the picture as it warmed up.

A rerun of an old sitcom was on, I don't remember which one, but when the towel was popped away from in front of the screen, their reaction was unbelievable. They all simultaneously sprang to their feet and began screaming, pointing at the television, and running around. It was instant chaos.

Three of the older boys ran to the television and tried to look inside from the top, sides, and back. One of the boys tapped it on the side and seemed to be trying to talk to it. Then I realized what was happening. The children thought the characters on the screen were alive inside this magic box on the table.

To calm things down and regain control of our ice cream party gone wild, I reached over and turned the television off. In an effort to restore calm, team members made repeated shushing sounds. After everything became quiet, I went and found Light to help me explain the wonder of television to the children who we had just inadvertently yanked into the twentieth century.

The next day, we were still laughing about our attempt to entertain and amuse the Montagnard children. All of the Americans seemed to enjoy sharing their culture with the villagers, who were quick to return the gesture by sharing theirs with the team.

I'm not sure who had the toughest time adjusting to the other's customs. Some of the Montagnard women felt no need to cover their breasts in our presence. But, as unsettling as that was at first, we got used to it and they were all treated with respect and given shirts to wear.

Something equally difficult to adjust to was sight of children smoking. The first time I saw a child with a pipe I thought the small boy was a dwarf. Even after getting very close to him I still wasn't sure he was a child, but he was. The young boy, who was only five years old, smoked his father's pipe like he had been doing it for years. As I stared, he smiled, then offered me the pipe. I shook my head back and forth and coughed, indicating what would likely occur if I accepted. He just laughed and put the pipe back in his mouth and continued to puff. He appeared to enjoy his pipe more than our ice cream.

CHAPTER 23

One More Time

DURING THE DAYS WHEN we waited to return to the village, my already developed affection for the Montagnards continued to grow. They were a relatively quiet people and kept to themselves. They seemed comfortable in their temporary surroundings and, even though primitive, possessed the courtesy to express appreciation for the care that they received at Trung Dung.

Whenever wandering through the tent area where the Montagnards were housed, I often looked for Mang Quang's children. Frequently, before going to visit, I would go through the goody boxes sent from home by my mother to look for something they might enjoy. My entire supply was depleted in only three days because I also took things to share with other children who learned to look at my pockets carefully when they saw me coming. It amused me how short the learning curve was for these children who had been born and raised in the jungle when it came to identifying objects in my pockets. They were able to detect a protruding candy wrapper or the outline of cookies at amazing distances.

While partial to the children, Mang Quang's in particular, I had warm feelings for all of the Montagnards. To me, they had become a tangible symbol of why American soldiers had come to Vietnam. They were a warm people who wanted nothing from anyone other than the opportunity to live in freedom in their small, generally isolated village communities.

Because of my affection for the villagers, a Vietnamese soldier who acted jealous with all the care and attention the Montagnards were receiving from the American team members drew my ire. He walked up beside me with a question one afternoon during one of my many trips to visit the Montagnards, "Trung Uy . . . why Americans give so much help to Montagnards? They are *jungle* people," he said.

There was already reason not to like or trust this particular soldier, and his question only served to increase my distaste for him. His attitude regarding the American advisors had almost always been negative, and I had once caught him sneaking around our teamhouse. Since we already knew that our camp CIDG units included VC sympathizers, it had crossed my mind that he may be VC. Unfortunately, we weren't able to prove our suspicions.

In response to his question, I looked straight into his eyes. "We help *them* for the same reason we came to help *you*," I said.

It is unlikely that my answer meant anything to him, but he didn't say anything else and simply walked away.

◆ ◆ ◆

The morning prior to our third and final trip west to the Montagnard village, interest in the operation began to spread beyond the walls of Trung Dung and the Dien Khanh Citadel.

Frank Orians called to say that Associated Press and other media agencies had contacted him, as had one of the three major television networks.

In 1968, there were only three major television networks for news. CNN, Fox, and the others were still two decades and more away.

Orians said the news agencies were interested in the Montagnard rescue and would probably be out within the next day or so to cover

the story. He was surprised, then enthusiastic, when I told him there
might be even more to report because we were going back to the village—one more time.

"Why?" he asked.

"In an attempt to retrieve families that are still missing," I said.

Even Frank, who was a Special Forces–trained PIO, recognized the
seriousness of returning to the village a third time.

"Isn't that risky?" he asked.

"Yes, but what can we do, leave them out there? We're all agreed, even
our support units. Leaving them out there is simply not an option."

"When are you going?" he asked.

"Tomorrow morning, as soon as there's enough light to see where
we're going."

He wished us luck and said he would be out not later than the next
afternoon to prepare a release on the story. I told him we would be
glad to see him and would introduce him to our new friends.

By later that afternoon, word of our return to the village had spread
around Fifth Group Headquarters in Nha Trang. A lieutenant colonel
from Operations called to ask if he could go with us the next morning. He said he had been behind a desk too long and wanted to get
into the field. "This sounds like something I would very much like to
be involved in. Do you mind if I tag along, Lieutenant?" he asked.

I told him we would be glad to have him along and suggested that
he catch a ride out with the 281st the next morning.

Preparing the operations order and coordinating plans for the mission helped pass the day. Somewhere in the midst of our planning session, Sergeant Roy King, who was capable of producing nearly anything you needed, presented me with a plasticized map that included
the Montagnard village area. "I don't want you to get lost," he said as
he handed it to me.

"Where were you a week ago?" I asked.

Sergeant King laughed and said, "Just be glad you have it now."

In was evening by the time I finished plotting positions and making notes on my new map. I folded it so that the cornfield was in the center and headed for the teamhouse. Having missed dinner, I went searching for something to eat in the kitchen. Upon opening the refrigerator door, I was surprised to see a plate with my name on it, LT ROSS. One of the cooks had covered a plate of food for me. I took it to my room and, after finishing it, had absolutely no problem falling asleep.

◆ ◆ ◆

There was just a glimmer of daylight when I slung my web gear up over my shoulders and fastened it in place. The screen door at the end of the teamhouse slapped shut behind me as it had many times before, and I started walking toward the airstrip. I was only halfway there when Tracer zipped overhead, followed by the 281st. They were early. It seemed there would be as much enthusiasm about our third trip west as there had been for our first.

When I reached the airstrip, the choppers were already on the ground. The Wolf Pack was circling overhead, and Tracer was now off in the distance making a turn.

I looked down toward the lead chopper and could see a familiar figure approaching, but was still a little surprised to see him. It was Frank Orians, and he was in his combat gear. I waved and went to meet him.

When close enough for him to hear me, I asked, "What are you doing here?"

"Go look on the lead chopper," he said. "I brought you a surprise."

"Oh, really?" I responded, having no idea what his surprise might be.

Following his direction, I walked up to see what he had brought. Upon reaching the front chopper, I found it full of press representatives along with the colonel from Fifth Group Operations. As they exited the helicopter, Frank introduced me to David Culhane from CBS News, his cameraman, and his soundman. He then introduced me to Don Tate, a Scripps-Howard war correspondent and staff writer. There was also a man from another major print publication and a female reporter. Their names, I am very sorry to say, I have forgotten.

The female, however, looked remotely familiar, and while she flashed credentials I don't recall what organization she said she represented. But that would be of little consequence because, while I have forgotten her name, I will never forget my encounter with her. She taught me something very important about the fortitude and courage of women.

The young female reporter had a camera hanging around her neck and a pad and pencil in one of her hands, with which she had already been taking notes. She was attractive, with short auburn-colored hair, bright, penetrating eyes, and appeared to be in her twenties. While her posture and conduct suggested self-confidence, she would soon demonstrate her assertiveness and her ability to represent herself.

Immediately after our introductions, I asked the female correspondent to step aside from the others with me. I pointed through the opening in the hill and told her that the Montagnards were just beyond it and that A-502 team members would be there to help her with her story. "I'll visit with you when we get back," I said.

Peering at me intently with a quizzical look on her face, she responded firmly, "What do you mean? I'm going *with* you."

"That's not possible," I quickly countered. "You're going to have to stay her until we return."

"Are they going?" she asked, gesturing toward Culhane, Tate, and the others.

"Yes, they are," I said.

"Then, why am I not going?" she demanded.

"I don't want you to get hurt," I said sincerely and with some feeling in my tone.

"Do you want them to get hurt?" she exclaimed, again gesturing toward the male reporters.

"No, I don't want them to get hurt either," I replied, noting the fire in her now slightly squinted eyes.

"Good! Then, leave them here with me!"

She was obviously extremely upset, so I didn't laugh. But, the others, who were positioned behind her after she turned to face me, either smirked or grimaced. Then they moved away to give us some space to discuss the matter.

Taking her gently by the arm, I asked her to walk with me. As we started to walk, I spoke with a relaxed voice.

"I know that you want to go with us. But . . . I must tell you, it is difficult enough for me to think of any of our troops down, wounded or dead, if something happens out there. We were very fortunate the last two times that no one was hurt. But, the thought of you or any other woman being injured or killed out there is one I don't care to deal with."

"Look, Lieutenant, I understand and I'm glad you care about my safety," she said quickly, "but this is my job. I've been all over this country, and I'm not afraid!"

"I believe that," I said. "But I am. I'm afraid of how I might act or react with you out there. I would be wondering where you were and how you were. And, if something happens to you I will feel responsible."

"But, you aren't responsible for me. I am responsible for myself, and I came to Nha Trang just to cover this story."

It seemed obvious she was prepared to argue the matter all day if necessary to get herself on what would become the press chopper. In my mind, though, that simply wasn't going to happen.

"Well, I can tell right now that we could go back and forth about this . . . probably till dark," I said. "But we've got to get this mission off the ground now." Then, I turned and started back toward the choppers.

She was following me back as we walked, so I talked over my shoulder.

"Look, it may be because of the way I was raised. I grew up in the South and was taught that ladies are special and to be treated with respect. I don't know; I just can't take a lady into a combat situation. I'm very sorry, but you'll have to cover the story from here."

When we reached the chopper, she marched around in front of me and positioned herself firmly.

"Damn it! I'm no southern belle!" she snapped.

I turned to Orians, Tate, Culhane, and the others.

"Okay, let's go. You all get on that one," I said, pointing to the second chopper from the front.

"Once we're sure it's safe," I continued, "we'll bring you in."

Then I signaled down the line that we were ready to go, and everyone began to load.

With the choppers powering up for lift-off, I turned back to check on the female reporter. She was standing with her arms tightly folded and didn't appear very happy.

"Look," I said. "Why don't you go up and begin visiting with the Montagnards? You can get a head start on your story."

Just then, Thieu Ta Ngoc walked up. He had come down to see us off.

"Having trouble with a woman, Trung Uy?" he asked.

"I don't know, Thieu Ta. I suppose I am. *"And that's one thing I never expected to happen over here,* I thought.

He laughed as we turned and walked toward the lead chopper. As we walked, Thieu Ta quipped, "You know, Trung Uy, we have this problem in Vietnam also. You are a good advisor. Can you advise me about this subject?" He was obviously amused by my dilemma.

"No, I don't think so, Thieu Ta. It doesn't look like I'm doing such a good job for myself."

When we reached the chopper, I briefed the 281st flight leader and Thieu Ta on plans for this mission. Thieu Ta would not be going because of work on another operation, but said that if we got into trouble he was again prepared to take command of any reinforcing unit.

I told him I hoped we wouldn't need him and looked down the line of choppers to see if we were ready. Everyone was loaded.

Turning back to Major Ngoc, I gave him a salute and told him we would see him later. He returned the salute and wished us good luck.

✦ ✦ ✦

Even though we had made this run twice before, I felt my heart rate increase as the choppers increased power and began to lift off.

Adrenaline was already beginning to flow. As we started down the short runway, I glanced back toward the ground to locate the female reporter. I didn't see her along the runway and assumed she had taken my suggestion to begin visiting with the Montagnards.

✦ ✦ ✦

Our chopper took the lead as the wedge formation of helicopters once again headed west through the early morning sky. Mang Quang wasn't with me this day as he had been on the two previous trips. I left him back at Trung Dung with his family. He had done enough. Instead of Mang, a squad of about ten of Thieu Ta's best men were with me. Our unit would go in first to secure the original cornfield LZ.

Just prior to reaching the LZ, the flight leader directed the other choppers to orbit and wait for instructions while we continued ahead.

On this trip, rather than approaching from the north as we had done previously, we were going to make a low approach from the east. We would make our first pass perpendicular to the ridgeline, in case 18B, the enemy unit controlling the area, had returned or in the event that the enemy soldiers left in charge of the village had organized resistance. If either scenario were true, we expected our flight might draw some ground fire.

If we received more than light fire that the Wolf Pack could not suppress, we had other response options this time. F-4s were available and on standby in Cam Ranh Bay along with "Spooky," the customized Air Force C-47 gunship carrying powerful miniguns that pour out red streams of hot copper and lead. The deep droning roar of Spooky's guns was a welcomed sound to friendly troops on the ground. However, for enemy soldiers, it was often the last sound they heard.

While powerful air support was available, any battle would make our effort considerably more challenging and prevent the insertion of the media. I hoped our luck would hold out one more day.

As we passed over the ridge just east of the LZ, our ship was at the point of a diamond-shaped formation. There were two gunships just to our rear on our left and right and one directly behind us, but further back than the other two. The flight leader led the formation down to near treetop level as we approached the cornfield.

We passed directly over the LZ as we made our east-to-west pass across its northern edge. From my position in the left door I had an excellent field of view. Quickly scanning the tree line that surrounded the cornfield for muzzle flashes or enemy troops, neither was in evidence.

"I didn't see or hear anything. Did anyone else?" I asked, radioing my question to everyone in the formation.

All the responses came back, "Negative."

"Okay, let's go back over it one more time," the flight leader said. "If it still looks clear, I'll come around quickly and put you in."

"Roger," I responded.

With that, he turned and we made another pass over the LZ toward the east.

As we cleared the field on our second pass, Flight Leader said, "I didn't see anything, did you?"

"No. Go ahead and put us in."

Once again, he brought the chopper around, descended quickly, and made his approach. And, as he did, he called in the other orbiting choppers.

The gunships, as if synchronized, swung around behind us and changed formation to provide cover. If you had to be out in the middle of nowhere, the Wolf Pack gunships were, without question, the men to have protecting you. They stayed right with us, then circled overhead as we settled in on the LZ.

Just before pulling my radio headset off, the pilot passed me his last message.

"Be careful."

"I will. And, remember, if anything happens, we're going to head downhill and we'll call you when we reach cover," I said.

I yanked my headset off and hurried the last troops off and moved to the front of the chopper where I could be seen. From there, I gave the pilot a thumbs-up, indicating he was clear to leave. He lifted off as the squad fanned out to various points around the LZ. Almost immediately, the other slicks began arriving.

The chopper with the media people arrived first, and the pilot checked in to see if we were ready for them.

"Zero Two, this is Bandit. I've got your press folks on board. Are you ready for them? Over."

At that point, there were only eleven of us on the ground, and the LZ was not secure enough.

"No, I'm not. Circle back and let us get all the troops in first. Then bring them in. Over."

"Roger. We'll be back."

As he responded, he rolled his chopper out of the incoming formation so there would be no delay in the landing of the one following him.

Troops from the incoming choppers helped secure the LZ, just as they had on the two earlier missions. Then, after the last troop-carrying chopper landed, the one with the media checked in once again.

"Zero Two, this Bandit on approach with the press. Are you ready? Over."

"Roger, Bandit. Bring 'em in."

After marking a set-down location for them, I pulled my collar up and turned my back to shield myself from the blowing dirt and grass.

When the chopper lifted off, I turned back to make sure everyone had gotten off safely.

They had, *everyone*—including the female reporter who I thought was safe at Trung Dung.

I was only slightly surprised when I saw her running out from under the chopper in the whirl of sand, grass, and cornstalk pieces. During take-off back at Trung Dung, when she wasn't anywhere to be seen along the runway, I guessed that she had gone to visit the Montagnards. But, on the way out as I considered her tenacity, another thought came to mind, *What if she jumped on the chopper anyway?*

Well, that was exactly what she had done, because there she stood.

While concerned for her safety, I wasn't really disturbed when she appeared. She had convinced me that she was probably very capable of taking care of herself. But, because she was by herself, I was concerned that we might lose track of her if something unexpected happened. So, while the chopper lifted off, I went over to speak with her.

Even when I got close enough for her to hear me over the roar of the chopper's engines and the loud beating sound of its blades, I still had to speak loudly. Squatting down beside her, I shouted a question.

"Lose your way to the Montagnards?"

Smiling as she shouted her response, "Yes, I suppose I did. Are you going to shoot me?"

"No, but the NVA or VC might. You know I could easily send you back on that chopper," pointing toward the one that was just lifting off of the LZ.

"Are you?" she asked.

"No, you can stay," I said.

As I spoke to her, the wash of air from the departing chopper poured over us and was blowing her hair across her face. I watched her as she tried to pull strands of hair away from her eyes and from between her lips. Now I was experiencing distracting emotions for which there was no time and certainly not in this place. Regaining focus, I finished my statement to her.

"But, now that you're here, don't let your presence be a danger to any of these men."

She nodded that she understood as I continued.

"Stay up on the cornfield, don't get anywhere near the jungle. If anything happens, we may not have time to look for you."

Again, she nodded.

"If anything does happen," I told her, "find me or one of the other Americans and stay with him."

"No, I will. I promise. And . . . I'll stay up here. I just wanted to be out here so I could cover the rescue from beginning to end. Truly, I won't get in the way. You won't even know I'm here."

"No, I'll know you're here. Just take care of yourself."

"I will, and thank you for letting me stay."

"Yeah, right."

Standing up as the press chopper cleared the LZ, I walked over to the edge of the cornfield to a point where the hills and valleys to the west and north could be observed.

If our delay in returning has convinced the VC we weren't coming back, I thought, *it may have convinced the Montagnards as well.*

I was concerned that those we had come for may have decided to seek safety even deeper in more remote areas somewhere out there in front of me. I knew there would be little likelihood of finding them.

I yelled over to Sergeant Sotello, our medic who was running wires to a large set of speakers we brought with us.

"Doc, when you get those hooked up, bring them over here." Then, pointing toward the northwest, I continued, "and aim them out that way first."

The valley floor ran in that direction, and it was probably the easiest path for moving families.

While Tracer would fly over that area as well, we were going to support his effort by using one of the other villagers whose family was still missing. He would broadcast our message from the ground, with his being another familiar voice to ring out over the valley.

From my vantage point on the ridge, the last chopper could be seen lifting out of our second LZ after depositing the final load of troops into that location. I didn't have a clear view of the LZ itself and was wondering if they had started up the ridge when Light walked up.

"Trung Uy, those guys just called. They said they are moving into the jungle."

"Good," I said. "Let's go help Doc get the speakers going."

It only took a few minutes to finish hookups and position the speakers, a much shorter time than it took to yield results.

Unlike the quick response we had experienced during the previous two trips, after an hour or so of broadcasting, we still hadn't seen the first villager. While squad-size patrols were out around the LZ for security and others were searching for villagers as they had done previously, the colonel from Fifth Group Headquarters, Frank Orians, and the media had little to do but wander around on the cornfield.

David Culhane and his crew were filming background footage of the valley and security troops around the edge of cornfield. Don Tate and the others made notes and snapped an occasional picture of our surroundings.

I watched the lone female correspondent as she confidently walked the cornfield in search of her story. Occasionally, she would stop and shade her eyes as she scanned the surrounding jungle for emerging villagers that were yet to be seen. One time, when she was very near the jungle edge, she turned as if to get her bearings. When she saw me watching her, she waved me off as if to say, "Quit watching me, I'm okay."

But she wasn't okay. She was unarmed and too far out, so I waved her back. Evidently remembering her promise to stay near the center of the cornfield, she shook her head in submission and started back.

After still more time passed, I was beginning to be concerned that the media representatives wouldn't have a story to photograph or tell about the rescue beyond that which had already occurred. Obviously, the same thought had occurred to Frank Orians because he walked over with Culhane and some of the others.

"Lieutenant Ross, since not a lot is happening, can you give these folks some background information on the operation?" Frank asked.

Recognizing that it wasn't a question, but a request to give them something to report, I said, "Absolutely. What can I tell you?"

The very first question required the creation of an answer and was posed by David Culhane: "What is the name of this area, Lieutenant? Where do I say we are?"

Pulling my map out of my web gear, I looked for a location name, but there was none. *Do I make up a name?* I asked myself. Then, thinking for a moment, I responded with an honest answer, "Well, we've flown so far west of the populated areas that there is no specific name for this place. However, on previous observation missions that weren't quite this far out, I've seen tigers either along the river or crossing open fields near the river. So, I suppose we could call this entire area the Valley of the Tigers."

"Great name," he said, "That's what I'll use for my report."

✦ ✦ ✦

It was interesting to discover many years later that CBS had cross-filed the raw footage of Culhane's rescue report in their archives under "Rescue in the Valley of the Tigers."

✦ ✦ ✦

The questions after "Where are we?" were easy. They wanted to know how the rescue effort had been initiated and asked why we were here today. Since things were quiet, we discussed much of what had occurred over the past several days. During our visit, I suggested that they talk to some of the other advisors for additional background information. They were also told that, if and when villagers appeared, they could use any of our Montagnard interpreters to obtain firsthand accounts for their reports.

There was virtually nothing newsworthy left to discuss when things finally started to happen. As our mini–press conference was breaking up, Light walked up with word from one of our South Vietnamese patrols. The patrol surprised four or five VC sitting along a trail and had captured them and their weapons without a shot being fired.

✦ ✦ ✦

Early in the first mission, everyone, Vietnamese and American, had been cautioned about shooting too quickly. We knew the Montagnards might appear almost anywhere, and many were dressed in black pajama–type clothing very much like that worn by VC.

The patrol making the capture had done their job under extremely difficult circumstances and with great restraint. Once they identified the individuals on the trail as VC, they could have easily opened fire. Rather, they chose the more difficult and dangerous option of capture and had been successful.

◆ ◆ ◆

Shortly after receiving news of the VC capture, one of the Vietnamese soldiers on the perimeter alerted us to a small group of Montagnards who were approaching from the lower part of the ridge. All of the media people immediately ran for cameras and equipment and headed over the hill to begin documenting the story that finally seemed to be developing.

At almost the same time as the first villagers emerged from the jungle, one of the patrols radioed with a report that they had encountered several others trying to make their way to the LZ.

As villagers popped onto the cornfield from various points around our perimeter, the CBS team moved here and there on the LZ, filming as they made their way up the hill. Other members of the media were taking either notes or pictures as they watched the arrival of Montagnards who carried belongings in baskets on their heads, backs, or under their arms. Men, women, and children were hurrying onto the cornfield.

There was new fervor in the voice of the villager who, via the loudspeaker for the past few hours, had been encouraging his friends and family to come to the LZ. Then, just as his effort was renewed, the speaker went dead. Something had happened to it: either the batteries had become weak or it had overheated from use, but that didn't stop the villager. He grabbed a bullhorn we brought with us and continued to encourage his people to try to reach the cornfield.

His aggressiveness paid off. One of the next people to emerge from the jungle was his brother. The NVA and VC had kept them separated for months.

The opportunity to witness their reunion was a heartwarming experience for the media to see. Of course, they loved it. Even the colonel from headquarters walked over to say how glad he was that he made the trip. "This one event made the trip and the wait worthwhile," he said.

✦ ✦ ✦

Villagers continued to arrive on the cornfield while others were found by our patrols in small groups of twos, threes, and fours. This continued until just before noon when I asked for a count. Three more had just arrived, and according to my tally we had forty-two people, which accounted for everyone. Based on our final discussions with the Montagnards, we were expecting to find between thirty-six and forty-two more villagers. So, when the count totaled forty-two, everyone was very pleased.

"Great!" I said. "That's everybody. Let's get everyone in and get out of here."

We still had a unit on the ridge west of us, and several security patrols were still roaming the area. Rain was approaching from the east, so we needed to start moving the villagers, the media, and troops back to Trung Dung before the rain closed in.

We had been very lucky to that point. To my great surprise, we had been able to find all of the villagers and had captured seventeen VC suspects without serious injury to either them or us. There was no need for our luck to change this late in the mission, so all of our units were recalled.

Next, I called the Bandit flight leader and asked him to request the slicks for extraction. We would start moving the Montagnards while we waited for our other unit and patrols to arrive.

Culhane was standing nearby and heard the call.

"Lieutenant, I'd like to interview you before we leave. Is that all right?" he asked.

"Sure, let me know when you're ready."

"How about right now?" he asked.

"Fine, let's do it."

He gave his crew some quick directions, and in just a few minutes he was ready.

"Lieutenant, we're set. Would you stand right here, please?"

✦ ✦ ✦

Culhane had barely finished his interview when the Flight Leader called to let me know the slicks were off the ground and on the way.

With all the Montagnards accounted for and about to be picked up, Tracer's work was done. Looking out over the valley to see where he was, I could see him running the valley bottom, and he was still broadcasting.

"Tracer, Zero Two. Over."

"Roger, this is Tracer. Go ahead, Zero Two."

"We've got 'em all, Tracer. You're clear to head home."

"Roger, understand. I'm coming up."

Tracer pulled up sharply out of the valley bottom and turned toward the cornfield. As his plane got closer, I pointed toward it and told some of the media people who were standing nearby about his role in the rescue.

"That guy is one of the people who made this mission a success."

"What's his name?" Don Tate asked.

"I don't know, but we can find out easily enough," I said.

"Tracer, this is Zero Two. Before you disappear into the clouds, we'd like to know your name, over."

"I'm Major Ken Moses," he responded.

"Ask him where he's from," someone else said.

"One of the reporters wants to know where you're from."

"Rush City, Minnesota," was his proud-sounding answer to the question.

He rocked his wings as he passed about two hundred feet over our heads, then turned east toward his base in Nha Trang. In only seconds, he had disappeared into clouds that were gathering along the coast.

✦ ✦ ✦

Since that day, I've thought about him many times and what he did. But I've never met him face-to-face and never spoke to him again after that last day of the rescue.

Tracer had only been out of sight for a few minutes when one of our patrols called in. They had spotted a small VC unit, but also reported seeing regular NVA troops with them. That information disturbed me. I was concerned that the 18B unit, which had been using the village as a base camp, might be returning. We didn't need a fight at that point; villagers and members of the media were all over the cornfield. The mission was essentially complete, and extraction choppers were due at almost any minute.

Because the report had come from a Vietnamese patrol, I had one of the other advisors call the Americans with the unit on the ridge west of us to alert them to the situation.

That the VC/NVA unit had been spotted moving up the gully between us didn't disturb me. If there was going to be a fight, they made a serious mistake. They had moved to a position between our two units. We could block the gully from above and below with patrols we already had out and then simply close in on them from both sides, if that became necessary.

What did disturb me was the fact that since they knew the area well, it was unlikely that they would make such a mistake unless they were unaware of our unit to the west. They may simply have been trying to distract us while a supporting unit maneuvered around us. Under the cover of the thick jungle growth, almost anything could be occurring.

To determine exactly what was happening, a couple of our patrols were redirected in an attempt to discover the size of the unit encountered. We also began preparing to move the Montagnards back to Trung Dung quickly.

I called the flight leader, who was flying a large circle overhead, to check on the slicks. "Bandit Leader, Zero Two. Over."

"Roger, go."

"Bandit, what is the ETA on the slicks? Over."

"Look over to the northeast. They're on the way in now. Over."

"Roger, I see them. Perfect. And, Leader . . . keep the guns in close. We have at least one unfriendly unit in the area. Over."

"Roger. Understand. I'll move them down now. Over."

"Roger, thank you. Out."

With the slicks on approach, I asked Sergeant Trujillo, who was among our American advisors, to mark a touchdown location for them when they arrived. Then, the media people were told to get ready.

"You folks will be going back with the villagers," I said.

✦ ✦ ✦

While everyone else was gathering equipment, Culhane walked over to me.

"Lieutenant, I'd like to stay a little longer, if that's possible," he said.

"I don't think that's a good idea. We've been told that there is an enemy unit moving around at the base of the ridge. You may get more of a story than you bargained for, but if you want to stay a while, I'll let that be your call. If you decide to stay, just let me know when you're ready to go, and we'll put you on the next chopper out."

"Fine, I will . . . and I'll keep my crew out of the way."

He told his crew they were staying and directed the cameraman to start filming the slicks, which were about to touch down in the area that Sergeant Trujillo was marking for them.

As the slicks began arriving, I encouraged everyone to help get the villagers aboard as quickly as possible. We didn't need a disaster to occur at this last hour in our nearly completed mission.

When the families crowded around the chopper doors, team members and door gunners helped lift women and children aboard. But, even as they helped the Montagnards onto the slicks, they kept glancing up to keep an eye on the jungle around the chopper.

As each slick arrived and departed, the Wolf Pack gunships wove themselves in and out of the air traffic so tightly that the LZ was always covered. I stood in awe as the sky appeared to be packed with spinning airships. Some were ferrying the villagers out while others provided an umbrella of protection over those of us on the ground. *God, don't let them run into each other,* I thought.

Under cover provided by Wolf Pack, the Bandit pilots and crews worked so quickly and efficiently that the Montagnards, the media representatives—except for Culhane and his team—and a small security unit were gone in a matter of minutes. I was relieved to see the cornfield relatively clear of people and particularly pleased that the female correspondent was on her way back to Trung Dung.

The last time I saw her before watching her get on the chopper back to camp, she was moving through the huddled Montagnards writing on her notepad. Seemingly undaunted by our location in the middle of nowhere, she moved from one family grouping to the next, snapping an occasional picture and making notes. Even though unarmed, I never saw any sign of fear—only a bold confidence in her ability to do her job.

At one point, as I watched her work, it occurred to me that she might have been the woman I saw taking pictures of combat action in Nha Trang the first day I arrived. If not, the women were similar in their capacity to display courage. It was easy for a man of that era to don the trappings of courage—the gun, the camouflage, even the green beret—but the courage of the women I met in Vietnam manifested without these types of props. Outfitted with only a camera, a notebook, or a powder-blue uniform, these women exuded a powerful dignity and bravery that equaled or exceeded that of soldiers. Once again, I found myself inspired by a woman.

In Vietnam, inspiration emanated from a wide variety of sources. But, in 1968, sources of inspiration in the United States were more difficult to encounter. So, as I stood and watched the clouds thicken around the LZ, my hope was that if any of the media reported on the mission, our country might find a measure of confidence in its soldiers and some inspiration in what had occurred in the Valley of the Tigers.

◆ ◆ ◆

With the last of 165 Montagnard villagers on the way back to Trung Dung, we reinforced our perimeter and waited for our ride home.

CHAPTER 24

A Promise Fulfilled

WITH THE VILLAGERS ON their way to safety, my attention turned to the security of our troops and getting them back to Trung Dung. No recent reports of VC or NVA sightings had been made, but that was no reason to delay our consolidation of forces. Our unit on the ridge west of us was given the direction to continue moving toward the cornfield as quickly as possible while our patrols continued to circulate around our position. Since we needed both security and early warning, they would be the last elements to be withdrawn from the jungle.

◆ ◆ ◆

Our incoming unit was about to turn east off of the ridge on which they were traveling. They were planning to cut across the small gully between us when their point unit discovered several huts. At the outer edge of the small complex, they encountered what they believed to be the VC/NVA unit spotted earlier further down in the gully. There was a brief exchange of light weapons fire and then quiet. The VC unit had disengaged and quickly retreated back up the ridge.

My Vietnamese counterpart, Trung Si Nguyen, radioed his men and told them to burn the huts and supplies to prevent the VC or

NVA from using the facility as a base camp in the future. Nguyen also told his men to cross the gully and continue toward the LZ as soon as the village was burning.

When the village was ignited white smoke filtered through the dark green jungle treetops and billowed over the ridge. As our unit continued to destroy the huts, the small enemy unit moved back into the area and, evidently trying to savage supplies, began sniping at our troops. With the huts well involved in fire, the unit was told to clear the ridge rather than reengaging the enemy. We had other plans for them.

After the unit was given time to move down off the ridge and clear the area, Wolf Pack gunships were called in. They were told to use the smoke as a reference point from which to begin firing onto the village complex. Their fire would also provide cover for our unit as it made its way across the gully to the LZ.

As soon as they were given their instructions, the three Wolf Pack gunships immediately rolled around and, in single file, began their attack. One by one, they fired rockets and .30-caliber miniguns into the mountainside. The rockets left thin lines of white smoke as they streaked into the treetops where they disappeared and then exploded. The miniguns created a deep humming sound as they rained fire into the jungle canopy.

Wolf Pack's continuing attack successfully shielded our unit from enemy pursuit. It wasn't long before the point element emerged from the jungle. They had crossed the gully without having had any further enemy contacts.

However, as our sister unit continued to arrive on the cornfield, one of our patrols at the base of the hill encountered another small enemy unit they believed to be NVA. But, again, there was only a momentary exchange of gunfire, and the enemy quickly disappeared into the jungle with which they were intimately familiar.

Within minutes of the enemy contact report, the rear guard of the incoming unit cleared the jungle and almost simultaneously the slicks began arriving back on station. So, as quickly as they reached the LZ, our remaining troops were loaded and transported back to Trung Dung.

✦ ✦ ✦

With turnaround time at about forty-five minutes to an hour, it was well into the afternoon by the time the process neared completion. While the last choppers in the current lift were loading, I decided to walk the western edge of the LZ since our perimeter was growing thin and we knew of at least two VC/NVA units in the area.

With the helicopters and most of the troops gone, the rugged mountainside became very quiet. Only the call of jungle birds could be heard along with the occasional roll of distant thunder.

After spending almost an hour along the western side of the perimeter, I walked back up toward the center of the LZ to wait for the slicks that were due to arrive at any time. Back on level ground and able to see across the LZ, I was surprised by what I saw.

There, near the center of the cornfield, stood David Culhane and his crew. When I left to go down over the hill, they were packing their gear. I was certain they had been taken out on the last lift. After getting close enough to be heard, I asked, "Why are you guys still here?"

"I told you we wanted to cover this operation as close to the end as possible," Culhane said.

"Yeah, well, this isn't close to the end. This is the *very* end. This isn't safe for you. It isn't safe for any of us. If there had been two more choppers, we would all be gone," I said.

"But the choppers are due back about now, aren't they?" he asked.

"Yes, they are . . . but, do you realize we're down to two squads or about sixteen men?" responding with a question of my own.

It was clear from the change in his facial expression that he understood the reality of our situation as I continued, "And those sixteen men are only very loosely deployed around our entire perimeter to provide security until we are extracted. There are a lot of holes in our fence."

Culhane said nothing, but exchanged glances with his crew. As the three contemplated what they had just heard, Light and Ahat walked up.

"Trung Uy, Bandit Leader wants you on the radio," Light said.

"Good." I said to the others, "We'll find out where they are."

Taking the handset from Ahat, I responded, "Roger, Bandit, this is Zero Two. How far out are you?"

"A long way," the voice said.

It wasn't Bandit, though. It was the radio room at Trung Dung, and it sounded like Miller. The radio snapped and crackled as he spoke, so I wasn't sure who it was. Something was causing interference.

"Bandit is still on the ground, Zero Two. The rain is pouring down here and in Nha Trang, he asked us to relay. He has been trying to reach you for some time. He has no visibility and can't fly. Over."

"Roger, understand. Any idea how long before he can get back up? Over."

"No. The rain is pretty heavy here right now."

Turning toward the east, it was very easy to see the clouds. While still in the distance, they were thick, very dark gray, and appeared to be moving our way.

"You know these storms," the unidentified radio man continued. "It could blow right through. Bandit says they're refueled and ready to go. He said he was just going to sit and watch it for now. Over."

"Roger, we'll be standing by. Zero Two, out."

Giving the handset back to Ahat, I turned to Culhane, who had been listening to my conversation with Trung Dung.

"I told you. You should have gone when you had the chance," I said.

"Yeah, I guess you're right. What do you think? Any idea how long we'll have to wait?" he asked, not seeming overly distressed.

"Do you want a straight answer?" I asked.

"Yes, of course."

Pointing toward the east, I said, "See those clouds? They aren't our only concern. It's going to be getting dark soon. Whether or not we get out of here tonight depends on how quickly those clouds move."

"Sure, okay . . . I understand," he said.

Now he seemed more anxious. Frankly, I wasn't very excited about our situation myself. We had become a very small unit, now with absolutely no support and a very long way from home. On top of that, we were in an area that was a very familiar landscape to the enemy. Despite our dilemma, until there was reason for concern, there was no need for Culhane or his crew to worry unnecessarily. I did what I could to reassure them. Then, trying to lighten the moment, I told them we might have to give them some quick jungle training.

"You may get more of a story than you came for," I said.

There were a few weak smiles and the cameraman said, "No, the story we have is great. Just get us outta here with it."

I laughed and again assured them we would be fine whether or not the helicopters made it back. Deep down, I couldn't be certain.

✦ ✦ ✦

Lieutenant Sullivan, who was also still waiting for extraction, said he would keep an eye on the perimeter. He headed down over the hill.

Still on the LZ with Culhane and his crew, there was little for me to do but wait and watch the distant clouds roll closer and closer. I did what was possible to keep spirits elevated. Eventually, though, clouds filled the valley. It was difficult to imagine how the choppers would be able to fly through their dense accumulation.

As the wind began to blow and rain started to fall, an extraction before dark began to seem extremely unlikely. Since the VC/NVA knew exactly where we were, and for a number of other reasons, it was apparent that I needed to start thinking about moving our small unit off the LZ and into the jungle.

Pulling my map out, I looked down toward the valley bottom. Running my finger along the map, a route was traced down to a clearing that was barely visible in the distance. If we weren't extracted before dark we would spend the night in the jungle and move toward the clearing in the morning. It would serve as an LZ for our extraction the next day.

With a contingency plan prepared, I refolded the plasticized map Sergeant King had given me and slid it back into my web gear. There were times when I thought King was psychic, and this was one of them. His map was already proving useful. Looking up and out across the cloud-filled valley, I became aware of the light rain blowing in my face. *At least my map won't get wet,* I thought.

The rain was cold, which was a strange feeling. I couldn't remember feeling cold at any time during my many months in Vietnam.

Maybe it's cold because we're in the mountains.

Turning to Culhane, I asked, "Everything okay?"

"Wet, but okay," he replied. "Lieutenant, you know this film is valuable, and we need to get it out of here as soon as possible. This is a story I'll enjoy telling. There aren't many of those, you know."

It seemed increasingly unlikely to me, as cold rain dripped off my nose and chin, that any of us would be going anywhere by helicopter that day. But, until such was a certainty, being pessimistic wouldn't help our situation. So, my attitude continued to be cautiously optimistic when I responded to Culhane.

"I understand," I said. "And you shouldn't worry. I want to get your film and our hides out of here as quickly as possible. Believe me, I don't want to hang around here any longer than necessary. But, with the rain and clouds, it may take them a little longer to get back to us. Even if they could fly it would be difficult, if not impossible, for them to find us now."

"Well, I just hope we're not here too much longer," Culhane said.

✦ ✦ ✦

It had been about thirty or forty minutes since we communicated with Trung Dung when my radio began to snap and crackle again. It sounded as if someone was trying to call, but we could only hear bits and pieces of the transmission. Light turned the volume on the radio to its highest setting. To make things worse, the radio battery was getting weak, and we had already used our last spare.

Mixed with interference, we could hear, "—ro Two—house—ver."

Hoping Trung Dung or Bandit was trying to reach us, I tried to establish contact with whoever was calling.

"Station calling Bunkhouse Zero Two, I am unable to read your transmission. Over."

Unfortunately, enough of the response, which was again mixed with interference, could be understood to make the message clear, "—ro Two—Bandit. Still unable—fly."

It was Trung Dung telling us that Bandit was still on the ground. A response was made to let them know we had received the transmission and understood the situation. "Roger. Understand Bandit unable to fly. Zero Two, standing by. Out."

The response was repeated a couple times in case they were having the same difficulty with reception that we were.

Well, I thought, dropping the handset on the ground next to the radio. *We're going to be spending the night away from home.*

No problem, I thought. There had been many nights out before. While unique, this one would simply be added to the list.

Other overnighters had always been planned or, at least, the possibility anticipated. And, on the others we were typically within range of support units that could provide an arsenal of weaponry. More often than not, we were also in an area where reinforcements could reach us. In the past, communication was essentially taken for granted. We were rarely in an area where communication wasn't possible, but on this occasion it seemed everything had gone to the devil. We had civilians with us and were in communication with no one, since reaching Bunkhouse had become virtually impossible. Our situation in the Valley of the Tigers had definitely changed, and we were very much on our own.

Without the civilian presence our situation wouldn't have been an issue at all. We would have simply moved into the jungle and waited out the weather. If the rain didn't let up, as was sometimes the case, we would have taken on the role of a long-range patrol and merely walked back to Trung Dung.

A month or so earlier, I had been out on a ten-day patrol and had returned with a short beard. While this would have been a much shorter trip, it would have been very difficult for the civilian media, who didn't seem inclined toward such an adventure.

With some feelings of regret for not making sure Culhane and his crew had gone back with the others, I began to feel very responsible for the three-man media team. I didn't want them to have to walk all the way back to Trung Dung and didn't want to think about what would happen if we encountered an enemy unit along the way.

From the mountainside, I looked out over the still thickening black sky. With the cloud cover and rain as it was, darkness was probably less than an hour and a half away. It was becoming more apparent that we were going to have to move, civilians or not. We weren't going to be able to secure the large LZ adequately with our small unit, and we didn't need to be wandering around in the jungle on Charlie's turf after dark. If we moved out soon, Sergeant Nguyen and I agreed we could find a relatively safe and defensible location to consolidate our troops for the night.

As we stood in the rain and prepared to move our small unit, I pondered about how significantly our situation had changed since morning. We had come with the morning light as rescuers, but as darkness drew near we were the ones in need of rescue.

✦ ✦ ✦

Turning to go back toward the radio, I thought about the unopened box and letters on my bunk. The box and one of the letters was from my family. It was a certainty that the box contained more good things to eat. The last one they sent had been filled with chocolate chip cookies baked by my mother. They were broken into a hundred pieces when they arrived, but that didn't seem to bother the Montagnard children who had helped me empty the box.

The letters and box back at camp were still unopened because we had been so busy with the Montagnards there hadn't been time to open them.

Funny, I thought, *the Montagnards are closer to the box and letters than I am, and we are now where they had been . . . and virtually in the same situation.*

✦ ✦ ✦

Once more I reached down and picked up the radio handset.

"Bunkhouse, Bunkhouse, this is Bunkhouse Zero Two. Over."

The interference was still very bad, but an answer was audible.

"Bunk—Go."

"Roger, Bunkhouse. Ahh . . . our situation here will be untenable after dark. So, we are preparing to move. Over."

Bunkhouse's next transmission was still very scratchy and weak, but at least all of it could be heard.

"Roger, Zero Two, understand. Wait one, while we check with Bandit. Over."

A couple minutes passed, then Bunkhouse called back.

"Zero Two, Bandit would like you to stand by a little longer. He says the weather appears to be breaking in there. Over."

"Roger, that's good news, but relay to him that our situation becomes more untenable the longer we wait. Over."

"Roger, Zero Two. If you haven't heard from us in thirty minutes, make your move and we'll contact you for new coordinates in the morning. Over."

"Roger, Bunkhouse. We'll be standing by. Zero Two—out."

✦ ✦ ✦

Culhane was walking over to ask me about the choppers and had overheard the last part of my transmission to Bunkhouse.

"Are they on the way?" he asked.

"Well, the weather in Nha Trang is breaking, so they may be able to get off the ground soon."

Looking back out at the sky, I'm not sure I believed Bandit would ever get off the ground. In fact, I was fairly convinced he wouldn't and thought about calling everyone in and heading downhill into the jungle. But, if Bandit was going to try to fly in that weather, we could wait another thirty minutes. An extraction before dark was certainly the desired conclusion to our mission. Even though I had only known

Bandit for a short while, he seemed to be the kind of guy who would fly if he could.

✦ ✦ ✦

Culhane had walked back over to update his crew when Sullivan came up to where Trung Si Nguyen and I were standing.

"What's our situation?" he asked.

"Well, if they can make it in the next thirty minutes, we'll fly back. If they can't, we'll secure a place in the jungle tonight, then move to another pickup point in the morning."

"A ride today would be nice," he said.

"You're right about that. We're all soaking wet and cold," I observed.

Turning to once again survey the clouds to the east and north, one of the two directions from which Bandit would approach if he was airborne, I said, "Look at that stuff. I don't know how he'll get through it."

From a rock I found to sit down on, I watched as the rain over the LZ diminished to a cold drizzle and the ceiling overhead begin to lift. But as the minute hand on my watch moved from marker to marker, it appeared that there would be no significant improvement in the weather before dark.

Getting up off the rock, I slapped my rain-soaked hat against my leg and repositioned it on my head. I shook the rain off my M-16 and told Ahat to put his radio backpack on. It was almost time to move.

Walking over to Trung Si Nguyen, I asked if any of his men had reported any enemy activity. He said that two of his men on the western perimeter had seen movement and said they could hear people talking, but couldn't see anything clear enough to fire. He had told them earlier, when it began to appear we would be out here overnight, that he didn't want them wasting ammunition. He said that was the reason they hadn't fired.

The fact that the detected movement was on the west side of the ridge was good news for me. When we moved out, we would be heading down off the ridge to the northeast. Hopefully, the enemy wouldn't be in front of us, but since they knew the area very well, they could turn up almost anywhere.

Trung Si Nguyen wasn't any more excited about moving down into the jungle than the rest of us. He had grown up west of Dien Khanh and knew that area very well, but he didn't know at all the mountain area where we were presently located. He felt uncomfortable about that and told me he didn't like being in a place the enemy knew better than he did.

Nguyen and I had decided we couldn't wait on Bandit any longer. It had already been about forty minutes since the transmission with Trung Dung. It was time to leave.

We had picked up our gear and were preparing to move down over the hill when the radio on Ahat's back boomed with Bandit's voice.

"This is Bandit Leader, Bandit Leader . . . looking for Bunkhouse Zero Two, Zero Two. Over."

His transmission was still a little scratchy, but it was clear and loud enough that I knew that he was up there somewhere. And he was close.

There were spontaneous cheers of "Okay!" and "All right!" from those of us standing at the edge of the LZ.

I responded immediately, "Roger, Bandit Leader. This is Zero Two. Where are you? Over."

"This is Bandit. I'm not exactly sure. We're still in the rain. We've been using the river as a reference and feel like we are near and to the north of you. Can you see us? Over."

"He's out there somewhere," I told everyone. "Look for him."

There was a sea of clouds over the valley. I scanned the swirling mass from west to east, focusing at various distances hoping to see him. Nothing, I couldn't see anything but clouds.

"Does anybody see him?" I asked.

There was an assortment of negative responses. Then, off in the northeast at some distance, I thought I saw something moving between the clouds. Looking further ahead for what I hoped was Bandit, I waited to see if he would fly across my line of sight.

✦ ✦ ✦

What happened next was extraordinary. Hollywood would have difficulty depicting it as dramatically as it occurred.

While I'm reasonably certain it was caused by the reflection of light from the setting sun penetrating the clouds, I have never disregarded the possibility of divine intervention. But, between two clouds directly in the center of my line of sight there was a bright, swirling, starburst flash of light that was clearly visible—for only a split second. The flash was as bright as any lighthouse beacon I've ever seen. Even though it was probably the reflection of sunlight on the wet, clear plastic nose assembly on Bandit's helicopter, the occurrence was remarkable!

"I've got him!" I shouted to the others.

Then, quickly, I called Bandit.

"I've got you, Bandit! Break southwest. We're at your ten o'clock position. Over."

"Roger. Breaking. We're coming around now," he answered.

Then, alerting Trung Si, "Call your men in quickly. We *didi*."

"Yeah, good, Trung Uy. I tell them now."

✦ ✦ ✦

Taking the only smoke grenade I had with me, a red one, from my web gear, I pulled the pin and threw it up the hill behind us.

"Bandit, we've got smoke out. You should have no problem spotting us when you break through the clouds. Over."

"Roger, we're coming out now."

There was a short pause.

"Roger, I've gotcha. I assume all that red smoke belongs to you, Zero Two. Over."

"Roger, it does. We didn't want you to miss us. Over."

"Not a chance. Get ready. We're comin' down and don't want to be there any longer than we have to. Over."

"Roger, no problem. We're ready. Come on in."

✦ ✦ ✦

Almost immediately, Trung Si Nguyen's men began gathering. Since there were so few of them it wasn't taking long. They were now forming a large oval around the very top center part of the LZ to provide security for our unit and the incoming choppers.

To determine how we would load onto the helicopters I radioed Bandit for a count on the slicks.

"Bandit, Zero Two. Over."

"This is Bandit. Go, Two."

"Roger, Bandit. What's your count on slicks? Over."

"Our count is two. Over."

"Roger, Bandit. Zero Two—out."

As the entire flight cleared the clouds, we could see a lone Wolf Pack gunship moving from the rear of the formation to take the lead. The count of slicks was easy enough to confirm. There was only one behind Bandit.

With only two slicks, we were going to have to get eleven men on each one. The load for one of those choppers was normally about six to eight Americans with combat gear. However, I had once seen a Huey take off effortlessly with twelve Vietnamese troops on board. Because of their smaller size, there was less weight to lift.

We hadn't brought a lot of gear, and with sixteen of the troops being Vietnamese, I felt sure we would fly. We just needed to split the six Americans between the two slicks.

The choppers were less than a half mile out when I checked on Culhane and his crew.

"Are you all ready?" I asked.

"Yes, we are," he said. "And, Lieutenant, thank you for getting us out of here."

"I'm not the person to thank." Pointing toward the incoming choppers, I said, "Those are the guys to thank. And, when they get here, I'd like you and your crew to get on the first one down, okay?"

"Sure, we'll be glad to. We're ready to get out of here," he said.

They all seemed relieved that we wouldn't be going into the jungle.

Still soaking wet and cold, I know I was glad to be flying rather than walking.

"Good, I'll see you back at Trung Dung," I said, and added, shaking his hand, "Thank you for coming with us."

When I looked back to see where the choppers were, the gunship appeared menacing and seemed to approach with attitude as it swooped directly over us less than fifty feet. He was low, very low.

Then immediately behind the single Wolf Pack gunship came Bandit Leader and the other slick. As they were touching down, I gave the signal to load and yelled, "Let's go!"

Standing beside Bandit's chopper, I counted as Culhane's crew and Nguyen's troops loaded. When there were eleven on board, I motioned the other troops to the second one and waved Bandit out. He nodded to me and powered up immediately. While running back to the second slick, I looked around the LZ to make sure we weren't leaving anyone. When I jumped on the crowded chopper, I asked Nguyen if we had all his men. When he said, "Yes," Sullivan yelled for the pilot to "Go!"

Leaning out the side door, I looked for Bandit. He was gone. *Great,* I thought. *We are gonna fly.* Then we lifted up and off the cornfield, rotated to the northeast, and flew down and out into the valley toward the river.

◆ ◆ ◆

On the way back to Trung Dung, our sky route took us through and around many clouds. And, as we flew, I thought about how extremely fortunate we had been. During our attempt to help the Montagnards, many things could have happened that would have yielded very different results. With that in mind, as we passed through the heart of one particularly thick cloud, I whispered a brief prayer of thanks that we were all returning safely.

◆ ◆ ◆

After we landed at Trung Dung, I walked up to Bandit's chopper. Certainly, he needed to be thanked for coming after us. Upon reaching his ship, I climbed into it and moved to the spot between Bandit and his copilot.

"Well, I guess you know what you did was above and beyond," I quipped.

He laughed.

"Well, we decided we weren't going to leave you guys out there either."

"No, what you did was absolutely not required. You know it and I know it." Then I added more seriously, "You might have saved our lives. We were a long way from home, and all of us know you didn't have to come. Thank you."

We shook hands, and as I turned to leave I offered an observation, "Birds don't even fly in weather like that. We owe you one."

"No," he said. "You owe us nothing. We were proud to have been a part of the mission. Just take good care of the villagers for us."

"It'll be a pleasure," I said.

Stepping down on the skid, I leaned back in and asked Bandit and the copilot to thank everyone from the 281st who had been involved for their tremendous effort.

"We could never have done what we did without them," was my final expression of gratitude for what the unit had done.

✦ ✦ ✦

The two choppers were at full power and were lifting off as I reached the small rise at the entrance to the airstrip. I stopped and turned around to watch them leave. The lone Wolf Pack gunship was circling overhead, waiting for the two Bandit ships to take flight.

How can "thank you" be enough for what they did? I thought, waving as they left over the south wall.

✦ ✦ ✦

I wouldn't learn about the competition until sometime later, but the pilots and crews of the 281st lift platoons had created a contest. The crew that could extract the most Montagnards would be declared winner of the contest, and the count was reported as "souls on board." I don't know who actually won the competition. In my book, they were all winners.

For the men of the 281st, the rescue was obviously more than simply another mission. After flying the Montagnards to Trung Dung, they shut down their choppers and helped them carry their children and belongings to a welcoming area prepared by A-502 team members. Then the chopper crews enthusiastically posed for pictures with those they had ferried to safety (see page 276).

◆ ◆ ◆

On the way back to the teamhouse, I stopped at the Montagnard camp, as I had many times the last few days. Mang Quang, his wife, and his children were sitting on a bench just inside the tent. They were laughing and trying to throw small rocks into an empty C-Ration can.

A couple of days earlier, I had asked one of the interpreters to teach me a few key phrases that could be used when speaking to the children. So, when close enough for them to hear me, my greeting was something roughly approximate to, "Hello, little ones," in Montagnard.

The reaction from the children would probably have been the same regardless of their nationality or what language was used. They became very quiet and began acting very bashful.

With some prompting from his father, Mang's small son, who looked to be near four or five years old, responded with his own equivalent of "hello." Then, much as a shy child would from anywhere in the world, he nuzzled close to his mother, who was on the bench next to Mang Quang.

Then, Mang, with one arm on his son's leg, reached for his daughter with the other. Gently, he pulled her close and held her snugly. She couldn't have been much more than eight years old. After her father whispered something to her, she showed me a tiny, but wonderful smile. I returned her smile and turned to leave. As I did, Mang caught me by surprise when he said, "Thank you, Trung Uy."

This time, no translation was necessary for me to understand what he had said. Mang Quang had obviously asked for a language lesson of his own. His simple gesture of thanks was very important and deeply touching to me. I smiled, nodded, and headed for the team-house to get out of my wet uniform.

Along the way I looked back over my shoulder at Mang Quang and his family, then beyond them to some of the other families and indi-viduals who were now safe at Trung Dung. Among them was a baby girl who had been born the day before we arrived as well as a woman in her eighties. It was a warm and gratifying sight for which Mother Nature could have provided the only appropriate backdrop (and she did. In the west, beyond the villagers, deep golden shafts of light from the setting sun pierced thinning clouds and caused the horizon to glow. It was a remarkable and fitting close to a day that couldn't have been much brighter for the men of Special Forces Detachment A-502 or for me. We had fulfilled a commitment to three mountain villagers who had sought our help by simply carrying out the Special Forces motto *De Oppresso Liber*, to free the oppressed.

Turning back, I took my floppy wet field hat off and stuck it in my web gear. Then, reaching down into one of the leg pockets on my fatigue pants, I pulled out my rolled beret, which was only slightly drier. Positioning it on my head, I continued walking toward the teamhouse. While I couldn't wait to change, and even though this one was soaking wet, I was never prouder to be wearing the uniform of an American soldier.

✦ ✦ ✦

A few days later, news of the rescue began to break in various media forms. David Culhane broke the story of the Montagnard rescue mis-sion in the Valley of the Tigers on CBS's *Evening News with Walter Cronkite*. He closed his story by saying, "This is a rare occurrence in this war, an act designed to give life and freedom in a place and time noted mainly for death and destruction."

MY TOUR COMPLETE, I was once again sitting on my duffel bag on the blazing asphalt runway at the Nha Trang air base. This time, I was waiting for the helicopter shuttle that would ferry me back to Cam Ranh Bay, where I would board my flight home to the United States. Since sitting in that very spot nearly a year earlier, much had happened. My time in Vietnam had been an incredible experience, and I left with many things to ponder and for which to be thankful. Most importantly, I survived the experience.

Just as I noticed the incoming helicopter, an air force airman walked out to the edge of the runway where I was sitting and pointed toward the inbound chopper.

"Lieutenant, that's your shuttle on approach."

"Great. Thank you."

♦ ♦ ♦

A collective cheer arose as the wheels of the big transport jet lifted off the runway in Cam Ranh Bay. Everyone on board seemed very happy to be headed back to the United States. As we turned east out over the South China Sea, I looked back to watch the Vietnam coastline drift off beneath us. A year in the place that I first imagined to be a tropical paradise left me filled with many impressions, both good and bad. Turning to look ahead along the way home, I began to think about my arrival back in Pensacola. My homecoming would be quiet—very different from the one my family had planned for me.

During the course of the year, my mother often wrote about the plans that she and my father were making for my homecoming. They had arranged for a band from one of the local nightspots to welcome me at the airport. I, however, didn't want a band or any other fanfare at my homecoming. There was now too much controversy over our country's involvement in Vietnam. All I wanted or needed was to see the faces of my family and have a quiet trip home from the airport. For those reasons, I hadn't told my parents when I would be returning, so they had no way of knowing that I was already on my way.

✦ ✦ ✦

After a very long flight back to the west coast of the United States, a long coast-to-coast flight still loomed ahead of me. After a plane change in St. Louis, we finally turned south. In late afternoon, we landed in Birmingham, Alabama. We were scheduled to be on the ground just long enough to drop off and pick up passengers. For that reason, everyone who was continuing to Pensacola and beyond was asked to stay on board the plane. When we took off again, it would only take about thirty minutes to reach Pensacola.

Knowing my mother would barely have time to get to the airport in Pensacola before I did, let alone organize a reception, I thought my family should probably know that I was near. Going to the front of the plane, I introduced myself to a flight attendant and told her that I needed off for just a few minutes to call home and explained why. A voice from the cockpit said, "Go ahead, Lieutenant, we'll wait for you. Just make it as quick as you can." One of the pilots had overheard my request.

When my mother answered the phone at home, I asked, "Do you have a place for a tired soldier to lay down?"

Taken by surprise, her voice began to quiver, "Oh, my God. Is that you, Tom? You sound so close. Where are you?"

"Birmingham," I said.

"Oh, thank God," she sighed. "But we wanted to do something special for you." Then, as other mothers glad to have children home from war, she started to cry.

"Mom, I have to go. The plane is ready to leave. I'll be home in about forty-five minutes to an hour. Will you call Dad and let him know I'm coming home?"

"Yes. Are you all in one piece?" she asked in a concerned voice.

"Yes, I'm fine. Mom, I have to go now. I love you."

"I love you, too. I'm so glad to get you back from that terrible place."

✦ ✦ ✦

About forty-five minutes later, the propeller-driven Eastern Airlines Silver Falcon touched down on the runway in Pensacola. Then, as we taxied to the terminal, I could see my mother and sister, Polly, at the gate. I had barely cleared the bottom of the steps before being rushed and smothered in their embraces. I was home.

After collecting my bags, we went to see my father at work. He was in the back of our family business and had his back to me when I walked in. When he heard the door, he turned, and in an instant his face lit up. He beamed with a huge smile.

Such was my homecoming, the only one I wanted.

✦ ✦ ✦

During the first few days after my return to the United States, I was surprised by the degree of anger being expressed over the Vietnam War. The true nature of the descent hadn't been this clear to me before I came home. I read the paper every day and watched the evening news every night. The news broadcasts were often painful to watch. There seemed to be protests everywhere, sometimes with rioting and fighting in the streets. For me, the situation was extremely distressing.

As I watched and listened to various reports on the Vietnam protests, I found the abuse leveled at military personnel difficult to believe. When I heard some of the terrible epithets hurled at Vietnam soldiers and veterans, my heart sank and my stomach turned. I now understood why my mother was so relieved to have me home.

Almost every time after reading, watching, or listening to news reports, I found myself filled with agonizing feelings and emotions that were contradictory. Even though I had served in the military, I began to understand the anger and frustration on the civilian side of the controversy. The more I learned, the more my own grave concerns grew regarding the validity of our involvement in Vietnam.

On the day the South Vietnamese government collapsed and Saigon finally fell in 1975, I watched all of the television coverage. By that time, all I could do was shake my head. *This can't happen again*, I thought. I was now certain we had made very serious mistakes, not only by becoming involved, but also by waiting so long to withdraw.

Over three million American men and women served in Vietnam during the years of our presence there. Of that number, more than fifty-eight thousand did not come home alive or were declared missing in action. As one who served, I feel a very deep and sincere regret for the loss of so many lives. I also regret the life-altering physical injuries and mental scars brought home by those who survived the Vietnam experience.

It was not only soldiers who had been affected by what occurred in Southeast Asia. When the Vietnam War was lost, it was obvious to me, as it was to most Americans, that we as a country and a people had suffered very deep wounds. Healing those wounds would take a very long time. But, with our wounds also came learning. As a country, we learned many lessons in Vietnam. Perhaps the single most important one was that our leaders who commit our military to forces to combat must do so with far greater wisdom and prudence.

I am convinced that those who died and those missing in action did not give their lives in vain. The memory of those lost in Vietnam has already resulted in more thought and planning being given to the commitment and withdrawal of our military forces. I am also personally strengthened and comforted in the belief that the Vietnam-era sacrifices will save countless lives in the future. For that reason, as well as a deep personal appreciation for their great sacrifice, I dedicated this book to, among others, each of the more than fifty-eight thousand who died or were declared missing in action in the Republic of South Vietnam.

While our involvement in Vietnam may have been ill conceived, there is no doubt in my mind about my reasons for serving my country. I am still at peace and perfectly comfortable that my decision to serve was the correct one for me.

While many admittedly and unquestionably dark stories persist about Vietnam, uncounted thousands of tales glow with brilliant luminescence. The stories told here are not as remarkable as many of those yet to be told. This book is offered as encouragement to others to tell their stories of dedication and patriotism. By so doing, our country and the families of those who served in Vietnam can know that the great majority did so with honor in the belief they were attempting to deliver the gift of freedom.

The opportunity to represent our country as a part of the team involved in the Montagnard rescue mission was a privilege. The chance to serve with American men and woman such as those I met during my time in Vietnam was another. Combined, they remain privileges of war.

The Men of U.S. Army Special Forces
Detachment A-502

Team members are listed by the year they joined the detachment.

1964

Day, Kenneth J.
Chastain, Joyce F.
Combs, Harold J.
Fields, Arthur
Foxworth, Louis G.
Grabey, Stanley G.
Hobby, Oscar L.
Johnston, James M.
Miner, Louis F.
Spradlin, Earnest J.
Wilson, Carl L.
Wilson, Gerry W.

1965

Batteford, Frank P. Jr.
Berg, Charles L.
Chestnut, John
Cincotti, Joseph G.
Foshee, Edgar E. Jr.
Grady, Clyde E. Jr.
Hughes, James E.
Mallare, Gerald E.
McClellan, Henry
Moore, George R.
Peters, Larry J.
Rice, Homer L.
Schreiber, Robert D.
Smeltzer, William L.
Switney, Robert
Watson, Roger

1966

Chaplin, Robert W. Sr.
Charest, Robert A.
Chase, James E. Jr.
Clow, James L.
Deason, Robert L.
Gumper, Victor W.
Johnson, Dean B.
Johnston, Charles W.
Jordon, Richard W.
McKitrick, Michael L.
McMenamy, Charles W.
Rouse, Glenn R.
Salsman, Berney
Shreck, Raymond D.
Shriver, Jerry
Sturm, Henry B.
Tocci
Young, James W.

1967

Anderson, Roger L.
Andree, Martin E.
Arrants, Jerry C.
Ballou, Richard D.
Bardsley, Richard W. Jr.
Barnes, James M.
Blake, John H. III
Brooks
Castillo
Daly, John J.
Cox
Everett, James L.
Freedman, Lawrence N.
Geronime, John F. III
Gilmore, Gordon S.
Goff, Robert E. Jr.
Goodwin, Donald J.
Herbert, John
Homitz, Ronald D.
Jackson, Hugh
Jarvies, James Y.
Kentopp
Key, John C.
King, Roy
Koch, Paul L.
Lee, Wilbur L.
Madera, Edward
Miller, James H. Jr.
Morace, Albert T. Jr.
Munoz, Ferdinand
Noe, Frank R.
Puckett, Wayne R.
Reynolds, Robert W.
Sanderson

Sotello, Juan
Stewart, Mitchell G.
StMartin, Joseph E. B.
Sullivan, Michael E.
Sweeney, Robert T.
Vasquez, Jose E.
York – Yourk

1968
Allen, Manuel B.
Armstrong, Edwin D.
Bachelor, Hardy E. Jr.
Beeler, David E.
Brandon, John C.
Brown, Edward
Burruss, Tommy
Caldwell, Herschel E.
Campbell, Charles E.
Cheston, Elliott B. Jr.
Childs, Benjamin B.
Darragh, Shaun M.
Dawkins
Drennan, Dennis P.
Dubovick, Richard R.
Dukovic, Gary V.
Egan, Jan C.
Gray, Darrell W.
Harrell, Robert L. Jr.
Harris, Edward D.
Hawley, Robert L. Jr.
Hicks, Archibald G.
Hillard, Sidney H. III
Hines, Robert M. Sr.
Holland, James D. Jr.
Hubbard, Lyman L. Jr.
Juncer, Dennis A.

Kerestes, Paul A.
Knorr, James R.
Land, Kenneth D.
Lane, William K. Jr.
Lane, Terry V.
Lavaud, Jean P.
McGill, Charles A.
McKay
Ochsner, Robert L.
Olt, Timothy F.
Oxenham, Randall
Palmer, Charles P.
Phalen, William C.
Phillips, William J.
Pope, Alonzo D.
Robertson, Juan P.
Ross, Thomas A.
Rupp, John N.
Sanford, H. C. Jr.
Sellers, Lawrence P.
Sheppard, Andrew D.
Sipots, Carl A.
Strong, Tully F.
Trujillo, Louis A.
Webb, Carlton E.
Weller, Richard O.
Wilson, Thomas E.

1969
Abraham, Anthony G.
Bemis, Donald W.
Carlson, John E.
Cooper, Gerald L.
Cottrel, George A. Jr.
Cottrel, John R.
Crabtree, Donald L.

Crockett, Charles D.
Deschamps, John T.
Dinnel, Michael L.
Ditton, William L.
Downs
Eastburn, David R.
Estrada, Pedro B.
Funk, George C.
Gebhart
Gigliotti, John L.
Guerrero, Francisco T.
Hearst, John R.
Hefferman, William F.
Hein, Charles
Hoffman, George P.
Home
Jenkins
Jones, James
Kemmer, Thomas J.
Kirby, Wickliffe B. III
Lindsey, Gene B.
McBride, John B.
McCandless, Kerry M.
Merletti, Lewis
Mika, Michael J.
Miller, Franklin D.
Mitchem, James W.
Overby. Morris C.
Payne, Thomas R.
Roush, James E.
Saganella, Eugene V.
Sheridan, William E.
Short, Harlow C.
Shutley, George F. Jr.
Stucki, Gary W.
Tolbert, James E.